PIRATE STATE

PIRATE STATE

INSIDE SOMALIA'S TERRORISM AT SEA

PETER EICHSTAEDT

Lawrence Hill Books

Library of Congress Cataloging-in-Publication Data
Eichstaedt, Peter H., 1947–
Pirate state : inside Somalia's terrorism at sea / Peter Eichstaedt.
p. cm.
Includes bibliographical references and index.
ISBN 978-1-56976-311-7 (hbk.)
1. Maritime terrorism—Somalia. 2. Piracy—Somalia. 3. Hijacking of ships—Somalia. I. Title.
HV6433.786.S58E43 2010
364.16'4—dc22
2010015506

Interior design: Jonathan Hahn
Map design: Chris Erichsen
All photos courtesy of the author

Published by Lawrence Hill Books
An imprint of Chicago Review Press, Incorporated
814 North Franklin Street
Chicago, Illinois 60610
ISBN: 978-1-56976-311-7
Printed in the United States of America
5 4 3 2 1

CONTENTS

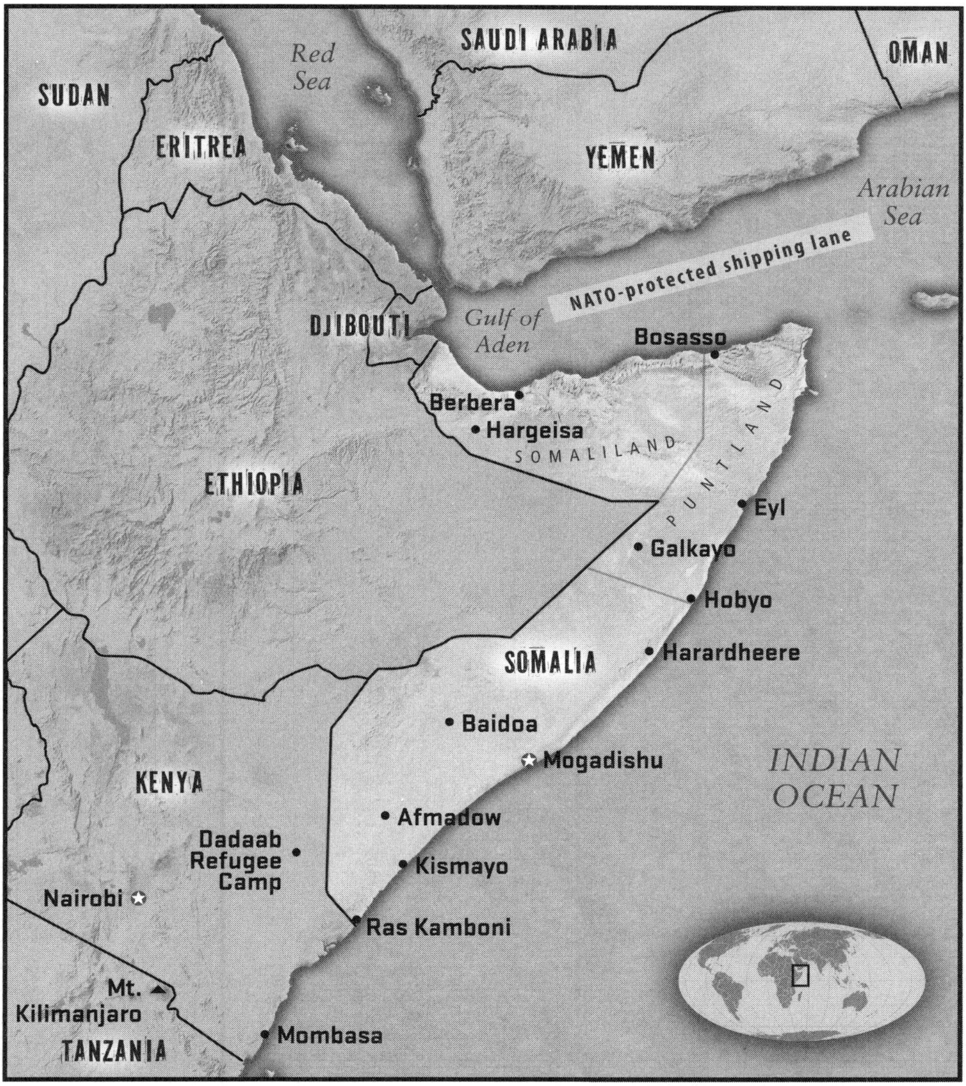
SAUDI ARABIA
OMAN
Red Sea
SUDAN
ERITREA
YEMEN
Arabian Sea
NATO-protected shipping lane
DJIBOUTI
Gulf of Aden
Bosasso
Berbera
Hargeisa
SOMALILAND
PUNTLAND
ETHIOPIA
Eyl
Galkayo
Hobyo
SOMALIA
Harardheere
Baidoa
Mogadishu
INDIAN OCEAN
KENYA
Afmadow
Dadaab Refugee Camp
Kismayo
Nairobi
Ras Kamboni
Mt. Kilimanjaro
Mombasa
TANZANIA

PIRATE STATE

PROLOGUE

THE PIRATES' CALL

Silence grips the gritty streets of Khartoum in early December 2008, as if the city has fallen into a deep sleep. It is Eid al-Adha, the Festival of Sacrifice celebrating Abraham's willingness to slay his son Isaac at God's bidding. Even the trinket peddler who camps in the hotel lobby has taken the day off. I retreat to my room and read the magazine on my hotel room desk, its cover curiously depicting a U.S. naval ship, a heavily armed man on the deck of a freighter, and an army tank. The story rails about the notorious Ukrainian ship, MV *Faina*, hijacked months earlier by Somali pirates. The armed man is a pirate draped in chains of bullets and brandishing a high-caliber machine gun.

I am not in Sudan's capital because of the Somali pirates. Rather, I am conducting a workshop for journalists from Darfur about the International Criminal Court in The Hague, Netherlands, which has indicted two ranking Sudanese accused of orchestrating the death and destruction in Darfur.

Yet the Somali pirates are with me in Khartoum, beckoning and taunting, a menace to the glut of oceangoing cargo carriers and pleasure cruisers that sail the East African waters between the Horn of Africa and the Arabian Peninsula. The pirates attack anything of value that floats: oil tankers, freighters, cruise ships, and private yachts, collecting handsome ransoms for their work. That dozens of desperate Somali fishermen harass global shipping magnates, holding them, their crews, and world trade hostage is as amusing as it is outrageous. And it all takes place under the watchful eyes of the world's largest and most powerful navies, including those of the United States, Russia, China, Japan, and half a dozen European countries.

The hijacking of the MV *Faina* was more than a random splash of publicity for the Somali pirates, and the ripples were felt throughout the region. The MV *Faina* set sail on the Black Sea in late August 2008, bound for the Kenyan port of Mombasa, carrying thirty-three T-72 Soviet-designed tanks, 150 grenade launchers, six antiaircraft guns, and pallets of ammunition. On September 25, gun-toting Somalis cranked up their slender skiffs, hooked their ladders to the sides of the ship, and climbed aboard. The *Faina* was theirs. How could the Somali pirates get so lucky? This had to be part of something larger.

Soon after the ship was seized, word leaked that the weaponry was headed for South Sudan. The article inside the magazine, a piece of Sudanese propaganda, revealed that the Sudan government was seething. It accused South Sudan of trashing the shaky peace deal the two parties signed in 2005. Sudan was right to be worried. I had arrived in Khartoum from South Sudan just days earlier, where I had seen about a dozen similar tanks at a military post in Wau, just 125 miles from the South's border with Sudan. It was clear that South Sudan was arming, fully expecting to fight Sudan as it did from 1983 to 2005 in a bloody and woefully underreported war that claimed some two million lives and displaced four million others.

The war this time would have new stakes. It would be over not only South Sudan's independence, to be voted on in 2011, but its untapped oil. War in South Sudan is a prospect no one wants to admit. But the South Sudanese know who they face in the people and the party behind Sudan's president, Omar al-Bashir, even if the world has failed to recognize the realities of Darfur. As the fate of the weapons ship hung in the balance, it was painfully obvious that Somali pirates had become players in a larger and more dangerous global game. The pirates have become a headache not only for East Africa but for the world.

America has been keeping tabs on Somalia. The psychic wound America suffered in the Battle of Mogadishu, fought in October 1993 and highlighted in the book *Black Hawk Down* and film of the same name, had scabbed over but never fully healed. That two-day battle claimed the lives of eighteen U.S. soldiers and wounded seventy-three others. It also killed an estimated one thousand Somali militia fighters. In the wake of that battle, Somalia descended into chaos as competing militias and militant Muslims grappled for control. In northern Somalia, the former British colony of Somaliland broke away and declared itself a republic that is still unrecognized by the world today. Encompassing the Horn of Africa was the politically autonomous heartland of piracy, Puntland, so-named as the Biblical source of frankincense and myrrh, once known as punt. For nearly twenty years, southern Somalia had smoldered and frequently burned out of control.

When the MV *Faina* was taken, U.S. attention was momentarily drawn to the region. The United States has quietly been supporting South Sudan, a move that can help contain and control recalcitrant Sudan. But with the MV *Faina* anchored off the Somali pirate enclave of Hobyo along with its array of weaponry, a crisis erupted. A U.S. warship was dispatched to prevent the weapons from falling into the hands of Islamist militants on shore in Somalia or, worse yet, reaching Khartoum. The warship positioned itself between the MV *Faina* and the Somali shoreline, ensuring that the tanks and everything else stayed on the ship. While the blockade was largely successful, some small weapons were reportedly smuggled away as the pirates routinely moved from shore to ship with supplies.

The hijacking of the MV *Faina* ended in early February 2009 when a ransom pegged at $3.2 million clunked on to the *Faina*'s deck. A week later, the MV *Faina* chugged into Mombasa, its twenty-member crew exhausted, disgusted, and deeply homesick. After nearly five months of captivity, the crew stumbled down the gangplank, bedraggled and clad in grimy clothes. The only casualty of the incident was the Ukrainian captain, who died of an apparent heart attack from the shock of having pirates storm aboard. His body was kept in the ship's freezer. The sailors described how they were locked in a stuffy room and allowed out once or twice a week, leaving little chance for escape. They were watched by jumpy Somali gunmen habitually chewing khat, the green leaves of a mildly narcotic plant that grows all over East Africa. The sailors were deprived of water and fed just enough spaghetti to keep them alive. The crew believed it would be executed once, when it was marched on deck and lined up along the rails. Only later did the crew learn that the pirates were complying with a request from the U.S. Navy to show that all were still alive.

Then, on April 8, 2009, the United States was hit broadside by Somali pirates who attempted to capture the U.S.-flagged ship the *Maersk Alabama*. The hijacking failed when the crew overpowered one of the pirates and arranged a deal in which the pirates fled in the cargo ship's lifeboat with the captain held hostage. When the drama ended with the killing of three pirates by military snipers, the Somali pirates were no longer just a menace to pleasure cruises and cargo carriers on distant waters. They had thrust themselves into the floodlights of the world stage.

Were these pirates truly a legion of desperate fisherman bloodying the noses of global shipping companies on a daily basis? Or was this the work of organized crime syndicates? Was piracy connected to the madness that gripped Somalia? In late 2009, I crisscrossed much of East Africa to find the answers to these questions. I met with pirates in Somaliland prisons. I attended pirate trials in Mombasa and visited sprawling Somali refugee camps. I held clandestine meetings with Somali pirates and their bankers. In the dark corners of Nairobi I interviewed a former fighter with the brutal Islamist al-Shabaab militia.

While the plague of piracy demands immediate and aggressive action, it is a symptom of a much deeper problem: Somalia itself. The potential of Somalia metastasizing into something worse than it already has become is more than worrisome. In late September 2009 I met in a quiet Nairobi coffee shop with Bruno Schiemsky. As the former head of the United Nations panel of experts monitoring the UN's weapons embargo on Somalia, he was intimately aware of the situation in Somalia on land and at sea. As we sipped coffee, Schiemsky described the links between the pirates and elements of the extremist al-Shabaab militia that controls southern Somalia. The tentacles of such terrorist groups extend across the Gulf of Aden into Yemen, Saudi Arabia, and the freewheeling port of Dubai, ultimately reaching Pakistan and Afghanistan. In Africa, those tentacles stretch throughout Somalia and across the porous borders of Ethiopia and Eritrea, and to Sudan, Egypt, and Libya. The pirates, he suggested, are at the edges of an underground network determined to make Somalia not only a haven for madness but a platform for a global jihad. Turning a blind eye to piracy and Somalia is to invite disasters of horrific proportions.

The West is about to commit the same egregious mistake in Somalia that it did in Afghanistan. After the Soviet Union was defeated in Afghanistan in 1989, when the so-called threat of creeping communism was removed, the United States set Afghanistan adrift, letting it descend into a chaotic and bloody civil war that gave rise to the Taliban. Ultimately, the Taliban gave shelter to Osama bin Laden, who hatched the plot that resulted in the September 11 attacks. Since then, the United States and its allies have been fighting wars in both Afghanistan and Iraq in an increasingly desperate attempt to contain extremism and terror.

Somalia duplicates Afghanistan. The country has been wracked with war since 1991 due in part to the United States' hands-off policy that followed the Black Hawk Down debacle and made the country ripe for an extremist takeover by militant Islamists. Doing nothing to bring stability and sanity to Somalia is inviting another 9/11, only the next one could be much worse. Doing nothing will also allow Somali piracy to flourish and grow, and as of this writing, it was already spreading far into the Indian Ocean. Modern-day piracy does not resemble the depictions that come out of Hollywood studios. These pirates are desperate and dangerous men who will do just about anything for money. They are increasingly linked with global financiers and religious fanatics prepared to kill themselves and countless others on the promise of paradise in the afterlife. These links to a disturbing and growing network may ultimately affect people around the world in ways they can't imagine.

1

ATTACK ON THE ALABAMA

Two men stand on the bridge of the U.S.-flagged ship *Maersk Alabama* as it churns through the Indian Ocean some three hundred miles off the coast of Somalia. It is Wednesday, April 8, 2009, and in the growing light of dawn their eyes follow a blip on the ship's radar.[1] They scan the steely gray sea, and in the distance a small boat races toward them, bouncing madly on the waves. Not again, they think. In the past twenty-four hours, the ship has been approached twice, the last time being just hours earlier, when navigator Ken Quinn was on watch. The *Maersk Alabama* had passed what Quinn suspected was a pirate "mother ship," a larger boat from which the pirates launch their armed attacks using skiffs powered by outboard motors. "They were telling us on the radio to pull over," Quinn said later. "They kept saying 'Stop ship, stop ship, Somali pirate,' but we just kept going."[2]

An earlier attack had come the afternoon before, when pirates bristling with weapons had trailed the ship. Captain Richard Phillips had ordered evasive measures and speeding up and left the pirates in their wake. "The little boats couldn't catch up to us," Quinn said.[3] Initially, the two men on the bridge, First Mate Shane Murphy and Captain Phillips, were not alarmed at this third attack. "I see pirates attack ships all the time," Murphy explained.[4] But as the speeding craft closed in, each man drew a deep breath and squinted as the morning sun glinted off the rippling sea. The boat was coming "faster than anything" they'd see before, splashing through the waves. "This one didn't feel right," Murphy said later, recalling his sense of helplessness.[5] Their heavy cargo—4,100 metric tons of corn and soybeans, along with 990 metric tons of vegetable oil—had lowered the deck to less than twenty feet off the surface. Phillips and Murphy realized that if the pirates came alongside, they would have little trouble climbing aboard. Ironically, the *Maersk Alabama* was headed for Mombasa, Kenya, with food aid for millions of malnourished Africans who would suffer due to Somali pirates bent on hijacking it and holding it for months, if necessary.

When Phillips sounded the alarm, Quinn jolted awake, having left his watch shift just hours earlier for some badly needed sleep. He sensed trouble. "I was sleeping," he recalled. "I got off watch at four in the morning and I went to bed." With the alarm blaring, Quinn pulled on his clothes, grabbed his radio, and ran to the ship's safe room, where he made a head count. The first pirate boarded quickly, Quinn said, using a ladder that was easily hooked onto the side of the ship. A wiry young man brandishing an AK-47 that he fired repeatedly, he scampered up several flights of stairs to the bridge and confronted the captain.[6] Fourteen of the nineteen crew members were already in the ship's safe room. Phillips and two others remained on the bridge.[7] Murphy and Chief Engineer Mike Perry were already gone. Murphy had ducked into the interior corridors, where he secured as many of the ship's locks and doors as he could. He stopped short and swallowed hard when Phillips yelled over the ship's radio and intercom, "Shots fired! Shots fired!" When Murphy and the crew heard this, they knew they faced their worst nightmare. "They were coming aboard," Murphy told himself. "It's going to be a fight." But he refused to surrender. "I wasn't willing to give up the ship to these guys yet."[8]

On the bridge with Phillips were Third Mate Colin Wright and crewman Zahid "ATM" Reza, who prepared to confront the pirates. The lead pirate, later identified as eighteen-year-old Abdiwali Abdiqadir Musi, and his accomplices leveled their guns at Phillips, Reza, and Wright. "You just hope you don't get killed," Wright said later of the ordeal.[9] The pirates ordered Phillips to stop the ship and gather the crew.

Murphy and the crew could monitor the conversation over the ship's radios. Phillips spoke in a calm, cooperative voice, but the tension was undeniable. "You could tell he had a gun pointed at his face," Murphy said later.[10]

After Musi and the attackers quizzed Phillips about the ship and crew, they began to cheer. Learning that the ship and crew were American, they believed they'd hit the jackpot. Musi and his accomplices reassured the three hostages that if all went well, they would survive unharmed. "Don't worry. We just want money," Musi said.[11]

The pirates then ordered Phillips to assemble the crew. Unknown to the pirates, however, the crew had a password that Phillips would use when the coast was clear. When he didn't use it, the crew hunkered down in their stifling confines.[12] Minutes dragged on. When no one showed, the pirates again demanded that Phillips gather the crew. Phillips made another call, but when no one appeared, the pirates angrily threatened to kill their captives. The pirates then sent Wright to find the crew members and bring them to the bridge. Instead, Wright used this opportunity to disappear, and he remained hidden for the rest of the ordeal that day.[13]

Moments after the pirates had boarded, Perry had told the helmsman "to try to swamp the pirate boat."[14] It was a maneuver they'd done before and involved fishtailing the behemoth cargo ship from side to side, creating a downdraft of water as the ship slid sideways. The roiling waters sucked the pirate skiff under. The move turned out to be critical. The four Somali pirates were left with no means of escape, should the hijacking fail. With their skiff gone, the control of the *Maersk Alabama* had already begun to slip away from the pirates.

Suddenly the *Maersk Alabama* was dead in the water as Perry shut down the ship's engines, leaving only an emergency generator running that powered a few emergency lights. Determined that the pirates would have nothing at their disposal, Perry stealthily raced about the ship and, reaching the backup generator, turned it off as well. The ship fell silent, its interior passageways pitch black. Perry's actions were strategic. He knew the pirates probably planned to take the ship to the nearest Somali port while negotiations took place.

But out at sea, the pirates were far from help and were vulnerable. Meanwhile, the crew huddled in the suffocating darkness of the safe room with no food or water as the temperature steadily climbed to 125 degrees Fahrenheit.[15]

As Perry and Murphy hustled about the darkened ship, the pirates realized they had to force Phillips to gather the crew to get the ship moving. The pirates renewed their demand that the crew surrender. Knowing this was impossible, and with Wright gone, Reza engaged the pirate Musi in a conversation, explaining that the crew members had instructions to hide and would do so as long as they suspected they were in danger. Reza, a Bangladeshi, used their shared Islamic faith to convince the young pirate leader Musi to cooperate with him. "I told him, 'Trust me. I am Muslim; you are Muslim.'"[16] Sensing he might be able get a jump on Musi, Reza agreed to help Musi find the crew but only if Musi left his AK-47 and pistol behind. Musi agreed. It was a fateful decision.

As Musi and Reza plunged into the darkened passageways of the ship, they were unaware that Perry, armed with a thick-bladed pocketknife, had taken up a position near the engine room. Anticipating that sooner or later the pirates would search the ship for the crew, Perry knew they would ultimately pass the engine room. His hunch proved correct when he heard the footsteps of Reza and Musi, lighting their way with a flashlight. Suddenly the light was in Perry's face. Perry retreated just enough to gain the advantage, then stopped as he rounded a corner. Musi gave chase, and Reza followed. As the light came closer with each of Musi's steps, Perry waited until the last moment before grabbing Musi and holding his knife at Musi's throat.[17]

With Reza's help, Perry wrestled Musi to the ground, and in the process Musi's hand was sliced badly. "I held him. I tied his hands and tied his legs. He was fighting me," Reza said of the struggle. "There was a lot of yelling, shouting, and screaming. I was attempting to kill him. He was scared."[18]

The struggle took place just outside the safe room door, Quinn explained later, leaving him and the rest of the crew to listen helplessly at the scuffling just inches away. "We could hear a commotion out in the engine room, and that lasted about fifteen minutes. I was right up against the door listening to see what was going on," Quinn said. "Then I heard voices, and I could tell the chief engineer was in there, and I could hear [the hijacker's] voice. Then [Perry] said, 'Dinnertime, suppertime, open the door.' That's our code word. We opened the door and he said, 'I've got this prisoner, and you guys are going to have to watch him.' So he pushed him in with us. The guy kind of went crazy at first. They pushed him down on the deck because they were mad. They said they were searching him for weapons. I won't go into the details. They had their knives out, and I was going, 'Remember, the mother ship could be here any minute. We don't want to mess up their leader too bad. I mean, if they show up with twenty more pirates, they're not going to be happy.'" The crew backed off, realizing that Musi was a valuable bargaining chip.[19]

The loss of their leader did not sit well with the remaining three pirates, who again threatened Captain Phillips, saying that unless their colleague was freed, Phillips would be killed. "They said they would shoot someone if their friend did not come back," First Mate Murphy recalled. It was a threat that he and the others had to take seriously. There had been incidents in the past, Perry explained, in which pirates, high on khat and bored with long, drawn-out negotiations, forced captive crew members to play Russian roulette. "I was never going to go that way," Perry said, and he didn't want anyone else to go that way either.[20]

With their leader now gone, the remaining three pirates grew increasingly scared and desperate. "For me, that was the toughest moment," Murphy recalled. Yet the crew had little choice but to hide and wait. With three pirates still on the bridge, Murphy collected what food and water he could from the galley. Seeing the crew's breakfast on the tables and untouched, he realized how crazy the situation had suddenly become. "It was kind of eerie," he said. Despite the tension, Murphy knew it was foolish to panic. "Our minds are the best weapons."[21]

After delivering the food and water to the safe room, Murphy found the ship's emergency beacon and decided to send out a distress signal in addition to what had already been sent. To do that, he had to get to the highest possible point on the ship. Wrapping the transmitter in a blanket, he rambled down the darkened passageways. Passing the captain's quarters, he paused at Phillips's desk to scrawl a note on a yellow legal pad: "We have one pirate in steering gear." But Murphy didn't get much further before he heard the voices of Phillips and a pirate approaching. He ducked into the ship's medical room, where he hid under a desk. Since Musi had not returned, Phillips had been forced to lead one of the pirates on a room-by-room search for the crew. "The pirate was so close I could see his foot," Murphy recalled.[22]

"See, there's no one here," Phillips told the pirate. Murphy chuckled to himself as they disappeared down the passageway. Murphy scrambled and soon found the high point he needed for the emergency signals. Knowing that the crew could now end the standoff, Murphy took the offensive and grabbed the ship's intercom. "I told them I was in charge now, and I had their friend." If they wanted their friend back, they would have to negotiate, he said.[23]

Realizing that the ship's hijacking had been badly botched, the pirates conceded and said they wanted to get away from the ship and back to shore as soon as possible. With their skiff gone, Phillips offered the ship's lifeboat, a red-orange, rigid-hulled craft. As part of the deal, the pirates could take the ship's cash—a stash of some thirty thousand dollars—and agreed to exchange Phillips for Musi.[24] It had been nearly twelve hours since the hijacking began, and a deal had been struck. Victory seemed near. But for the deal to move forward, the lifeboat had to be lifted off the deck and dropped into the water. This required an electric winch, and the winch needed power. The crew agreed to abandon the safe room if it meant getting rid of the pirates. As the pirates waited, the *Maersk Alabama* slowly groaned back to life.

With their leader, Musi, back among them, the pirates took advantage of a moment when Phillips agreed to show the pirates how to operate the motor and other devices. Instead of letting Phillips join the now free crew, the pirates kept Phillips, thinking that if they couldn't ransom the ship, they could ransom Phillips. "I thought he was going to jump" from the lifeboat, Murphy said later.[25]

With Phillips as hostage, the pirates fired up the lifeboat engine and headed for the Somali coast. With Murphy now in command and Quinn at the helm, the *Maersk Alabama* followed the lifeboat closely. "I maneuvered the ship. I chased the lifeboat to get him even with the gangway, but it looked like they were headed for Somalia. I kept trying to cut them off with the ship," Quinn explained later, by steering the ship in front of the lifeboat to slow and divert it until help could arrive. "I was trying not to run over the lifeboat, but I kept it pretty close."[26]

Word Spreads

Once an attack or hijacking is reported, the information is relayed to shipping companies and the navies on patrol in the Gulf of Aden and the region. Among them were U.S. warships patrolling the Gulf of Aden as part of a multinational force. The nearest U.S. ship was a guided missile destroyer, the USS *Bainbridge*, which reversed course and headed back toward Somalia. The *Bainbridge* was about 345 miles away from the *Maersk Alabama*, a trip of ten to twelve hours at best. Ironically, an advisory had been issued that day warning merchant ships that pirates were now operating much further from shore than in the past. The *Maersk Alabama* became the sixth vessel to be hijacked that week.[27]

Although such hijackings had been going on for years, the stories had been largely ignored by the American news media. This was different. That an American ship had been taken made it a hometown story. Better yet, the crew had apparently recaptured it. The story went global, riding the uniquely American cowboy imagery and the defiant bravery of the crew in the face of despised banditry. In the early scramble to get the story, the jumble of information added to the mystery and excitement.

"The crew is back in control of the ship," a U.S. official said at midday, some twelve hours after the attack. "It's reported that one pirate is on board under crew control—the other three were trying to flee." Another U.S. official, citing an interagency conference call, told a news agency reporter: "Multiple reliable sources are now reporting that the *Maersk Alabama* is now under control of the U.S. crew. The crew reportedly has one pirate in custody. The status of others is unclear."[28]

As reporters raced to find relatives of the now free sailors for comments, they swarmed into Underhill, Vermont, where Andrea Phillips, the wife of Captain Phillips, clutched a photo of her husband on her farmhouse porch. Her husband had sailed the Gulf of Aden "for quite some time," she said, so becoming a victim of piracy was "inevitable."[29] Even so, the family closely monitored television news and fielded telephone calls from the U.S. State Department. "We are on pins and needles," said Andrea Phillips's half sister, Gina Coggio, twenty-nine, who talked with reporters as a light snow fell. "I know the crew has been in touch with their own family members, and we're hoping we'll hear from Richard soon." Explaining how and why Richard was with the pirates, she said he had surrendered himself to keep the crew safe. "What I understand is that he offered himself as the hostage. That is what he would do. It's just who he is and his response as a captain."[30]

Meanwhile, the United States scrambled. The White House was notified and newly elected president Barack Obama was briefed. Strangely, this highly unpredictable event became the president's first test of military decisiveness as the new commander in chief of the world's most powerful military. While U.S. naval ships sped to the scene and Navy SEALs were alerted, an FBI team of negotiators was assembled.

The USS *Bainbridge* reached the *Maersk Alabama* in the dark hours of Thursday morning, roughly twenty hours after the hijacking, and found the crew safely aboard the ship with Murphy in command. Phillips was with the pirates steadily motoring to Somalia. Although armed guards from the *Bainbridge* boarded the *Maersk Alabama*, there was little they could do to help Phillips. As dawn broke over the sea some hours later, a U.S. Navy surveillance aircraft circled the scene and recorded it on video.

Back in the United States, FBI spokesman Richard Kolko said the agency's hostage negotiating team was "fully engaged," although the situation was at a standoff. There was little to do but wait and watch, which was exactly what the navy did. *Maersk* company spokesman Kevin Speers, meanwhile, told journalists in the United States that the pirates had made no demands but were in the lifeboat with Phillips. "The boat is dead in the water. It's floating near the *Alabama*. It's my understanding that it's floating freely."[31]

The drama surrounding the hijacking of the *Maersk Alabama* was also news in Somalia. Somali Foreign Minister Mohamed Omaar, part of the U.S.-backed Transitional Federal Government, told a news agency reporter that the pirates could not win against U.S. forces. Though his government was barricaded in a corner of the Somali capital of Mogadishu and fighting daily for survival against Muslim extremists, Omaar said the pirates were doomed. "The pirates are playing with fire and have got themselves into a situation where they have to extricate themselves because there is no way they can win."[32]

With the situation on the water at a standstill, a call was placed to the bridge of the *Maersk Alabama*, and it was revealed that the ship was now headed to its original port of call, Mombasa, Kenya. "We're moving," a reporter was told.[33] Although the crew was extremely reluctant to abandon Captain Phillips, there was little that it could do to help. The USS *Bainbridge* was trailing the lifeboat and communicating with the pirates, and two other ships were soon to arrive: the USS *Halyburton*, a guided missile frigate, and the USS *Boxer*, an amphibious assault ship. Additional lethal "assets," as they're called in military-speak, specifically navy snipers, were also coming. The best thing the *Maersk Alabama* crew could do was clear out. For the family and friends of the crew back in the United States, the ship's departure from the scene was good news. "From the standpoint of the families, we're ecstatic," said Murphy's father, Joseph. "The families, the crew themselves have been under a lot of stress."[34] But for the Phillips family, there was no such relief.

From the bridge of the USS *Bainbridge*, negotiations grew increasingly tense as the pirates renewed their threats to kill the captain unless they got two million dollars, a figure the pirates probably had in mind when they tried to hijack the ship. Although such ransom amounts have become routine as shipowners and insurers pay dearly for the release of their ships, this situation was wildly different. The pirates were dealing with a military force that had no authorization or intent to pay a ransom. The military wanted Phillips back alive and would use whatever force was necessary. For the time being, however, the standoff continued as four pirates armed with AK-47s and one hostage held the world's most powerful navy at bay.[35]

Nerves frayed as the U.S. warships trailed the lifeboat with resolve. Finally, around 2:00 A.M. Friday, something unexpected happened. The pirates' attention waned as three of them dozed, Phillips explained later. When another relieved himself over the side, Phillips took that rare moment to escape. He dove into the water and began stroking toward the ship. But the splash alerted the pirates, who fired at Phillips, forcing him to give up. The pirates pulled him aboard, beat him, and tied him up.

Unfortunately, the navy had no warning that Phillips was going to jump. If it had, SEALs could have been prepared to grab him and possibly sink or capture the lifeboat with the pirates aboard. Despite Phillip's failed escape attempt, his jump into the sea sent a message that was heard at the White House. Phillips wanted out of the situation, and the pirates were clearly prepared to shoot him. Phillips's jump was enough to convince President Obama that stronger measures needed to be taken.[36] Senior members of the National Security Council then met in the White House Situation Room and pored over options. Obama issued what was apparently his first order authorizing the use of lethal force.[37]

Yet the White House still hoped for a nonviolent end to the standoff, a senior military official explained later. "The president wanted the opportunity to say, 'Have we tried everything to make this reach a peaceful conclusion?' He wanted to be a check valve so that everybody was looking at all options."[38] The ability to use lethal force in the situation did not materialize, in reality, until a contingent of SEALs parachuted into the water near the *Bainbridge* at 5:10 A.M. Saturday. A second group arrived some twelve hours later.[39]

After three full days at sea, the situation with Phillips and the pirates reached a critical juncture as the Somali coast loomed beyond the horizon. It meant that the pirates, already armed with cellular phones, were coming within calling distance of their comrades on shore. Once in contact, their pirate colleagues and bosses could reinforce and resupply the pirates, escalating the situation and virtually negating any chance to rescue Phillips. Mayhem was in the offing. One of the U.S. ships tried to stop the lifeboat by spraying it with high pressure fire hoses to force it back out to the sea. At a minimum, the United States hoped the pirates would be forced to throttle up the engine and consume more of their dwindling fuel.

When the hosing failed, the navy launched a Seahawk helicopter that settled over the sea in front of the motoring lifeboat. The Seahawk's powerful rotors created a downdraft that stopped the lifeboat in the frothy water. But the pirates did not give up. They nosed the lifeboat in a new direction and tried to continue their run to the coast. But each time they moved, the Seahawk moved with it and held it back. This cat-and-mouse game continued for nearly a half hour until the pirates simply gave up. Frustrated, one of the pirates popped out of the lifeboat's front hatch and shot at the USS *Halyburton* with his AK-47. The navy didn't return fire, however, and the scene grew quiet as the lifeboat sat in the water.[40]

Now on board the *Bainbridge,* navy snipers positioned themselves and the SEALs readied their inflatable craft should they need to get to the lifeboat quickly. Unaware of the fate that awaited them, the pirates repeatedly exposed themselves, but the snipers held back. No action was to be taken unless Phillips was in immediate danger. The preferred goal was to convince the pirates to surrender and hand over Phillips.[41]

As Saturday faded into night, worries increased that the standoff, already in the fourth day, would continue. Spirits began to sag until a breakthrough came at dawn Sunday morning. The wounded pirate leader, Musi, called the ship and said he wanted to make a deal. The lifeboat was out of food and water, he said, and needed to be resupplied if Phillips was to live. And, Musi complained, the stab wound in his hand from four days earlier had become infected.[42] A SEAL team climbed into an inflatable boat and delivered the food and water, collected Musi, and returned to the ship. Musi was given clean clothes, and his wound was treated. It was a move calculated to convince the others to surrender. "Let's show these guys we are serious about the fact that if you give yourself up you won't be harmed," a military official explained. But, he later confessed, "It didn't have the effect we had hoped."[43]

Now on the *Bainbridge*, Musi tried to convince his fellow pirates to release Phillips. Promises were made, and Musi urged them to give up. But the remaining pirates refused, and negotiators feared that the pirates were becoming dangerously desperate. In fact, they were.[44]

Sunday dawned, and as the day warmed, another break developed for the rescuers. The wind picked up and the seas grew rough, setting in motion a series of events that would end the standoff in a way few imagined. The sea began to toss the now powerless lifeboat mercilessly, forcing the pirates back on the radio. The pirates agreed to let the *Bainbridge* tow them to presumably calmer water. It was a ruse that left the pirates thinking they might actually be able to complete their kidnapping of the captain. In reality, the thoroughly exhausted pirates had little idea what was happening.

Initially the pirates were at a distance of about two hundred feet from the fantail of the *Bainbridge*, which was the full length of the tow rope. But since the boat continued to bounce on the choppy waters, the pirates were hauled closer to the ship until the lifeboat was within about seventy-five feet of the fantail and riding calmly in the destroyer's wake.[45] This gave the snipers an unobstructed shot. "From that range," a military official said later, "they've got a fairly good margin of error." Another senior military official added, "Bringing them in closer gave them a smoother ride," which meant "the shot would have greater potential for success."[46]

Perhaps realizing the predicament and feeling powerless to change things, one of the pirates started yelling at Phillips. Negotiators on board the *Bainbridge* could hear the tension in the pirates' voices as they became more agitated. Then "they broke off the last communication," a senior military official said later. "And, again, they said, 'If we don't get what we are demanding, we will kill the captain.'"[47] It was a threat the negotiators had heard before, but the pirates were desperate, and darkness was descending.

Another long night loomed. The snipers were ready, having followed the pirates' every move in the small cabin. Phillips remained seated in the lifeboat's cabin, where, despite the close quarters, he was out of the line of fire. Two of the pirates were clearly visible in the windows of the lifeboat. But the third was elusive until he pushed open a side window and leaned his head out to get a breath of fresh air. It proved to be his last. One of the pirates then fired his gun, apparently by accident. Convinced that Phillips was about to die, the order was given to shoot. On a simultaneous count, the snipers squeezed the triggers. Three pirates were dead.

Within minutes, rescuers climbed aboard the lifeboat and grabbed Captain Phillips, ending a crisis that had captured the attention of the world. Phillips was immediately taken aboard the *Bainbridge*, given a thorough medical exam, and found to be in good condition for a fifty-three-year-old seafarer who has just survived a four-day ordeal. He called his wife, Andrea, and their two college-aged children at home, where outside dozens of yellow ribbons fluttered on a white picket fence and two small American flags waved on the lawn. He also spoke with President Obama. Thankful to be alive, Phillips praised his rescuers: "The real heroes are the navy, the SEALs, those who have brought me home."[48]

Phillips was taken to the USS *Boxer*, which headed south along the Somali coast, and arrangements were made for his return to Vermont.[49] When news of the rescue reached the crew of the *Maersk Alabama* in Mombasa, Kenya, whoops and shouts filled the air.

President Obama was briefed on the crisis at least eighteen times during the ordeal, including a National Security Council session on "hostage contingencies" just hours before the snipers took their shots.[50] When Phillips was freed, the White House quickly responded. "I share the country's admiration for the bravery of Captain Phillips and his selfless concern for his crew," President Obama said in a statement. "His courage is a model for all Americans."

The next day, Obama vowed to fight the plague of piracy off Somalia. "I want to be very clear that we are resolved to halt the rise of [piracy] in that region. We have to continue to be prepared to confront them when they arise. And we have to ensure that those who commit acts of piracy are held accountable for their crimes." But even as Obama's statements were broadcast, the prospect of million-dollar ransoms had spawned a new and lucrative industry populated not only by the pirates and their organizers and backers, but by a host of people who assisted in the negotiations and delivered aerial ransom payments. Calls were surging to security agencies that provided costly marine safety and training, despite claims by international law enforcement agencies that they were organizing to combat what one official said was "a level of organization to these pirates."[51]

Was piracy already out of control? As official statements were being issued, I made arrangements to go to East Africa to find the pirates of Somalia.

2

PIRATES AND PRISONS

THE DIMINUTIVE Somali with a pronounced overbite grinned in the glare of camera lights. A bandaged left hand cuffed and chained to his right, he wore blue prison coveralls as he was hustled along a New York sidewalk on a drizzly night in April 2009 by a phalanx of police officers. At just five feet two inches, with a slight and compact frame, Abdiwali Abdiqadir Musi did not cut the imposing figure of a pirate capable of stopping the *Maersk Alabama*, a behemoth of the world's waterways. Yet Musi maintained a smile as he was to become the first man in the United States to be tried for piracy since 1885.[1]

In federal court in the Southern District of New York, Musi faced ten counts of crimes prosecutors pulled off the shelves of moldering maritime law. Leading the list was "piracy under the law of nations," but there were many others: seizing a ship by force, hostage taking, kidnapping, and possession of weapons, as well as conspiracy to commit these crimes. Eight of the ten counts carried a maximum sentence of life in prison. Three of the counts carried a *minimum* sentence of thirty years. "From the deck of the *Maersk Alabama*, Musi fired his gun at the captain who was still in the bridge," alleged the federal complaint based on statements from FBI agent Steven E. Sorrells. Once on the ship's bridge, Musi "conducted himself as the leader of the pirates," the complaint said. As Captain Phillips was held hostage for four days, Musi bragged that he had hijacked other ships, Sorrells alleged. Given the wealth of evidence and likely willingness of the crew of the *Maersk Alabama* to testify against him, including the celebrated Captain Phillips, chances that young Musi would walk were slim.

When Musi appeared in a crowded New York federal courtroom in April 2009, he knew enough English to follow the proceedings, telling the judge that he was aware he had been appointed legal representation: "I understand. I don't have any money."[2] But the former gun-toting tough guy sobbed when his lawyers explained that only recently had he spoken to his family in Somalia. Defense attorneys depicted Musi as a frightened juvenile, not the violent criminal leader that federal prosecutors wanted to convict. "As you can tell, he's extremely young, injured, and terrified," lawyer Deirdre von Dornum told the court. "What we have is a confused teenager, overnight thrown into the highest level of the criminal justice system in the United States out of a country where there's no law at all," said Omar Jamal, executive director of Somali Justice Advocacy Center in Minneapolis, who had spoken with Musi's family during the *Maersk Alabama* standoff.[3]

The oldest of twelve children, Musi is the son of a woman who survives on a couple of dollars a day earned by selling milk in a local market in Galkayo, a sprawling, dusty town in central Somalia. Musi's father tends camels, cows, and goats that nibble the sparse vegetation of the arid, windswept highlands. They "don't have any money," explained Jamal. "The father goes outside with the livestock and comes home at night. The father said they don't have any money, they are broke." Although his mother sells milk most days, it takes a month to save the six dollars required for her son to attend school, Jamal said. She also needs to pay fifteen dollars a month for house rent.[4]

Expectedly, Musi's forty-year-old mother, Adar Abdirahman Hassan, was horrified when she learned that her son was in a New York jail. "I cried when I saw the picture of him," she told a reporter. "Relatives brought a copy of the picture to me. Surely he is telling himself now, 'My mother's heart is broken.'" She offered no explanation for her son's turn to piracy, except to say, "A young man, at his age, could say he needed money, perhaps. I used to give him his school fees because I could not afford more than that. But of course he needed money."[5] The boy's father, Abdiqadir Musi, was convinced that his son was lured into piracy. "He just went with them without knowing what he was getting into," the father said. It must have been his son's first outing with the pirates, he said, because Musi had left home only a week and a half before he surrendered at sea to U.S. officials.[6] Hassan described her son as "wise beyond his years," a studious child who passed on sports and preferred books. "The last time I saw him he was in his school uniform," Musi's mother said. "He took all his books the day he disappeared, except one, I think, and did not come back. He was brainwashed. People who are older than him outwitted him, people who are older than him duped him."[7]

Musi and his family live a life that few in the developed world can comprehend. Since much of Somalia struggles with scorching heat most of the year, farming in the sandy grit and gravel is virtually impossible. Sanitation and running water do not exist outside of a few major urban areas. One of every four Somali children dies before the age of five. Organized society in Somalia disappeared nearly two decades ago, leaving each community to govern itself as it saw fit, meaning that whoever carried a gun was the law. Musi's generation has never known a society governed by law, and what little order does exist is based on family, clan, and tribe. Musi's hometown of Galkayo is 450 miles north of the coastal capital of Mogadishu and part of the semiautonomous region of Puntland. Though Galkayo is far inland from the Somali coast, about 125 miles, Puntland is home to the vast majority of pirates and their leaders, organizers, and investors. That Musi would link up with pirates, given the grim future that he faced, is not surprising.

Ever since the early 1990s, Galkayo has been flooded with refugees fleeing the internecine violence that has wracked southern Somalia. In late 2006 and early 2007, Galkayo was again deluged by refugees from the south, swelling total refugee numbers beyond thirty-five thousand, creating yet another minor humanitarian crisis in the region.[8] The refugees there live a squalid existence in some fourteen refugee settlements surrounding Galkayo, where families cower from the pounding sun inside dome-shaped huts of sticks wrapped in white UN plastic tarps and scraps of fabric, creating a sea of desert igloos. Most scavenge in the streets and live with limited latrines, washing facilities, and potable water. Women beg in order to survive, or roam the sparse desert for scraps of firewood far from the settlements—a task that subjects them to rape, theft, and brutality.

Musi had it better than most. He studied English and was a fan of a dusty, outdoor cinema that he frequented after school, transfixed by the swirling dancers and singers in Bollywood dramas dubbed into his native Somali. His mother insisted that Musi was only sixteen, a claim dismissed early by a U.S. judge who ruled that Musi was least eighteen and would stand trial as an adult. Musi's mother admitted she had no birth records, because like most Somalis, "I never delivered my babies in a hospital."[9] A former classmate of Musi, however, supported what the judge had ruled: "I think he was one or two years older than me, and I am sixteen," said Abdisalan Muse. "We did not know him to be a pirate, but he was always with older boys, who are likely to be the ones who corrupted him."[10]

As his mother suggested, Musi may have been motivated by money. The first man to climb aboard a hijacked ship is known as the jumper and is paid a premium for the risk, according to an experienced Somali pirate negotiator. "That guy doing the jumping, he gets five thousand dollars extra because he's taken the risk of getting hit by anything coming from the crew. And it's something good for his CV, to show to other investors."[11] It is not surprising that Musi and his accomplices were ecstatic when they learned that the *Maersk Alabama* and crew were American. They'd hit the jackpot. "He was surprised he was on a U.S. ship. He kept asking, 'You all come from America?' Then he claps and cheers and smiles. He caught himself a big fish. He can't believe it," crew member Zahid Reza recalled.[12] When Musi confessed to Reza that he had always wanted to go to America, the irony was not overlooked. "His dreams came true, but he comes to the United States not as a visitor but as a prisoner," Reza said.[13]

On May 18, 2010, Musi pleaded guilty in the New York court to hijacking, kidnapping, and hostage taking. He reportedly faced more than thirty years in prison and was scheduled to be sentenced in October 2010.

Into Somaliland

SOMALILAND IS an independent, breakaway region of northwestern Somalia that remains unrecognized by the international community. A former British protectorate, it operates under a relatively stable and democratically elected government. To get there, I fly from Nairobi to the small republic of Djibouti, itself an independent, ethnic Somali enclave, where I can catch a short direct flight to the Somaliland capital of Hargeisa. On the morning of my departure from Djibouti, I climb into one of the many battered green and white taxis that ply Djibouti's sun-baked streets. Though I'm anxious to get to the Djibouti airport, the driver pauses at the gate, where a security guard tosses a used tire into the trunk, then waves us on. There is no such thing as a direct route in Africa. Going anywhere involves a stop or two, with people and cargo to be picked up and dropped off, especially if there's a paying customer inside.

Minutes later, we're caught in a snarl of traffic at an international school patronized by expats and well-to-do Djiboutis. We nose our way into the tangle of shiny SUVs driven by parents frantic to get a child or two to the school before the bell. They mutter, gesture, and slap their foreheads as a couple of Djibouti policemen blow whistles to manage the mayhem. Beside me, a wild-eyed woman pounds her steering wheel and shouts, "*Passé! Passé!*" French being the dominant language. This kind of anxiety, I muse, must be punishment for a privileged lifestyle in the midst of poverty.

At the airport, I'm the only one at the Daallo Airline check-in counter, a portable plywood desk painted white that fronts a rumbling baggage conveyor. I reluctantly hand over my bag when the agent, a plump young woman shrouded in a silky orange scarf, tells me that I must. After a customs officer flips through my passport, closely inspecting each page, he stamps my passport and sends me on with a flick of the wrist. At the top of curving stairs is a dingy and cavernous waiting room where a sign on the wall reads NO KHAT, with a red circle and slash imposed on a bundle of stems and leaves. I glance around the room. Not a chew in sight. Several Somalis are sprawled across hard plastic seats, fast asleep. Others talk or sullenly stare into the glaring sunlight on the cracked tarmac. On the far side of the airport, U.S. air force cargo planes and helicopters are hunkered down while fighter jets sporadically scream along the runway and rise into the hot air.

I delve into a paperback novel, trying not to think about how late this plane is going to be. The flight was supposed to leave at 8:30, but when 8:30 comes and goes, as does 9:00 and 9:15, no one seems to mind. Finally the woman from the check-in counter appears and barks, "Galkayo, Hargeisa," then begins to collect boarding passes. It is approaching 10:00 A.M. when we climb into a prop-engine Russian Illyushin II-18 aircraft, better suited for goats than humans. Most seats are broken and covered with stained, worn fabric, shiny with use. When the door is slammed shut, we sit on the runway for what seems an eternity as the temperature inside the plane soars. Sweat oozes, forcing passengers to shed jackets, making shirts stick and covered Muslim women frantically fan themselves. Eventually the hulking aircraft rolls and lifts off, and once airborne, a small trickle of cool air moves through the cabin.

As the plane taxis to a stop in Hargeisa and the doors are flung open, I hungrily inhale a refreshing blast of cool air. As I wait to deplane, one of the Russian pilots, wearing worn orange coveralls, barks at a passenger slumped in his seat with his feet sprawled on the collapsed backrest in front of him. The pilot says that the seat, when flat, is to be used for eating, not a footrest. The passenger rolls his eyes. I glance at the grimy, threadbare carpet and food-splattered walls, and I marvel at the Russian sense of humor.

I'm greeted by Yassin, a portly man with gold teeth and mirrored aviator-style sunglasses who has been helping me make arrangements. We shake hands, and he asks for my passport and seventy dollars. I hesitate. "Don't worry," he says. "The twenty dollars is for the visa, which I will get for you, and the fifty dollars you must change into Somali money. You will need it." We plunge into the cacophony of the cramped passport control, where Yassin bulls to the front of the line and returns with my passport stamped and three fat bundles of crisp Somaliland currency. He explains that the exchange rate is 6,300 Somaliland shillings to the dollar, and the denominations are all five-hundred–shilling notes.

Early the next morning, I'm picked up at my hotel by my translator, Mohamed British, so named because his father was British. He's a product of this former British colony. I climb into a gleaming Toyota Land Cruiser with a driver and an armed guard—a necessity for traveling anywhere in Somalia, including Somaliland—and we rumble down dusty dirt roads flanked by plastered security walls topped with glittering shards of glass, sturdy protective barriers for homes of the well-to-do and many government offices. We stop at a metal gate, where an armed guard eyes us suspiciously, then lets us into a chalky dirt compound. We park in the shade of a spindly tree. I follow British into the dark recesses of a low-slung building and am quickly ushered into the office of the Justice Minister, Ahmed Hasan Aki, who reviews my request to visit the Somaliland pirate prison with deep concern. After a few long moments, he leans back in his black chair and tells me that I'm more than welcome to visit the prison and talk to pirates.

Piracy is on the wane, he says, not because of the annual monsoon winds whipping up the seas at this time of year, but because of the NATO naval patrols. Somaliland's coast guard also is clamping down on piracy, he says, despite a desperate lack of equipment and patrol boats. He ticks off the needs: more boats, more facilities, more observation posts, more communication equipment, better training, and more courts, prosecutors, and jails. I offer my most sympathetic smile. The tenuous political situation in Somaliland is not exactly conducive to an influx of military aid, I suggest. Yes, he concedes, Somaliland elections have been delayed three times this year. "Power sharing is not working well," he says, a delicate balancing act between the state's three official parties. The election postponements have been caused by the lack of a valid voter list, he says. "People here are nomadic. They are not settled. We are a tribal society, and each tribe tries to overtake the other." For a wad of cash, election officials will produce voter cards, stacks of which are handed out to cooperative tribal members for use on election day. The system has to be scrubbed clean or, better yet, scrapped, he suggests.

While Somaliland dithers with voter lists, extremists are waging war in southern Somalia, I point out. Is Somaliland ripe for similar chaos? He nods reluctantly. "If they get a victory in the south," he says of the militant Islamist group al-Shabaab, "they will be here. If they're defeated, they won't. They will be here if they get the upper hand." The situation in southern Somalia is more urgent than most suspect, he says.

The Reluctant Pirate

After leaving the justice minister, we angle out of Hargeisa, passing through sprawling markets that crowd the road, and wide intersections marked by profusions of thick blade cactus sprouting with purple pears. We trail brightly painted buses spewing clouds of black diesel smoke, rocking from side to side as they negotiate the rough roads. A desolate expanse of scrub and stunted trees greets us at the edge of town, reminding me of the Sonoran Desert of northern Mexico. Herds of white goats roam the brush, some rising on hind legs to paw branches for a bite of succulent leaves. Clusters of camels meander, barely turning their heads as we speed past. In the distance, dark and barren hills rise from the desert floor of this antediluvian land.

As we settle into the drive to find the Madheera prison, my driver, Ismail Abdullahi Ibrihim, tells me that his oldest and closest friend is in the prison, serving a fifteen-year sentence for piracy. I say jokingly that Ismail, too, must be a pirate. He smiles and nods, proudly telling me he was one of the first. Finding pirates and getting them to talk, I have been told, has become difficult despite the growing number of convicted pirates. Somali clan lords have ordered convicted pirates not to talk, fearing that their murky network of piracy will be revealed. Yet here is Ismail, who has not been accused or convicted, and a ready raconteur.

Life's prospects were good in 1988, Ismail explains, when he left his home in Hargeisa to attend university in Mogadishu, intent on becoming a doctor. But not long after he arrived in the Somali capital, the smoldering civil war in northern Somalia between the army of former president Siad Barre and the Somalia Liberation Movement intensified, forcing Ismail's family into neighboring Ethiopia. He lost relatives in the fighting, he recalls, as well as what money the family once had for his education. Stranded, Ismail enrolled in a German-sponsored fishing management program that took him to the southern Somali coastal town of Kismayo. He was joined in this program by his best friend, Rashid, one year his junior. Though the training focused on freshwater fishing in the Jubba River, he and Rashid took their newfound knowledge to the sea. Securing a boat with the help of funds from family and friends, Ismail and Rashid hunted sharks in 1989, a lucrative business because of the high price for shark fins, highly prized by East Asians for shark fin soup. "We worked together, and we got a lot of money to feed our family in Ethiopia," he says.

After two years, Ismail had saved enough money to leave Mogadishu when the Barre regime was toppled, and he traveled to Ethiopia to join his family. Shortly after, Somaliland proclaimed its independence, allowing Ismail's family to return to Hargeisa. Soon he was back at sea and again teamed up with Rashid. He grins as he describes the abundance of fish along the Somaliland coast. Every day they went out, "the nets became full," he says. "We worked together. We ate together. If he had a cup of tea, I had half of it." The money they earned from fishing went to rebuilding the houses destroyed by the civil war, he says.

But their fortunes began to wane when Ismail and Rashid encountered fishermen from Yemen, which is little more than 110 nautical miles directly north, who regularly crossed the Gulf of Aden and dropped their nets in the Somali coastal waters. "In 1992 we saw Yemeni boats," he says. "At that time we had arms, three guns, so we could defend ourselves. Our aim was not to attack any other persons but only to defend ourselves." Boats were arriving from all over the world, he says, as word spread of the abundant marine life and unfettered access due to the breakdown of organized government in Somalia. Their catches dwindled. "They collected our animals from the seas," he says. "When we tried to fish, we didn't get anything. We became very angry. Everyone was coming. Where can we get our fish? So we decided to attack the Yemenis."

Their first act of piracy was to capture five fishing boats at gunpoint, Ismail says, keeping four that they brought back to shore in Berbera. The fifth boat was sent back with a message for the Yemeni fishermen. Ismail and Rashid stripped two Yemeni fishermen down, coated them with dark motor oil, and told them to leave. "The white men became black men," he says with a wide grin. "I saw it and I was very happy." As Ismail tells me this, I recall a conversation just a day earlier with a former government Somaliland cabinet official who complained that the Arab world, of which Yemen is considered a part, looked down on Somalis, considering them to have been diluted with African blood and therefore not Arab. While the physical distinctions are elusive to the casual observer, the undercurrent of racial and ethnic animosity runs strong and deep.

Such early acts of piracy did little to improve things, Ismail says. "The production was very weak. We didn't get enough sharks or fish." Their typical routine was to place the nets at sea in the afternoon or evening and either stay at sea or return to shore for the night, retrieving the nets and fish early the next morning for market. Far too often, their nets would disappear. Suspecting that the nets were being stolen, fish and all, or simply cut loose from the floats and let sink, they became desperate. "We stopped our work because we [didn't] have nets." Unwilling to give up, they sought sponsors. Only a couple of local businessmen agreed to advance them money, but it was enough to stay in business. Yet illegal fishing increased, he says. "We decided to attack."

Their first big foreign target was a German fishing trawler, he says, which he and Rashid were convinced had taken their nets. They attacked the trawler with guns blazing. "We shoot and shoot," he says, and they forced the trawler to stop. They confronted the captain, accusing him of illegally fishing in Somalia's coastal waters. The captain promised to pay them fifty thousand dollars if they would let him keep fishing there, pleading with Ismail and Rashid to release him so he could get the money. "We refused," Ismail says proudly. "Our aim [was] to make them stop. We [were] the first ones to take a ship." This particular vessel was doing more than fishing. While it had nearly three tons of fish, Ismail says, it was also loaded with motorcycles and heavy ropes, very useful in shipping and at ports. "I refused the money and told him to go into the port." Back in the port of Berbera, Ismail rounded up the local fishermen and told them to take the fish from the ship and sell the entire catch, saying, "These fish are mine." The port manager took the situation a step further, he says, and told the community to strip the ship of its cargo, which it did, and soon the motorcycles and rope were gone. "[The port manager] told them never to come back to our sea" and let the empty German trawler go.

Some three or four months passed, Ismail recalls, before he and Rashid encountered their Somali neighbors from Puntland. After sleeping at sea one night, a practice necessary to protect their nets, they spotted a fishing trawler. "They came to hunt sharks here," he says of the Puntland fishermen. Ismail and Rashid began shooting, so the Puntland fishermen returned fire. But Ismail and Rashid had three guns, he says, while the Puntlanders only had one. They captured the Puntland fishing boat and forced the fishermen to swim to shore, then hauled the boat to Berbera and called the owners in Puntland. "It was a big boat," he says, but as a point of honor, neither the boat nor the fish in it were touched. When the owners arrived, Ismail told them they could leave peacefully, but the next time they might not.

Despite their increasingly aggressive attacks on fishing boats, Ismail says, they could not slow the plunder of Somali coastal waters. "Many big fishing boats came. When we attacked, they just continued. I became very angry. If there is no government to control fishing, I was going to kill someone. But I preferred to leave." In 2001 he quit fishing altogether. It was not worth the effort, he says. From being able to collect three tons of fish in just a couple of hours, his marine harvest had dropped to about half a ton per week, he says.

Ismail is now a driver and works primarily for the United Nations. "Now I am in the city and I am happy," he says. He no longer feels like he is fighting a losing battle. In retrospect, Ismail would have done nothing differently. "What would you think if someone came to your house and wanted to take things?" he asks. "You're going to fight. That's it." Instead of being victims of illegal fishing, he says, "it is better to hunt." He has sympathy for the pirates who are now attacking large cargo ships, he says. "I like the pirates."

The Pirate of Madheera

THE MADHEERA prison in Somaliland is a rugged stone structure just a short drive off the paved road connecting the Somaliland capital of Hargeisa and the port town of Berbera. The prison holds some fifty convicted pirates, each serving a sentence of fifteen to twenty years. Here is where I meet convicted pirate Farah Ismail Eidle, a lithe man of thirty-eight, with darting dark eyes and a quick smile that reveals darkly stained teeth, many of which have rotted away, leaving only jagged points, due to a lifetime of chewing khat leaves. Khat is plentiful in Somaliland, as common as a cup of tea, and is one of the few pleasures, along with cigarettes, found in prison. We sit in the prison warden's office, a simple room with a concrete floor, a few straight-backed chairs, and a bench along one wall where Eidle hikes a leg up, around which he folds his Somali skirtlike wrap favored by men.

"It's difficult to see the sun," Eidle says, when I ask about life in prison. He explains that he was born not far from Madheera, though he has lived much of his life in other parts of Somalia, mostly in Puntland. I tell him he's come home but unfortunately is living on the wrong side of the prison wall. He laughs and shakes his head, saying he has been denied justice and wrongly convicted. "If I went to an international court, I would be innocent."

Though born just thirty miles from Berbera, Eidle learned to fish in Mogadishu and became a boat mechanic. After the collapse of the Siad Barre regime, he moved to Bosasso in 1995 to pursue fishing, leaving behind a small family, he says, a Somali woman born in Kenya, who bore him a son, now fourteen. He then migrated to the coastal town of Eyl, southeast of Bosasso, where the fishing was good and where he made "good money" from 1996 to 2004, eventually accumulating three fishing boats and a crew of twenty-four fishermen. Fishing is seasonal, he explains, and he could make from two thousand to ten thousand dollars a month, depending on the kind of fish. Most of his catch was shipped to Dubai. The more time he spent at sea, however, the more he encountered foreign fishing trawlers dragging their nets through Somali waters, he says. "During this time, there were big trawlers taking our fish illegally," and occasionally he would lose fishing nets and the fish they had caught. "Before that, I was just hearing of the complaints."

When the infamous Christmas tsunami of 2004 rolled across the Indian Ocean from Indonesia and slammed into the Somali coast, Eidle was one of the victims. His ships were among the 117 destroyed by the tidal wave, and it knocked him out of the fishing business for a while. A stroke of luck sent him back to sea, he says, when he won a United Nations lottery that gave away eight boats to fisherman who had lost their craft to the tsunami. It was a new, seven-meter-long boat, he says, but when he resumed fishing, "nothing was there." He and his friends were starving. "We were there like refugees waiting for something to eat." He quit the business, vowing, "I'll not be a refugee." He resorted to piracy, he says, out of frustration and desperation after trying to alert international news organizations to the plight of the Somali fishermen. "Nobody was hearing us," he says, so "we decided to attack the ships entering our waters illegally." At first the Somalis only wanted to scare the trawlers. But their attacks became more serious when the Somalis started to lose their fishing boats, he says, and soon they were hijacking foreign trawlers and collecting fees and ransoms. "We were hoping the international community would do something," he says, but nothing happened.

Although Eidle will sit in the Madheera prison for the next fourteen years, having begun his fifteen-year sentence in September 2008, he never successfully hijacked a large cargo ship. "As a sea pirate, I did many tries to hijack a ship but didn't succeed." He had hoped to hijack a tourist ship, which he says could have netted him fifty million dollars from all the money and jewelry he thought he could have taken from the cruise ship passengers. Motivated by the dream of millions of U.S. dollars, Eidle considers himself an entrepreneur of the uniquely Somali mold. In his first attack, Eidle's skiff bounced and splashed through rough surf only to be outrun as the churning propellers of a powerful cargo ship left him in the wake. "I became angry," he says, and he bought a bigger engine. Again he sped to sea, his hand firmly on the throttle as the skiff sliced through the surf. Brandishing AK-47s at an apprehensive captain and crew, perhaps even firing off a few shots, Eidle and his crew pulled alongside a bulky freighter. But when they realized their ladder was too short, they could only bemoan their fate. They were left to drift at sea for two days and nights as ocean tankers and cargo ships rumbled through the shipping lanes, any one of which could have crushed their small craft.[14]

The crew made it back to port, and after launching his first two attempts from the coast of Puntland, Eidle decided to try his luck closer to home and to the shipping lanes, preparing for his third attack from Berbera. But word spread in town that outsiders had arrived with weapons. In an early-morning raid, Eidle and his crew were taken into custody by the Somaliland coast guard and charged with piracy. The arrest included Ismail's old friend, Rashid, who says he was accused of being one of the pirates but in fact had only rented a room to Eidle and his crew. Eidle confirms that those captured by the Somaliland authorities were not involved in his plans and that he was able to warn most of his crew to run. "Those who were arrested were innocent."

While Eidle calls himself unlucky, he's proud that he was able to mount an assault by himself, financing his failed piracy by selling a fishing boat to buy a speedboat, guns, and satellite phones, depleting his earnings from a dozen years of fishing. He was too eager, he says. "We were not experienced at the time." Does he have regrets? He shakes his head, saying he would do it again because "there's nothing else to do." The Somali fishing waters are depleted, and even if he swore off piracy, it would have little effect on the overall problem. "If I stop, it's nothing."

I am curious as to why he, among the nearly fifty convicted pirates in the prison, is so willing to talk. "I'm talking for the fishing community," he says. What would it take to convince the fishing community to stop the piracy? "Give us compensation for what was destroyed," he says. When I suggest that it would be impossible to determine what was a legitimate claim and what was not, he says the international community should sit down with the fishing communities. "We should start talking to each other . . . and [try to] understand each other," he says.

The Lure of Success

Though Abdiwali Abdiqadir Musi was the sole Somali pirate in U.S. custody at the time, he was not the only Somali pirate to encounter an unlucky twist of fate. Compared to some other Somali coastal prowlers, including his now dead accomplices, Musi was lucky. Take the hijackers of the *Sirius Star*, for example, the Saudi oil supertanker carrying crude oil valued at sixty million dollars that netted pirates a reported ransom of three million dollars in early 2009. For a few fleeting moments the hijacking caught the world's attention when news channels showed the ransom container dangling below a parachute as it dropped gently onto the deck. The footage reinforced the dream of all pirates past, present, and future: easy riches coming from a skiff, raw nerve, and a handful of weapons. Joy was premature for the *Sirius Star* hijackers, however. According to an account by the Somali-based news site Somaliweyn Media Center, the pirates were "singing in colorful tones and exchanging some ridiculous words" as their skiffs pounded the waves on their way to shore, hearts pounding with glee and pockets bulging with dollars. Strong winds had kicked up, creating dangerously choppy seas. Driving their boats at maximum speed for the beach, the delirious pirates hit a wave, lost control, and flipped. Five pirates disappeared into the water. Only four of the original nine pirates survived, but they also lost their money. Later, the body of one pirate reportedly was washed onto the shore with a bag containing more than $150,000 in cash. *Time* magazine reported, "Pastoralists traveling along the shore have slowly collected dollars floating on the surface of the sea, and some brought by the ebb tide to shore."[15]

Neither threat of death at sea nor jail terms of two decades has deterred enthusiasm for piracy in Somalia. Some 250 miles to the east of Berbera is the Puntland port city of Bosasso, said by many to be the capital of Somali piracy. Toward the end of 2008, the prosperity brought by piracy became clearly evident in the multistory houses springing up where tin-roofed shanties once sprawled in what is called New Bosasso. "These guys are making a killing," said Mohamud Muse Hirsi, the former president of Puntland. Hirsi is reputed to have ties to the piracy, a charge he has vigorously denied. "We are the leaders of this country. Everybody we suspect, we fire from work," he said of pirate collaborators in the government. Puntland had taken aggressive action against the pirates, he insisted, and he pointed to those in Bosasso's main jail.[16] Yet most knowledgeable observers disagreed with Hirsi. "Top Puntland officials benefit from piracy, even if they might not be instigating it," said Roger Middleton, a London-based expert on Somali piracy. "All significant political actors in Somalia are likely benefiting from piracy."[17]

Piracy is also attractive due to the trickle-down economic effect. A shopkeeper in the Puntland town of Garowe said that the pirates were good customers and spent money, well, like pirates. "If they see a good car that a guy is driving," he said, "they say, 'How much? If it's thirty grand, take forty and give me the key.'" Local merchants benefit when a ship is captured because the hostages have to be kept alive for a ransom to be paid. Sheep, goats, water, fuel, rice, spaghetti, milk, and cigarettes are provided by locals at exorbitant prices as hostage negotiations drag on, often for months.

There is glamour in being a pirate, especially a successful one. Some in Garowe admire the swagger of pirates who drive big cars, run many of the town's best businesses, and throw really good parties. This flash and cash has grabbed the attention of young people who have known only poverty and deprivation. "We have heard of the risks, but the profit is too great," said a former pirate in Garowe. "Even now, pirates are marrying the most beautiful ladies, with nonstop dancing at weddings that go a couple of days. Some pirates are even sending their girlfriends to hospitals abroad to give birth. Imagine that," he said.[18] Fatuma Abdul Kadir, twenty-one, bragged about attending a two-day pirate wedding in July 2008 with endless dancing, trays of goat meat, and a band from neighboring Djibouti. "It was wonderful," she said. "I'm now dating a pirate."[19]

3

CAULDRON OF CHAOS

IN THE white light of day on the northern Somali island of Hafun, a turbaned man trots along the sand in rubber sandals, dodging debris of rusted car parts, suitcases, and discarded clothes. It is early January 2005, just days after the Christmas tsunami of 2004 surged from western Indonesia across the Indian Ocean and into the Horn of Africa, striking four hundred miles of the central Somali coast. The debris that covered the beach at Hafun was swept from the bottom of the ocean by the tsunami and deposited by a wall of water that also killed three hundred people, demolished thousands of homes, clogged wells, and left an estimated one hundred thousand Somalis homeless and hungry. When the United Nation officials arrived, they wondered what most of the Somalis did: what was this stuff and where did it come from?

In 2006, the United Nations Environmental Program produced a 144-page report on the damage caused by the 2004 Christmas tsunami. With a coastline of 2,450 miles, where 55 percent of the population lives, Somalia figured prominently in the report.[1] As UN investigators sorted through the beach clutter at Hafun, it was obvious that this stuff was not from Somalia. This was the detritus of the western world, not a country like Somalia where people find a use for every scrap of metal and piece of cloth. Investigators concluded that the dumping off the Somali coast was neither new nor benign.

> Starting from the early 1980s and continuing into the civil war, the hazardous waste dumped along Somalia's coast comprised uranium radioactive waste, lead, cadmium, mercury, industrial, hospital, chemical, leather treatment and other toxic waste. Most of the waste was simply dumped on the beaches in containers and disposable leaking barrels which ranged from small to big tanks without regard to the health of the local population and any environmentally devastating impacts.[2]

> The effects were severe.

> The impact of the tsunami stirred up hazardous waste deposits on the beaches around North Hobyo [South Mudug] and Warsheik [North of Benadir]. Contamination from the waste deposits has thus caused health and environmental problems to the surrounding local fishing communities including contamination of groundwater. Many people in these towns have complained of unusual health problems as a result of the tsunami winds blowing towards inland villages. The health problems include acute respiratory infections, dry heavy coughing and mouth bleeding, abdominal hemorrhages, unusual skin chemical reactions, and sudden death after inhaling toxic materials.[3]

The UN report said this dumping of nuclear and other toxic waste violated international treaties that were supposed to govern the export of hazardous waste—to Somalia or anywhere else—and was immoral. Investigators also unearthed an even more sinister fact when they noted that it had been "ethically questionable" that "hazardous waste disposal contract[s]" had been negotiated when Somalia was in the midst of a protracted civil war. Negotiated contracts? That such contracts existed was an indictment of the foreign companies and the Somali officials, whether they were warlords or the duly elected and appointed, who had arranged them. The Somali leaders had apparently poisoned their own people and sowed the seeds of piracy.

The early days of 2006 weren't the first time the United Nations had been on the Somalia waterfront investigating complaints of toxic waste. In May and June 1997, a consultant named Mahdi Gedi Qayad strolled the beaches of Somalia looking for signs of illegal dumping. Judging from the report, he appears to have done little more than meet with government officials—possibly the same ones who could have arranged the toxic waste dumping. His inconclusive six-page report acknowledged the allegations of illegal fishing, toxic dumping, and destruction of Somalia's coral reefs but said that he saw no signs of it. If there was a problem, he wrote, "on behalf of Somalia, the United Nations should issue a strong appeal to the international community against illegal fishing and toxic waste dumping into Somali waters." He further wrote, "The United Nations should devise ways of providing protection, monitoring, and surveillance of the Somali waters against abuse."[4] None of this happened.

The trash stirred up by the 2004 tsunami prompted a new round of accusations implicating Somali and European companies. "Somalia has been used as a dumping ground for hazardous waste starting about the early 1990s and continuing through the civil war there," said Nick Nuttall of the United Nations Environmental Program in Nairobi not long after the UN report was made public. "European companies found it to be very cheap to get rid of waste there, costing as little as $2.50 a ton, where disposal costs in Europe are something like $250 a ton. And the waste is many different kinds. There is uranium radioactive waste. There is [sic] leads. There is [sic] heavy metals like cadmium and mercury. There is industrial waste, and there is [sic] hospital wastes, chemical wastes. You name it."[5]

Death of a Journalist

ILLEGAL DUMPING off the Somali coast first drew serious international attention in March 1994, when a thirty-two-year-old Italian journalist named Ilaria Alpi was killed in Mogadishu. The prelude to Alpi's death was Siad Barre's departure from Somalia, which left the country crawling with militia fighters flush with victory but short on food and water. As chaos and starvation spread, the world descended on Somalia in 1992 with troops on a humanitarian mission to protect aid workers and ensure food distribution. This included the U.S. marines who walked ashore in December 1992. The multinational force had the situation somewhat in hand by the end of January 1993, but restive warlords provoked a series of confrontations climaxing on the disastrous day in October 1993 when eighteen American soldiers were killed when a U.S. military operation to capture a troublesome warlord, Mohammed Farah Aidid, went awry.

When the United States departed Somalia, its humanitarian mission gone sour, other western peacekeepers followed. Due to Italy's involvement in Somalia from colonial times, video journalist Ilaria Alpi was there to cover the Italian troops for Italy's RAI television network. It was a dangerous assignment to be sure, but there were other Italian and international journalists doing similar work. No one realized exactly how dangerous the assignment was until Alpi and her cameraman were gunned down on March 21, 1994. In the wake of their deaths, it became apparent that Alpi was doing more than reporting on the withdrawal of peacekeepers. She had been investigating not only suspected dumping of toxic waste in Somali waters but also gunrunning.

More than a decade later, Alpi's death provoked an angry outcry when, in 2005, a Somali environmental activist named Amina Mohammed charged, "She was killed because there were many things that she discovered. There are Italian companies. There is the Mafia. There are Somali warlords. There is a whole range of people, dealers, and brokers involved in this task." Mohammed was convinced that Alpi was killed while investigating allegations that Mafia-run companies in Italy were involved in the transport and dumping of industrial waste in Somalia. Mohammed claimed that Alpi had discovered that much of the waste was being carried from Italy to the shores of the former Italian colony aboard fishing vessels of a Somali-owned company. "This company was owned by the Somali government and it is now in the hands of a manager who is also presently a member of parliament," Mohammed said. The money the Somalis collected for the dumping in Somali waters bought weapons that fueled the country's bloody civil war.[6]

An American journalist working in Mogadishu at the time of Alpi's death, Michael Maren, spoke to her less than an hour before she was killed. Maren has written about her death and the inconsistencies between what Italian authorities say happened and known facts of the incident. Maren is the author of a critical book on foreign aid, *The Road to Hell*, based on his fifteen years of living and working in Africa. While the killing of journalists was a tragic phenomenon in war-torn Somalia, the events surrounding Alpi's death suggest that it was not accidental. Maren dug into the Alpi murder, and his report was eventually published online.[7]

Lurking in the not-too-distant background of Alpi's murder, Maren wrote, was an Italian exile living in Mogadishu at the time named Giancarlo Marocchino. A reputed former trucking company owner from Genoa, he had lived in Mogadishu since 1984 after apparently skipping Italy in the wake of tax evasion allegations, Maren wrote. Married to a Somali woman whose clan controlled north Mogadishu, Marocchino was said to have ties with Italian peacekeepers in Somalia. The U.S. military, in contrast, wanted nothing to do with Marocchino and had tried to toss him out of the country, convinced that he was supplying guns to warlords.[8] Somalia had been under Italian influence for much of the twentieth century, having been part of what the Italian dictator Benito Mussolini declared in 1936 was Italian East Africa and included Eritrea, Ethiopia, and Italian Somalia, which continued to benefit from Italian aid and business long after independence in 1960. One such aid project completed in northern Somalia was a highway linking the northern port town of Bosasso to Somalia's main north–south road, part of the Italian-built *Strada Imperiale*, which connects Addis Ababa to Mogadishu. Still in the trucking business, but now in Somalia, Marocchino benefited from the road.[9]

Italian journalists in Mogadishu took advantage of Marocchino's influence, accepting not only his hospitality but his protection and extensive contacts as well. But not Alpi. Yet Marocchino was well aware of her movements, Maren wrote. Among the stories that she pursued were such things as human rights abuses by Italian peacekeepers, and she reportedly possessed pictures of soldiers' abuses that were taken by the soldiers themselves.

The day Alpi died, she had just returned from a trip to Bosasso that had been hush-hush. She had taken a UN flight from Mogadishu to Bosasso, Maren learned, where she had interviewed a clan leader named Boqor [King] Musa, known as King Kong. Her taped interview was recovered after her death, despite the loss of her notebooks and camera. The conversation with King Kong was routine until she asked about arms trafficking. King Kong hesitated to answer, so Alpi told her cameraman to turn off the camera, which he did, but he continued to record the sound. King Kong acknowledged that some things "came from Rome, Brescia, or Torino." Brescia is an arms manufacturing center in Italy. King Kong then added, "Those people have much power, contacts."[10]

Maren wrote that even in the mid-1990s, the foreign fishing boats in Somalia's waters were forced to pay for the right to take fish. If the boat captains refused to pay, the Somalis seized the ships. As Alpi conducted her interview with King Kong, fishing trawlers were being held for ransom in Bosasso. One of the captive ships had been given to Somalia by the Italian government and had an Italian captain, two Italian officers, and a Somali crew. "Kidnapping and hijacking were business as usual in Somalia," Maren wrote, as early as 1994.[11]

When Alpi returned to Mogadishu from Bosasso on Sunday, March 21, she received a call. At 3:00 P.M. Alpi and her cameraman drove across the city's green line, a demarcation between two battling warlords, to the Amana Hotel, where she met an Italian news agency correspondent. They were driven by their regular driver, Mahamoud, and accompanied by their armed guard, named Ali. According to Maren's account, a group of men in a blue Land Rover followed Alpi's vehicle, parked outside the hotel, and drank tea at a nearby tea stand. When Alpi and her cameraman left the hotel, the men followed. Moments later they swerved their vehicle past Alpi's pickup and cut it off at an intersection at the bottom of a hill. Two men jumped out and began shooting.[12]

The official story was that Alpi's guard, Ali, fired first, not the men in the Land Rover. In the ensuing mayhem, Alpi and her cameraman were killed by stray bullets. But only Alpi and her cameraman were killed. None of the men in the Land Rover died, nor did Alpi's bodyguard or driver.

The official motive listed in the reports was robbery, but this raises the question, why would someone driving an expensive vehicle like a Land Rover want to rob a journalist or try to steal a pickup truck, neither of which required a gun battle? Italian police investigated but said none of the men in the Land Rover could be found. Alpi's bodyguard and driver later agreed that the whole thing was a robbery gone bad and their passengers had simply had a bad day. Though a suspect was eventually brought to Italy from Somalia, tried, and jailed for Alpi's murder, the convicted man's lawyer told Maren the whole thing was a deal to close the case and shut people up.

Photos of Alpi's body, taken by the medical doctor aboard the Italian ship where her body was taken after the shooting, could have provided critical information about how she died, but they disappeared along with the doctor's medical report. Despite the loss of such vital material, the medical officer who wrote the autopsy report told Alpi's parents that he thought she had been assassinated. Largely at Alpi's parents' request, their daughter's body was exhumed twice for autopsies. The result of the first was vague, but a second in January 1998 concluded that she was shot at close range. Alpi had curled up in the back seat of the truck and had placed her hands over the back of her head. The autopsy noted that the bullet took off the small finger of her right hand, indicating an execution-style shot to the back of her head. The autopsy was performed by a team of six doctors, three selected by Alpi's parents and three by the police. The report was unambiguous, yet the police refused to accept the conclusion that Alpi had died from a direct shot to the head.

On the evening that Alpi was killed, and many times after, Maren reviewed a videotape of the shooting scene taken by a cameraman for

ABC News who went to the site when word spread of the attack. In the video, Maren wrote, the bodies were being removed from Alpi's Toyota pickup truck and placed in a Land Cruiser owned by Marocchino, who had arrived at the scene within minutes of the shooting. One of the Somalis helping to remove the bodies collected Alpi's notebook and a pair of two-way radios and handed them to Marocchino, who was unruffled and turned to the camera, saying, "They were somewhere they shouldn't have been."[13]

Maren talked at length with a former colleague of Alpi's, journalist and author Maurizio Torrealta, who investigated Alpi's death. Torrealta was convinced that Alpi's death was linked to some hijacked fishing boats off Bosasso. Among other documents uncovered by Torrealta was a transcript of testimony by the Italian military commander in Somalia at the time, who said the military planned to recapture the fishing boats taken by the Somali hijackers. Why the military would be interested in those boats was unclear, unless, of course, the boats carried something that the military did not want to fall into the wrong hands.

At the time of Alpi's interview, King Kong apparently was negotiating the release of the ships, Maren wrote. King Kong was undoubtedly aware of what was on the boats, and Alpi may have known as well, but she needed him to say it on tape. Torrealta later traveled to Bosasso to interview King Kong, who reluctantly discussed the subject but said, "I know that in general, those companies involved in the fishing industry are also involved in other activities—especially those with Italian interests." When asked what those other interests might be, King Kong stammered, "I can't say. . . . I don't know." But Torrealta pushed him, suggesting that the ship may have had arms on board. King Kong responded, "It is quite possible, because it is evident those ships carried military equipment for different factions involved in the civil war."[14]

A New Battleground

One reason some in Somalia might have been touchy about a reporter looking into toxic dumping in exchange for arms shipments into the country was that in 1992 the United Nations had slapped an international arms embargo on Somalia in an effort to staunch the flow of blood by choking off the supply of weapons. It didn't work. The Somali arms embargo is probably the most violated in history. Foreign involvement in Somalia and its immediate neighbors has been rapacious yet largely ignored by the world until the hijacking of cargo ships off the Somali coast became an international nuisance. In the eighteen years since the embargo was imposed, Somalia has morphed into a battleground in the war on terror that has made the arms embargo an embarrassment.

In the wake of Siad Barre's defeat and the abandonment by western peacekeepers in 1994, Somalia devolved into a collection of warring clan-based fiefdoms. Just as the Taliban rose phoenixlike out of the ashes of a brutally destructive civil war between powerful warlords wrestling for control of Afghanistan in the wake of the Soviet Union's withdrawal, so arose the fundamental Islamic Courts Union (ICU) in Somalia. The ICU grew out of eleven regional religious courts that administered Islamic fundamentalist sharia law in Somalia, the only form of law that remained in the country. As religious courts, they operated outside of any political structure and could be notoriously brutal, particularly against women. Indian-made Bollywood films were banned as pornography, and a prohibition was imposed against watching soccer games. As the courts became more organized and influential, they also provided education and health care and ran local police forces with the help of businessmen desperate to reduce wanton crime.

As a source of basic social order, the Islamic courts drew public support. By 1999 the courts united and formed a militia that exerted control in Mogadishu. Inevitably, the ICU clashed with the clan warlords. Although they had once fought the U.S. forces there, the warlords reportedly found support from the CIA, which wanted to counter the Islamists due to their suspected ties to terrorists groups such as al-Qaeda. The public face of the ICU was Sharif Sheikh Ahmed, who was considered a moderate and insisted that the union was not a threat but an instrument of peace and order. In fact, the ICU not only restored order, it organized a garbage cleanup of Mogadishu, something the city had not had for a decade, then reopened Mogadishu's airport, which had not operated since international forces had left in 1995, and reopened the port at Mogadishu. The ICU, after extending its control far up the coast into Puntland, forebade piracy as being anti-Islamic and for a short time put an end to it.

Following the demise of the ICU at the end of 2006, largely at the hands of well-equipped Ethiopian invasion forces, the militant Islamist factions that remained declared a jihad against the largely Christian Ethiopians. Muslim-dominated Eritrea, meanwhile, which broke from Ethiopia in a protracted and bloody war, became the prime supporter and conduit of supplies for the Islamist militants in Somalia. The call for an international jihad against Ethiopia was heard by many in the radicalized Somali diaspora, including some in the United States who volunteered to fight in Somalia.

Militant Islamists clashed with Ethiopian and transitional government troops throughout 2007 and 2008, portraying themselves as a nationalist Islamist movement. Former ICU leaders regrouped, however, and became the Alliance for the Re-liberation of Somalia (ARS) in September 2007. But internal disputes between moderates and hard-liners divided the ARS. The moderate Djibouti-based wing of the ARS established ties with the western-backed Somali transitional government, and on February 1, 2009, the former ICU leader and chairman of the ARS, Sharif Sheikh Ahmed, was elected president of the transitional government.

Hard-line Muslim Somalis opposed reconciliation with the transitional government, considering it a tool of the western powers, especially Ethiopia and America. President Ahmed was quickly accused of being a traitor. Led by the former military wing of the Islamic courts, the al-Shabaab militia, which means the Youth, declared war on Ahmed's transitional government.

Fueling the Somali chaos was a steady supply of weapons into Somalia, the ingredient that allowed one group or another to exert dominance. The UN cease-fire and arms embargo had been so thoroughly trashed that the UN was forced to expose embargo violators in hopes that it might shame them into stopping. Coinciding with the rise of the ICU in 2006, Somalia had become a platform for the global jihad, the UN arms embargo monitors said. In its November 2006 report to the Security Council, the monitors revealed a sprawling underground network that provided weaponry, personnel, and training to Islamist militants in Somalia. It came from a host of well-known players: Iran, Syria, Libya, Egypt, and the Hezbollah militia in Lebanon. The report's vivid details of the violations painted a portrait of the global network of terror and set the stage for the rise in Somali piracy and the fears of piracy's links with militant Islamist forces in Somalia.

During the ascendency of the Islamic courts, monitors reported, "large cargo aircraft and oceangoing dhows have been clandestinely delivering arms and other forms of military support from states, arms trading networks, and others, almost on a daily basis." The deliveries included "a wide variety of arms (including surface-to-air missiles), military materiel, and motor vehicles (trucks and land cruisers used as mobile weapons platforms)." Individuals arrived who were involved in "the recruitment of new fighters and volunteers from foreign countries and establishing military camps and conducting formal military training."[15]

According to the report, Egyptian sources promised military training for 3,800 fighters by sending trainers to Somalia. Libyan sources promised to provide financial "incentives" for fighters and to pay for their training as well as upgrades to their facilities. Iran sent consignments of arms, ammunition, medical supplies, and the services of three medical doctors.[16] Though operating in Lebanon, the militant group Hezbollah recruited 720 Somali fighters provided by the ICU to fight in Hezbollah's thirty-four-day war in 2006 with Israel. Hezbollah offered money to the Somali fighters, paying their families two thousand dollars for their efforts and up to twenty-five or thirty thousand dollars if a fighter died. Upon return to Somalia, the fighters were to collect one hundred dollars a month as "hero money."[17] Initially, only about eighty of the Somali fighters returned to their homeland, followed by a second group of twenty-five who returned to Somalia in early September 2006, accompanied by five Hezbollah fighters. The fate of the more than six hundred other Somalis is unknown. Saudi Arabia was also reportedly involved, providing food and medical supplies for the ICU.[18] Syria provided arms, ammunition, and training.[19]

While regional players were deeply involved in the supply of weapons and money to foster the ICU, much of the support came via Eritrea, the monitoring group said, used as a conduit to, a platform for, and a coordinator of support for the Somali ICU. States using Eritrea for this purpose included Djibouti, the Libyan Arab Jamahiriya, Egypt, and certain Middle East countries. Despite the vehement denials from Eritrea, as well as all states said to be involved, the details were overwhelming.

> On 4 July 2006, four flights of Eritrean military aircraft landed at Esaley airport, located in the north-eastern part of Mogadishu. Two of the flights contained arms for ICU, and the other two were transporting approximately 500 military personnel consisting of Eritrean military and fighters from the Ethiopian insurgent groups Ogaden National Liberation Front (ONLF) and OLF.[20]
>
> Subsequent to their arrival at Esaley, all of the military personnel were transported to El Ma'an seaport. At El Ma'an, militant fundamentalist businessman and financier . . . made arrangements for the troops to be transported by dhow to the vicinity of Marka, Lower Shabelle [in southern Somalia]. The threefold purpose of the troop deployment to Lower Shabelle is to create an alternative headquarters in addition to Mogadishu and to establish both a new military base and a training camp for foreigners—both military trainers and fighters. The new facility is located near both the seaport and the airport of El Ahmed.[21]

And again:

> On 17 July 2006 a vessel using the name *MV Yohana* travelled from Eritrea to Somalia carrying food and arms, as follows: 3,000 tons of food . . . 30 82 mm mortars, 2,000 AK-47s and 100 RPG-7s.[22]

And then:

> On 20 July 2006 an Airbus A310-300 . . . departed from Assab, Eritrea, destined for Somalia. On board the aircraft were a variety of arms, as follows: B-10 antitank guns; heavy [large-caliber] machine guns; PKM machine guns, with magazines and telescopic sighting devices; AK-47 assault rifles; G3A3 assault rifles; Browning .30-calibre machine guns; 120 mm mortars; and rifle-fired grenades. On or about 21 July 2006 a second arms shipment, consisting primarily of a variety of ammunition, arrived in Somalia on board an Airbus A310-300.[23]

All parties named by the monitoring group denied violating the embargo, including the ICU. A letter signed by Sharif Sheikh Ahmed, chairman of the ICU's executive council at the time and now president of Somalia, called the report "misinformation" and accused Ethiopia of an "invasion" and "occupation" of Somalia under the guise of UN authority.[24]

The United States Strikes Again

KEENLY AWARE that Somalia had become a haven for radical Islamist fighters and a hideout for suspected al-Qaeda operatives, the U.S. maintained a clandestine involvement in Somalia that publicly appeared to be a hands-off policy following the Black Hawk Down debacle. The lid came off on January 7, 2007, and then again on January 23, when U.S. gunships struck the Islamist military training camps in multiple locations in southeastern Somalia.[25] The Pentagon confirmed the strike, with one U.S. intelligence official saying that al-Qaeda suspects had been targeted.[26] The target had been Fazul Abdullah Mohammed, the suspected head of al-Qaeda operations in East Africa. As word spread of the attack, it also became known that U.S. advisers were on the ground in Somalia and working with Ethiopian troops pursuing al-Qaeda in southern Somalia. American and Somali officials said U.S. special operations provided intelligence and support to Ethiopian and Somali fighting forces.[27]

Some six months later, a U.S. Navy warship bombarded the northern Somalia village of Barga, where al-Qaeda targets were thought to be hiding after making their way up the coast from the south. Missiles pounded hills where foreign jihadists had fled after clashing with locals, residents told a Reuters reporter. Barga is a small port town in Puntland that had been targeted by Muslim extremists because it had resisted coming under the wing of the Islamist fundamentalists. One Barga resident said that at least two uniformed U.S. military officers had arrived in the port before the attack and "were driven by Puntland troops and were carrying telecommunications equipment." A Puntland official told a reporter that the Islamist militants headed into the hills behind Barga after arriving by boat from Ras Kamboni, the coastal militant training camp on the Somalia–Kenya border. The group included thirteen foreign fighters, the locals said, and U.S. sources reported that among these fighters were al-Qaeda operatives working in Somalia, including Fazul Mohammed, who had been targeted in the earlier attacks, along with Sheikh Hassan Dahir Aweys, the hard-line leader of the ousted UIC who would eventually re-emerge as leader of Hizbul Islam, another militant Islamist group that would oppose al-Shabaab. A third suspect in that group was Aden Hashi Ayro, who was killed later on May 1, 2008, in a separate U.S. air strike.[28]

The United States' 2007 attacks did not escape the notice of the UN's embargo monitors, who wrote to Zalmay Khalilzad, then the UN ambassador for the United States, seeking an explanation. Khalilzad responded that the arms embargo banned the "deliveries of weapons and military equipment to Somalia," and, "We do not believe that these operations against known terrorist targets constituted the 'delivery' of a weapon."[29]

The shift in American foreign policy in Somalia became clear on September 14, 2009, when six U.S. helicopter gunships struck a suspected al-Qaeda convoy in southern Somalia that carried Saleh Ali Saleh Nabhan. A thirty-year-old Kenyan, Nabhan was wanted for his role in the November 2002 bombing of the Israeli-owned Paradise Hotel in Mombasa and the attempted downing of an Israeli jetliner with surface-to-air missiles at the Mombasa airport. The suicide bombing of the hotel killed three Israelis and ten Kenyans. Kenyan police also sought Nabhan for his role in August 1998 bombings of the U.S. embassies in Nairobi and in Dar es Salaam that killed 229.

According to reports, at least four U.S. helicopters strafed the convoy carrying Nabhan and other senior militants. With the target hit, two helicopters landed, prompting a firefight. Nabhan's body and two others were taken to a U.S. Navy warship waiting offshore. The attack was near the coastal town of Barawe, some 150 miles south of Mogadishu and deep inside territory controlled by al-Shabaab, the Islamist insurgent group. "This marks an evolution in U.S. operational and intelligence capabilities," explained Peter Pham of Virginia's James Madison University. "This is a setback for al-Shabaab and al-Qaeda in East Africa because Nabhan was the communication link with the wider al-Qaeda network in Arabia," Pham said.[30]

The attack came little more than a month after the two-day visit to Kenya by Secretary of State Hillary Clinton, who on August 6, 2009, had met with recently elected Somali president Sharif Sheikh Ahmed in a show of U.S. support. "President Sheikh Sharif's government has taken up the fight on behalf of the Somali people against al-Shabaab, a terrorist group with links to al-Qaeda and other foreign militant networks," Clinton said. "Al-Shabaab and its allies lack regard for human rights, for women's rights, for education and health care and the progress of the Somali people."[31]

While Clinton's remarks made U.S. policy in Somalia more public, the true boots on the ground were being worn by the soldiers of the African Union Mission in Somalia (AMISOM), a force of about thirty-five hundred soldiers from Uganda and Burundi, well short of the total eight thousand troops pledged by other African countries to help keep peace in Somalia. AMISOM has been heavily supported by the United States, including the mid-2009 delivery of forty tons of weapons to AMISOM soldiers, despite the UN arms embargo.[32] "We will also continue to provide equipment and training to the [transitional government] as well as humanitarian assistance to the Somali people where delivery is feasible and effective," Clinton said. Blasting

Eritrea for its support of al-Shabaab, Clinton called Eritrea a "destabilizing neighbor" and warned, "Certainly if al-Shabaab were to obtain a haven in Somalia, which could then attract al-Qaeda and other terrorist actors, it would be a threat to the United States."[33]

With the fight now public, militants of al-Shabaab wasted no time in striking back. On Thursday, September 17, 2009, just three days after the killing of Nabhan, suicide bombers riding in two UN vehicles said to have been hijacked months earlier detonated themselves inside the AMISOM headquarters in Mogadishu, killing seventeen Ugandan and Burundian soldiers and four civilians.

With everyone's cards seemingly on the table, war continued to rage in south Somalia, permitting the full flowering of piracy in Somalia.

4

METHOD TO THE MADNESS

As the hijacking of ships off the coast of Somalia spun out of control in 2008 and 2009, fueled by inflated ransoms, the UN Security Council's arms embargo monitors turned their attention to the Somali pirates, documenting methods, organization, and networks. "Piracy in Somali waters has rapidly evolved over the past twelve months from a domestic nuisance, aimed mainly at illegal fishing vessels, into a sophisticated and well-organized industry whose dramatic expansion poses a growing threat to international shipping," the monitors wrote in November 2008. "The extraordinarily lucrative nature of piracy has transformed ragtag, oceangoing militias into well-resourced, efficient, and heavily armed syndicates employing hundreds of people in northeastern and central Somalia. Some of these groups now rival or surpass established Somali authorities in terms of their military capabilities and resource bases. The acquisition of arms, ammunition, and equipment to sustain the growth of these maritime militias almost certainly involves violations of the arms embargo."[1]

By the time the report became public, the UN Security Council had adopted a series of resolutions that unleashed the navies of the world to go after the Somali pirates. Resolution 1816, adopted on June 2, 2008, permitted the navies to "enter the territorial waters of Somalia for the purpose of repressing acts of piracy and armed robbery at sea," and to use "all necessary means." But permission did not automatically translate into action, so on October 8, 2008, the Security Council formally appealed to countries "to take part actively in the fight against piracy on the high seas off the coast of Somalia, in particular by deploying naval vessels and military aircraft."

A third resolution further authorized navies to arrest pirates and urged the international community to sort out the jurisdictional questions surrounding piracy. This resulted in a European Union agreement with Kenya that effectively turned its High Court in Mombasa into an ad hoc piracy tribunal. Meanwhile, the chaos off the Somali coast escalated as pirates took to the sea in droves, their numbers swelling from several hundred to an estimated fifteen hundred who turned the vessels they commandeered into mother ships from which they launched small skiffs to attack yet more vessels.

The carnival-like shooting-gallery atmosphere that gripped the Gulf of Aden prompted observers and victims alike to ask how the pirates could have gotten so good at what they were doing so quickly. One answer is that some of the Somali pirates may have been trained by foreign security firms. The UN investigators noted that, beginning in about 2000, the fledgling Puntland coast guard was trained by a British company, Hart Security Maritime Services Limited. Formed ostensibly to prevent illegal fishing and dumping of toxic waste in territorial waters with an initial cadre of about three hundred sailors, the Puntland coast guard operated out of Bosasso using eight armed vessels to stop any and all foreign fishing boats they encountered. The guard financed itself by collecting cash fines and forcing the fishing trawlers to buy licenses. This practice had been observed by UN monitors, who in 2003 reported, "While there exists an urgent need to protect Somalia's maritime resources from foreign fishing vessels, there is also a clear risk that 'coast guard' operations of the kind organized by the Puntland authorities could in fact provide legitimacy for [arms embargo] sanctions-busting by local authorities and faction leaders. At the same time, the sale of licenses to foreign vessels in exchange for fishing rights has acquired the features of a large-scale protection racket, indistinguishable in most respects from common piracy."[2]

In a news report broadcast by the Al Jazeera network in September 2009, Richard Bethell, head of the Hart Group, confirmed that his company had trained the Puntland coast guard personnel but insisted that his company had nothing to do with the rise in Somali piracy. Instead, the Hart Group was providing protection services to ships traveling through pirate-infested waters. Even so, Al Jazeera's story included a Puntland man who claimed the training he got from Hart gave him the confidence he needed to capture ships at sea.[3]

A stronger motivation for piracy, however, was the general sense of grievance against foreign exploitation that became part of the popular, if mistaken, justification for the pillaging of international cargo. In a deeply divided, impoverished, and lawless land, the lure of piracy was virtually irresistible. The unarmed cargo ships were helpless prey due to the "right of innocent passage," a long-established principle that allows a merchant ship to freely enter ports around the world as long as it is unarmed. And in the Gulf of Aden, most ships were heavily loaded and rode low in the water, making them easy to board, even from a small skiff.

The route through the Gulf of Aden and into the Indian Ocean is possibly the most important sea lane in the world, with an estimated thirty thousand vessels passing through each year, carrying much of the commercial products consumed in Europe and North and South America. The narrowness of the Gulf of Aden creates a bottleneck for the seagoing behemoths and makes hijacking ships like shooting fish in a barrel. Somalia and Yemen are separated by only 170 nautical miles at the Gulf's widest point and as few as 100 nautical miles at other points. Add million-dollar ransoms and the absence of punishment for piracy to the mix, and you have the ingredients for the explosion of Somali piracy.

Ransoms paid in 2008 totaled about fifty million dollars, a tenfold increase over previous years, and mushroomed in 2009 as Somali pirates attacked about one ship per day during the first half of 2009. On one April day they reportedly struck at four vessels. Somali pirates eventually collected about eighty-two million dollars in ransom during 2009, according to UN estimates. But all of this was not profit, of course. Costs had to be deducted, but still, piracy provides a high profit margin for backers and financiers compared with the risk faced by the pirates themselves.

With more pirates working farther out at sea, the taking of international fishing trawlers for use as mother ships from which the smaller skiffs are launched became all the more important. Capturing a well-equipped trawler relieved the pirate organizers of paying for high-tech gadgetry such as GPS, radar, and sonar, estimated to be as much as fifty thousand dollars per trawler. Other pirate expenses include satellite phones at eight hundred dollars per unit and costly airtime. Arming a pirate with an AK-47 might cost two hundred dollars. Add pistols at one hundred dollars each, with ammunition, and the costs could mount. Machine guns, of course, are more costly, as are rocket-propelled grenades, which are usually carried but used sparingly. Food and housing for pirates and the hundreds of hostages who were taken during 2009 also required piracy payoffs to be big. Assuming that costs were about 30 percent of the business, Somali piracy probably cost about twenty-five million dollars in 2009. But with ransoms totaling eighty-two million dollars for the year, that would leave a profit of about fifty-seven million dollars.[4]

Clan-Based Business

The organization and composition of Somali pirates and piracy, including the key personnel and organizers, have never been a secret. However, the complete picture of the pirate networks has never been clear. The vast amount of information that is readily available raises questions about how seriously anyone, including the global shipping industry, views the problem of piracy in Somalia. UN arms embargo investigators found that while news reports suggested the pirates were a formidable force, "they are for the most part loosely organized and poorly trained, and their membership is fluid. Their strengths are the depth of their motivation and their adherence to a common code of conduct."[5]

That said, the size and scope of the piracy operations demand business savvy. For piracy to flourish, financiers operate in the background, like master puppeteers hovering over a watery theater in and around the Gulf of Aden. These pirate masters include business and political figures, some with fishing assets, within the region and without, the UN investigators found, who provide the seed money for the often far-flung maritime assaults. The financiers provide the boats, fuel, arms and ammunition, communications, and salaries for the pirates. Pirate groups have metastasized into regional networks, the monitors found, some with contacts working in ports around the region who relay details on what ships are carrying, when, and where. "Increasingly, these advance teams appear to be benefiting from intelligence provided by contacts who monitor major ports in neighboring countries," according to a UN report.[6]

Once a merchant ship is successfully captured, and if the pirates don't already have a supporter, then one or more financiers are found to underwrite the costs, monitors said. The organizer of the hijacking arranges for the captured vessel to be harbored in a port where provisions and protection can be provided. For this, a host of other players are needed: a negotiator with foreign language skills, local officials and even tribal and community elders, along with senior government officials who provide political cover and protection, and money launderers to move the ransom payments into the right bank accounts.

After a ransom is agreed on, the money is delivered to the pirates on board the captured ship, who divide it then and there. Portions may vary, but UN monitors found that the hijackers get 30 percent, distributed equally among all members. The first pirate to board a ship, the jumper, gets a double share or a bonus, such as cash or a vehicle like a Toyota Land Cruiser. Pirates who fight with other pirates are fined. Compensation is paid to the family of any pirate killed during the operation. Those on the ground at the port who provide security get 10 percent. The local community gets 10 percent, and this includes the elders, local officials, and residents who may host the pirates and their friends. The financier gets 20 percent and often shares the earnings with others, such as political allies. The hijacking sponsor gets 30 percent.[7]

There are two large pirate networks, the UN arms embargo monitors found: one based in Puntland, mainly of the Majerteen clan, and a second based in central Somalia and controlled by the Habar Gidir clan. The port town of Eyl has become the most important locale for piracy, although other pirate groups operate from Bosasso and much smaller coastal communities as well. The central Somalia piracy network operates out of the town of Harardheere and is dominated by the Saleebaan subclan of the Habar Gidir, but monitors noted that clans and subclan piracy networks often overlap when they cooperate.[8] UN monitors reported that clan leaders Mohammed Abdi Garaad and Mohamed Abdi Hassan "Afweyne," based in Harardheere, worked with a third, Farah Hirsi Kulan "Boyah," based in Puntland, having organized piracy projects together on and off since 2005. In early 2008 the clan partners based themselves in Eyl, and UN monitors indicated that Boyah has evolved as a major backer of piracy.[9]

Afweyne, an impudent nickname that means "big mouth," acknowledged his role in hijackings in a French Press Agency report as early as August 2006 and claimed to have taken a variety of ships. Not surprisingly, arms embargo monitors reported that Afweyne was also involved in the weapons trade via Eritrea.[10] The other Harardheere-based pirate leader, Garaad, was reputed to have been behind the 2007 hijacking of South Korean–flagged fishing vessels and described his role in the hijacking to a Somali radio station after he had threatened to kill hostages when his accomplices were caught by the U.S. Navy. In Mogadishu, UN investigators found that some pirate attacks had involved port security personnel, and in one 2007 case, hijackers were government-hired security guards.[11]

Most worrisome to the UN arms embargo investigators was the deepening involvement of piracy groups in the weapons trade that armed militant Islamists that controlled southern Somalia. "The Monitoring Group has repeatedly received allegations that ransom payments obtained from hijackings have been used for the purchase of weapons. The use of Harardheere, Hobyo, and Mogadishu for weapons imports and acts of piracy creates opportunities for both pirates and arms embargo violators."[12]

An Insider Talks

WITH A wealth of detail about Somali piracy in mind, I am anxious to talk with a pirate negotiator when I land in the Somaliland capital of Hargeisa. It is here that I meet a man initially identified to me as Mr. Ali, whom I would come to know as Abu Suleiman. I'd found him through a series of unlikely connections. Suleiman had assisted a Danish shipping company executive to negotiate a ransom for the release of a captured ship, the details of which I explore in the next chapter. Suleiman lives in Hargeisa and agreed to tell me about piracy from his insider's perspective. He's also an easy man to talk with, since he spent about thirty years in the United States. We meet often during my time in Somaliland.

"Angry fisherman [are] not the reason and cause of piracy," Suleiman says adamantly. "It is a purely selfish business." Piracy flourishes in Somalia "because of lawlessness and extreme poverty." Piracy may have originated with the fishermen, he concedes, but piracy has been going on for so long that the loss of fishing grounds is but a distant memory. "Maybe initially there were fishermen from some areas taking Yemeni dhows," he says, and collecting thirty or forty thousand dollars per ship, but no longer. "It's only greed and ignorance" that fuel the explosion in piracy. Despite the efforts of the international community to control piracy, it will take years, perhaps decades, to eradicate. He insists, "Piracy is not going to fade away." Piracy can only be stopped on land, and to do that will require a strong central government that can impose law and order in Somalia. "It will be fifty years to have another strong, centralized Somalia," he states.

Suleiman was first drawn into the murky world of piracy when an acquaintance asked him to help free a German couple, veteran sailors Juergen Kantner and Sabine Merz, who were abducted on June 28, 2008, as they sailed their small yacht through the Gulf of Aden. Taken to a remote location in the mountains of Puntland, they endured mock executions and deprivation until being released on August 9, 2008, when a ransom was reportedly paid by the German government. Kantner and Merz were reunited with their ship in the Somaliland port of Berbera but spent the next six months repairing it and replacing an engine. Suleiman tells me that the pirates took the German couple's yacht out of frustration. They'd been trying to find a cargo ship to hijack but had failed, so they grabbed the yacht because it was an easy target. "It was their last resort," he says. Suleiman frequently drove into the mountains to check on the couple and delivered information to the pirates on the progress of the negotiations. "I just hung in there," he states, until the couple was eventually released.

Ransoms for hijacked ships have more than doubled, from between $600,000 and $800,000 per ship to between $1.8 million and $2 million, he says. The money has allowed the pirates to change and adapt to antipiracy measures by the international community. Pirates are moving their bases of operations from some of the better-known coastal towns of Eyl and Harardheere to remote islands in the Gulf of Aden historically used by pirates and smugglers. Here they are able to stash weapons and equipment needed for hijacking, such as ladders, night goggles, and satellite phones, and they also use these islands as outposts to watch ships passing in the gulf. One of the prospective new bases for the pirates, he says, is the desolate northern coast of Somalia along the sparsely populated region between eastern Somaliland and western Puntland. This area affords direct access to shipping lanes and removes the need to take hijacked ships around the Horn of Africa to the eastern coastal fishing villages, a trip of three to four days at sea.

Suleiman has been involved in more substantial ship hostage negotiations but insists he does not do it for the money. He wants the people and ships released and sees himself as a facilitator. If, as some suggest, piracy is the product of well-organized crime syndicates, does the impetus for an attack come from on high? Suleiman shakes his head and says it's very simple. One or two guys who want to make some money "come up with the idea." It's not unusual, he says, because "the idea looms around with everybody." But, he cautions, "it is serious only with those who have money." With this in mind, a couple of would-be pirates might cook up the scheme, then seek backers who can provide a boat, weapons, communications, fuel, and, most of all, cash to get the process started. Investors, Suleiman explains, want to maximize their chances of success, so they look for "seasoned" pirates. "You need to have an experienced man to handle all the stuff," Suleiman says, and this includes an experienced jumper, the first one on the ship. But even more important than experience is the fearlessness of the individual pirate. "The main thing is if they are willing to die for it," he says.

A well-organized piracy attack requires two skiffs, Suleiman explains. One is called the stopper, which is a boat with heavily armed pirates who fire a rocket-propelled grenade across the deck of a ship to get it to stop. "If it doesn't stop, then he fires a warning shot at the bridge. They'll stop at that." The rewards are well worth the risks, Suleiman says. "If you make six thousand dollars or seven thousand dollars your first time at sea for just risking your life, the next time you will have your own crew."

The reality is that most of the pirates "don't know how to swim," which shows how desperate these men are. If a pirate survives his first hijacking successfully, he will find investors much more easily, Suleiman says, and then has the chance of making twenty or thirty thousand dollars for organizing a successful hijacking. Despite the lure of money, the business is very risky. "There are no guarantees."

After assisting in the release of the German couple, Suleiman was contacted by pirates who asked him to help negotiate a ransom for a cargo ship. "I knew this was something big," he says. "I knew experts were needed." That project turned out to be a lengthy effort to release a Danish-owned vessel that netted him some cash and also solidified his reputation. Reflecting what the UN experts had reported, Suleiman scoffs at the idea of a central pirate command in London or some large city. "Piracy is not organized in such a manner," he states. "There is another way. It is very stealthy." He admits that increasingly piracy includes "some elements of Islamic radicalism."

But it must be organized, I suggest, if pirates have spotters who identify potential targets as they pass through the Red Sea before entering the Gulf of Aden. "There is no way ships can be targeted in that way," Suleiman says. Instead, the pirates typically linger near their mother ships and watch as ships pass, looking for a slow-moving ship that is low to the water. "They will focus on one just like animals do in East Africa. They look for the loneliest one. They attack any ship that slows down [or separates] from the flotilla," he says, referring to the merchant-ship convoys escorted through the gulf by EU, British, and U.S. naval vessels.

A typical piracy operation will require at least ten to twelve men, and investors can estimate their costs at about five thousand dollars per day. This will cover the expense of equipping the pirates and then maintaining them, the ship, and the crew. So, for a typical hijacking, that means a sum that could reach $150,000 per month. Local community and clan leaders may charge a fee of $100,000 or more just for the right to let pirates anchor a ship offshore. Local merchants sell food and supplies to pirates at outrageously high prices, such as $25 for a pack of cigarettes, $250 for a goat, or $10 for a can of Coke. If negotiations drag on for two or three months, the costs can seriously erode profits. If investors in the piracy operation don't have the money they need, they obtain loans, even though the loans may come with an interest rate of 20 percent, Suleiman says.

Piracy networks are loose and purposely fragmented, he explains, for security purposes. Investors, backers, and the "people on the ship never meet each other most of the time." Once the ransoms are collected, the money is distributed quickly, and almost as quickly, the money is spent. The vast majority of the pirates, the foot soldiers in the piracy operations who get only about ten thousand dollars per hijacking, are not smart about their money. "Do they understand investment?" he asks. "They don't have a clue."

Because the piracy paydays may take months to materialize, frustrations can grow and cause arguments and jealousies. Fights and killings are common. Disgruntled pirates "spend their time creating havoc," he says. "With every crew [of pirates] you have one or two who get killed." Because of this, each piracy operation has a "master pirate," an experienced person to control and oversee the operation. Often this person is also an investor in the scheme or may have clan ties to investors.

The government in Puntland is deeply linked with piracy, Suleiman explains, to the extent that during recent elections, top officials solicited and received large donations from the clan leaders who orchestrate and conduct the piracy operations. "Each payment that comes through Puntland, the authorities get a piece of it," he says. Out of a recent $1 million payment, pirates only collected about $590,000 to be divided among themselves.

The current Puntland president, Abdirahman Mohamud Farole, sixty-three, is a former college history teacher who worked in Australia. He left Puntland in 2006 after reportedly falling out with the previous Puntland president over an oil exploration deal in Puntland still in the works. Farole returned to Somalia and in January 2009 became the fourth president of Puntland. He immediately vowed to tackle piracy head-on by cracking down on local authorities who have allegedly collaborated with pirates in return for a share of the profits. However, Farole reportedly received political contributions in excess of one hundred thousand dollars from clan leaders in Puntland, the same ones thought to control many of the piracy operations. Suleiman tells me that some top Puntland officials are reputed to have their own pirate crews.

Despite widespread doubts, Farole and others in Puntland say they're making progress against piracy. They have enlisted the support of Islamic clerics as well as gun-toting police to push pirates out of Eyl and other towns along the coast. "We've done a lot," Farole told a reporter in June 2009. "We're in full control of the major towns where they used to operate. But we would be more effective if the international community would help us to establish a taskforce. Piracy cannot be beaten offshore. It has to be eradicated on the ground."[13]

Although some ninety pirates had been tried and jailed in Bosasso by the middle of 2009, almost all had been delivered there by foreign navies. The culprits were kept in the cramped cells of a stone fortress just outside of town, where Bosasso's police chief, Osman Hassan Uke, said he was happy to slam the door on the pirates and throw away the key. "These pirates are thieves and cowards," he said. "We will defeat them. They are not organized in the way we are organized." Uke said the willingness of shipping companies and foreign governments to pay ransoms only encouraged the growth of piracy. "It is completely wrong," he said. "Whenever ten guys get paid ransom money, twenty more pirates are created."[14]

Moving Pirate Money

THE DIFFICULTIES and dangers of pirate life are minimized in a pirate's mind by the money that can be earned. Money motivates the pirates, as the Bosasso police chief explained, but how is it spent? Pirates and their friends reportedly are putting money into real estate, some of it in Nairobi, where a construction boom in the Somali neighborhoods has been attributed to the rise in piracy. One man who knows this well is Asad (not his real name), a thirty-seven-year-old former Somali bank employee. But it was not a regular bank where he worked. Rather, it was part of the global *hawal* system of money transfers, an off-the-grid banking network used by Somalis and pirates to move money in and out of the country and around the world.

One of the more successful institutions, Dahabshiil, offers a wildly popular method of money transfer by mobile phone text messaging. The system is quite simple. You just deposit money at an office in one country, and that office will confirm the deposit to an affiliated office in another country where the same amount of money can be picked up. It's all done by text messaging between the bank and the money sender, the bank offices, and sender and receiver. The system works much like Western Union and requires a certain amount of cash be on hand in the receiving locations.

Asad worked for such a system in Mogadishu for many years, starting as a bank clerk. "People used to send money through our system," he says when we meet in a quiet corner of Nairobi. He was recently fired from his job because he "asked a lot of questions."

While the system operates like any other banking system, it is not part of the international grid and therefore largely unseen by the prying eyes of most international investigative agencies. "We normally used computers," he says, which have links all around the world. And, like the inner workings of Somalia itself, the system is largely based on tribes, clans, and families. "We know who is who in Somalia. It's not hard for us to know what money belongs to whom."

Since Bosasso is a nexus of piracy, a lot of the money flowing through the system comes from there, Asad says. From Bosasso or other locations in Somalia such as Mogadishu, it is "sent to different locations" dictated by the clients. The system has direct links in Nairobi and Dubai. In Nairobi, the system has brokers who can legitimize or "wash" the money by buying real estate in the name of Kenyans or Kenyan firms. Even so, the Somali community knows who owns what. Once money is deposited with a bank in Somalia, he explains, a purchase order can be placed in Dubai for such things as shiny new Toyota Land Cruisers, house construction materials, or food supplies. "The majority of [clients] are businessmen," he says of the individuals ordering the larger money transfers. "The people who control the ports and the airports. They're all good clients."

Not all of the money is illegal. Money from the Somali diaspora flows into the country from all over the world, Asad explains, as expat Somalis send money to help take care of family and friends. "Sometimes we receive a lot of money from America." But significant amounts of money flowing through the system are from piracy. "Sometimes millions of dollars," he says, "sometimes all in one day." He is aware that some pirate ransom money has gone to support the militant Muslim group al-Shabaab, including the purchase of weapons. Some of the money comes from private businesspeople outside Somalia who support radical Muslim ideology. Asad says if pirate-financed construction goes on in an area of Somalia controlled by al-Shabaab, then the builder or businessman must pay a fee to al-Shabaab to do so.

Asad has been in Nairobi about a year and until recently was working in the underground Somali banking community. He was fired not only for asking questions but for talking to people about what he did, which is forbidden. "They don't want their secrets to be given. Sometimes there are a lot of threats." Because he was overheard saying the wrong things to the wrong people, he was warned to be quiet, a threat he takes seriously. "Now I have to run away." He feels he hasn't done anything wrong, however, and does not deserve to be threatened. "I was being honest. I never thought I was making a mistake. I was [fired] just like that" and then told "be careful for your life."

As he talks, Asad becomes increasingly nervous thinking about his family still back in Mogadishu. He left his wife and four children there, including three boys and a girl, the oldest being eleven and the youngest four. "So far they have not been affected by al-Shabaab," he says.

Even though the militant group has near total control of much of southern Somalia, it is generally despised because it supports and fosters terrorism, he says. Asad wants to take his family to a foreign country as refugees, but to do that he must first get them out of Mogadishu. That will require a stop at the sprawling Dadaab refugee camp in eastern Kenya, not far from the Somali border, he says. From there, he wants to bring them to Nairobi. He is grateful to be living in Nairobi, even if he has to live underground. "I'm happy to be in a peaceful country. I'm happy to tell the world about what is going on in Somalia," he explains. But he misses his former life in Somalia. "I was a middle-class earner," he explains, and he was building a life there. He does not want to become a refugee, saying he detests that kind of existence, but he sees no alternative.

Asad will go back to Somalia "if good government comes." Then, he hopes "people will be held responsible" for the crimes they've committed. His dream, like that of many other Somalis, is to go to the United States. "America could take me as a refugee." He looks at me with hope. "We think of going there. All of [Somalia] wants to go to America." His mood darkens as we talk about the life he left in Somalia. "It's hard for me to talk about Somalia," he tells me. "Foreign countries are giving guns to many people. Weapons come from some countries and go into the hands of innocent, primitive people. You can't expect a child to live in that. The situation is getting worse and worse." Justice may only come in an afterlife, he asserts. "All are answerable to God at some time."

5

INSIDE A HIJACKING

When the *Maersk Alabama* was hijacked in April 2009, it sent a shiver up the spine of Captain Andrey Nozhkin. He commanded the Danish-owned merchant ship the CEC *Future* when it was hijacked by Somali pirates six months earlier and held captive for two months. As Nozhkin followed the five-day hijacking of the ship and the climactic killing of three pirates and the surrender of the fourth, he could only shake his head. He knew all too well the nightmare Captain Richard Phillips had lived through.

On Friday, November 7, 2008, Nozhkin was at the helm of the CEC *Future* as it pushed through the Gulf of Aden. His heart sank when he saw the blip on the radar screen and spotted a small craft closing in from behind. "It was like a firecracker had gone off inside my head," he said later.[1] An experienced captain, Nozhkin, along with his crew, had anticipated this kind of trouble and had prepared the ship's powerful fire hoses, intent on blasting the pirates with water should they try to board. The ship was in contact with naval forces that patrolled the gulf. But the presence of the navy ships did little to help Nozhkin and his crew. Within minutes the speedboat, loaded with heavily armed men, was splashing closer to the ship. "We knew it was pirates. They were coming towards us at an angle so we accelerated and changed direction to make it harder for them to catch up," Nozhkin explained.

A rocket-propelled grenade smoked across the CEC *Future*'s deck. Nozhkin watched the pirates reload the grenade launcher. The next shot would not be a warning. "They were now aiming directly at us in the bridge."[2] Nozhkin decided that hoses were no match for grenades. He stopped the ship.

So began a harrowing sixty-eight-day ordeal for Nozhkin and his thirteen-member crew, all of whom survived but with agonizing memories. As stories emerged of their terrifying captivity, the mayhem of the Somali pirate world was revealed. Once on board, the pirates didn't force the captain to open the ship's safe. Instead, they ordered Nozhkin to steer the vessel directly to the pirate haven of Eyl, where he anchored it off the coast three days later. "Sure enough, Monday morning the ship drops anchor at Eyl, and we had our first contact from pirates," said Per Gullestrup, CEO of Clipper Projects, the CEC *Future*'s owner. "[A negotiator] called one of my colleagues and introduced himself as 'Mr. Ali,' and would we please pay seven million dollars?"[3]

In the fall of 2009 when I finally met Mr. Ali, he distanced himself from the pirates and made it clear that he was not "one of them," noting that he once had been held captive by pirates, an experience he did not relish. Suleiman proved vital to the release of Captain Nozhkin and his crew as he developed a working relationship with Gullestrup. "For thirty-six hours we did not get any feedback from the company, so we sent them a fax," Suleiman recalled of the CEC *Future* negotiations. "The pirates were saying, 'If we don't get an answer from you within a few hours, we will be forced to capsize the ship.'"[4] It was Suleiman's job to relay these messages, no matter what he thought of the pirates or their tactics.

The company, meanwhile, scrambled to respond, making emergency calls to its ship insurers and negotiators, some of the highly paid players involved in ransoming hijacked ships. "We brought in an adviser, a consultant who was helping us throughout, advising us on how to respond to them," Gullestrup tells me when we speak some months after the hostages and ship were released. Two days after the initial contact by the pirates, the company responded with an offer of a three-hundred-thousand-dollar ransom. The pirates countered with a demand of five million dollars, insisting that was as low as they would go. The pirates' outrageously high demand told the shipowners it would be a long and drawn-out process. "We decided it wasn't going anywhere. We told the pirates we didn't see any point continuing discussing. They could call us back when they decided to go below two million dollars," Gullestrup explained.[5]

While this might seem like a callous response by executives sitting in comfortable corporate offices far from Somalia, it was a calculated tactic and based on sound advice. "They know full well that they're never going to get it," Gullestrup tells me when we discuss the pirates' demand. Both parties knew that the game was over if the pirates violated their own rules and began killing captives. "One has to understand the nature of Somali hijacking," he says. "Never has a crew been purposely harmed. A few crew members have died inadvertently because of shooting among the pirates. There's been one incident of a crew member committing suicide. For the pirates to shoot the crew, the minute they do that, their business model is shot." Without a crew, the pirates have nothing to bargain with. And without hostages in the way, commandoes from any number of nations operating in the Gulf of Aden would not hesitate to storm a ship and eradicate the pirates, such as the French have done. Gullestrup understood this and used it. "It's not ideological people you're dealing with here. It's strictly a business. The minute they start shooting people, the international community will go in and do rescue operations."

After the initial exchanges, time dragged on as the shipping company held firm, and the pirates grew antsy and angry. They threatened the crew members and made their lives miserable, once cramming them into a ten-foot-by-ten-foot room for twenty-four hours. Nozhkin was forced to call the company and say, "Very soon the pirates plan to remove us to the shore. . . . That means the jokes are finished. Please, please, I ask you, please, let's do something." In recordings of the calls, the captain's voice was clearly strained, according to reports, and his words seemed prompted by someone close by. This pirate scare tactic was difficult to endure, Gullestrup said, because the company did not want to lose anyone. "The crew [is] foremost for us, so when we heard the captain's distress it was difficult." Yet advisers encouraged Gullestrup to stay strong. This was standard pirate procedure, the advisers said, assuring him that the crew would be released unharmed.[6]

November and December passed slowly, and the company faced the prospect of a long winter with a crew drifting dangerously close to the edge of despair. Then, a breakthrough. "I was having a cup of tea at home with my wife when my mobile phone goes, and it was [Suleiman] introducing himself," Gullestrup recalls. Until then, Gullestrup had been out of the negotiations, his role limited to observer and adviser. Frustrated with the endless delays, he eagerly accepted Suleiman's offer: "Nothing's happening; I want you and me to do the deal." The pirates were ready to cut their demand to a so-called reasonable level, and Gullestrup, too, was ready to negotiate. A deal was struck within days. The exact amount has not been revealed, but the company said the ransom was between one and two million dollars. A private firm dropped the money from a small plane as it swooped low over the ship. Dangling below a parachute, the ransom splashed into the water, and the pirates scrambled to pull the watertight container on board their ship, anxious to divide the cash.[7]

As the ordeal was about to end, the danger escalated. "It was very hot, ten in the morning," Suleiman says, recounting the bizarre and violent events that quickly followed the ransom drop. "All of the pirates came into the captain's cabin. Everybody with a gun." Dozens of people from Eyl had crowded onto the ship: shopkeepers, businessmen, and creditors, each desperate to be paid for the supplies he had provided to keep the pirates and the crew alive, most of it on credit. Heated arguments broke out, followed by bloody knife fights. "There was total chaos," Nozhkin said later, having witnessed the chaos. The pirates frantically cut open the container of money, and the bargaining began. "Those accused of trying to take too much had their hands slammed in doors as a punishment. Then some of the pirates started shooting; some were fighting with knives," Nozkhin recalled. "Then other boats started arriving, trying to get on board, and people on the boat began shooting at them."[8]

It took sixteen hours of bloody and bitter fighting for the money to be divided, but finally the shopkeepers and creditors left, each thousands of dollars richer. The pirates then divided the remaining ransom money among themselves and shinnied down ropes dangling from the ship, abandoning the crew after sixty-eight days of captivity. But the madness was not over. The festering animosities between the pirate leaders and their underlings did not fade when they reached land, Suleiman explained, having witnessed the aftermath. A couple of the pirates followed one of the pirate leaders and shot him dead on the shore. The other leader was also tracked down and killed.[9]

SPEAKING WITH me some five months after the release of the crew, Gullestrup says he would have preferred to handle the hijacking negotiations personally. "We chose to have a communicator," he says, but it didn't work. "We ended up in [a] dead-end situation. He decided to call me directly," Gullestrup says of Suleiman. Because progress had stopped, "I felt I was fully prepared to deal directly with them. In retrospect, I probably would do the communication myself going in. You may lose something in translation, and you may lose some opportunity in the negotiations." After all, "it's all negotiations. It's not one-size-fits-all." Because many personalities are involved, a personal touch can be important for a successful outcome, he says.

Gullestrup's company has two hundred ships that make about one hundred transits of the Gulf of Aden each year. But the risks his ships face are small compared with other, larger companies with many more ships making many more transits. This left Gullestrup wondering why shipping companies don't collaborate to fight piracy, just as the various pirate groups cooperate to increase their chances of success. Instead, shipping companies remain secretive, leaving each to fend for itself and often flounder. As a result, ransoms have risen. "I became frustrated by the secrecy of it all," he says. "It's nonsense. Once you accept the premise that this is a business and understand that pirates are good about sharing information, then [the shipping] business should be doing the same thing," he argues. "Instead of having information sharing, and industrial organizations collecting and deciphering information," they're all operating independently. Each time a hijacking occurs, "we have to start all over with a blank sheet of paper. I didn't see any reason for the cloak and dagger game going on. We decided to come out swinging."

Gullestrup has been public about the hijacking details in an effort to change the corporate cult of secrecy that surrounds ship hijackings. "We've done a lot to try to raise awareness. We just decided we were not going to be another one lying down and taking it. We need to try to put a cap on the ransoms paid. The more the ransom creeps up, the more you encourage the pirates. We have no problem telling the pirates to go fly a kite." Shipowners should act collectively, he says. "Someone needs to come in and hold the shipowners' hand."

While Gullestrup admits that the pirate groups cooperate, they're not like well-oiled business machines. "I don't buy into them being sophisticated and well organized. I don't accept that premise from what I've seen. The clans are working together. It's part of the culture. The clans will syndicate the hijackings," he says, dividing the attacks among themselves, rather than one clan trying to dominate. "Our speculation is they're doing that to cover their flanks," so that clans don't start fighting among themselves. "Kinda spread the wealth." When I ask about pirate moles in various ports who provide shipping information to pirates, he agrees it is possible. "I have heard that's true, there are pirates spotters along the line who will alert [others] some ship is coming," but how that translates into successful hijackings is unclear. He cautions, "Don't give them more credit than is due."

Into the Lion's Den

THE PORT town of Eyl on Somalia's eastern coast is not high on anyone's must-see list, even for the most cavalier of seasoned travelers. But for much of 2008 and 2009, it was the destination of choice for Somali pirates, becoming the mecca of piracy. Eyl sits some 250 miles southeast of Bosasso, Puntland. To get to Eyl, one takes the road south from Bosasso about two hundred miles to Garowe, then another ninety miles east on rugged dirt roads to the coast. Here the dusty road drops down the side of a crusty canyon and follows a small river that empties into the Indian Ocean. Non-Somali visitors usually are accompanied by heavily armed guards, lots of them, as was one BBC reporter who traveled there in mid-June 2009 with six soldiers provided by the Puntland government. Even that was no guarantee of safety since soldiers in such countries often go unpaid, succumbing to murky motives and mixed loyalties.[10]

The town of Eyl is a quiet, unassuming, and rock-strewn collection of low-slung homes plastered with dried mud. That millions of dollars in ship ransoms had passed through the town was evident only in occasional dusty Toyota Land Cruisers parked in the searing sun. Perhaps piracy was a blessing for some in this fishing village, but don't ask Abdul, an Eyl fisherman who was repairing his fiberglass skiff, much like those used by pirates. "Night and day, they drive their cars up and down," he grumbled to a reporter. "It's dangerous for our kids. These criminals have brought nothing but harm to our town." From the beach, Abdul and others eyed two large ships, a merchant cargo carrier and a fishing trawler, anchored beyond the breaking waves. "Those have been hijacked by pirates," Abdul explained with a wave of his hand. "We don't know where they're from. The pirates bring them, then get their ransom, then take them off somewhere else. It's a cycle."

Rather than praising the pirates, most in Eyl couldn't wait for the scourge to be gone. "We are all against the pirates here," said Abdi Hirsi, a local businesswoman. "They have brought bad culture here. They come here with their shiny cars, collect their money, and leave. We worry that our children will be attracted to crime." While the wild and brutal life of pirates was a problem for the tradition-bound locals, there were other, perhaps greater, fears. Some worried that eventually, the international community would take its revenge by attacking the coastal villages that had been invaded by the pirates. "We are very fearful of the pirates and of the international community," she said. "We hear reports that the West will launch air strikes against our town."[12]

Pirate with a Problem

AT THE age of forty, Khalil (not his real name) is old for a pirate. He has a wife and three children living in Bosasso. "I'm here because of them. I want to go back as soon as I can," he says. Khalil sits in the darkened recesses of a hotel bar in downtown Nairobi wearing a zip-up sweater and jeans to fight off the seasonal chill. He sips an orange Fanta, often squinting at my questions as if they're painful to hear. The meeting has been arranged by my colleague, an ethnic Somali and Kenyan journalist whom I will call Aziz. He has extensive contacts in the burgeoning Somali community in Nairobi and speaks a variety of languages, including English, Somali, Swahili, and some Arabic. Aziz is also well versed in the complexities of Somalia and Somali piracy, having recently traveled in and out of Somalia.

There is tension to this meeting. Khalil and his companion, Asad, the Somali bank employee described in the previous chapter, are in Kenya illegally. We meet downtown because I am working alone and am unwilling to meet with them in a "secret" location in the Somali community. That's fine, Aziz explains, because they also don't want the risk of being seen with a foreigner in their community, suspecting I could be an intelligence agent. Being seen with an American could only raise suspicions by others in the community. Our meeting room fronts a busy side street, has a couple of pool tables, and is quiet except for the steady noise spilling in from the street, until someone turns on the flat-screen TV hanging on the wall to watch a cricket game between Sri Lanka and India.

Khalil has lived in Nairobi for nearly three months after making an arduous trip from Bosasso to the Somalia–Kenya border by truck. From there, he made the fifty-five-mile trip into Kenya, arriving at the Dadaab refugee camp, home to some three hundred thousand Somalis who have fled the violence in southern Somalia. He spent a month in the camp before continuing on to Nairobi.

Khalil is on a mission. He's chasing down a distant relative who has a sizeable chunk of the money Khalil earned from piracy and has disappeared. Khalil is not angry—yet. Before things get ugly, he wants to exhaust all possibilities. "I know his family and his close relatives," he explains, and the two men have talked by phone. "He talked to me personally. I didn't make any threats. But if that money is not coming, the threat will be made." The man's relatives have told Khalil not to worry, that he'll get the eight thousand dollars he is owed.

Khalil explains that he collected thirty-five thousand dollars as one of a group of pirates who hijacked a ship. Of that money, he spent fifteen thousand dollars to build a house in Bosasso and another ten thousand dollars to pay off debts accumulated by him and his extended family. He then gave eight thousand dollars to his relative in Nairobi to be invested, keeping two thousand dollars in reserve. But after not hearing anything for several months, Khalil came to Nairobi only to learn that his relative was in Dubai. This left Khalil with little choice but to appeal to the man's clan elders for help. Khalil is patient, he says, and will wait for things to evolve.

The thirty-five thousand dollars was not easy to obtain. "I got it through my own sweat and hard work," Khalil says, and that money was his payoff for his participation in a hijacking. "I did it once, and that was all." Khalil does not like being a pirate but feels that most Somalis like him have little choice. When the Siad Barre regime fell in 1991, people along the coast made money by "protecting our ocean" from foreign fishermen, he says. Today most pirates are much younger than he, mostly men in their late teens or early twenties attracted by the quick money, despite the dangers.

Khalil was drawn into piracy by a friend who, like many others, envied the tangible results of piracy. "I was fishing and selling fish," Khalil says. "I used to enjoy it." But that changed as his fishing income dwindled. "I was influenced by a friend" who kept telling him that with piracy "you will either die or you will get rich." The prospect of riches began to outweigh the risks, Khalil says, because fishing became increasingly difficult. Somalis don't eat a lot of fish, and his market was limited, as was the supply due to overfishing of Somali waters by foreigners. Meanwhile, the pirates in town were driving new cars and building new houses. He decided to get involved.

As Khalil describes the events surrounding his hijacking, I surmise that he was one of the pirates who hijacked the infamous weapons ship the MV *Faina*, the same ship loaded with the tanks and machine guns that had been bound for Juba, South Sudan. It was the hijacking that I had read about in Khartoum nearly a year earlier. The ship was released for a reported ransom of $3.2 million, and Khalil was one of those who shared in the bounty. As I relish this bizarre connection, I realize I don't really know who Khalil is. I have had to trust my contact Aziz completely. But as we talk, my confidence grows.

"It was a totally dangerous job," Khalil says. "No coward can do it." He saw a lot of U.S. soldiers. "They're tough guys," he says of Americans. "They will either fight you or give you money." Though amusing, the comment puzzles me until I recall that a U.S. naval ship, the *Ticonderoga*, had been positioned between the *Faina* and the Somali shore to prevent the cache of weapons from falling into the hands of the Islamist extremists of al-Shabaab. The ship was harbored off the coastal town and pirate haven of Harardheere. I ask him who was behind the hijacking, but all he can tell me is that the sponsor was "a businessman from the village" and was a negotiator.

The hijacking was a big undertaking, Khalil explains, and the assault was conducted by about a dozen pirates in different skiffs that attacked the ship from various directions. It was a "very successful mission for me," he says, in part because the ship's crew did not resist. "Those guys surrendered. We kept them for some time." Khalil did not stay on the ship but guarded it on land from outsiders trying to steal the cargo. "I was among the security. We were [preventing] other people from taking those weapons by force."

Some of the weapons may have been spirited off the ship during the early stages of the hijacking, however, before the U.S. ship was in place. According to the November 2008 issue of *Terrorism and Security Monitor*, published by Jane's, "The pirates who hijacked the MV *Faina* . . . have given some of the weapons on board to the Khalid bin Walid Brigade, a relatively new insurgent group that seem to be affiliated to Hassan Turki." Hassan Turki is thought to be a senior Islamist commander in southern Somalia once loyal to the Islamic Courts Union.

"There was no way they could escape," Khalil says of the Ukrainian crew. "We tried to give them what they needed. We were not ready to kill." Had the crew resisted and put up a fight, however, he confessed, "they would be killed."

Since he remained on shore, Khalil says, "I was an outsider," but he was ready to respond to a crisis on board. "If there was trouble inside the ship, we got some hand signals."

Khalil is vague about the length of time that the ship was held, telling me it was about two and a half months, when in fact it was four months, and is unclear about the crew, telling me he thought they were Ukrainians. He then admits he can't tell one European from another in terms of nationality. While this again raises my suspicions, Khalil enthusiastically describes the weapons on board. When I tell Aziz that Khalil could have learned about the ship hijacking from television, the Internet, or talking with friends, Aziz says the *Faina* was hijacked exactly a year before our meeting, which is why some details are fuzzy. Khalil obviously speaks no English, nor does he understand it, relying on Aziz's translations.

More relevant is that Khalil's pirate money is gone, Aziz says. "I've not saved anything," Khalil admits, which is why his eight thousand dollars is so important now. His family never wanted him to join the pirates in the first place, he says, so he tried to invest the money, hoping it would generate enough income for him to forgo piracy. But, if his investment is not recovered, he may return to piracy. "I have an ambition to go back," he says.

But at forty, I ask, why consider returning to such dangerous work? There are few alternatives, Khalil responds, explaining that if the international community truly was interested in eradicating piracy, it would help rebuild Somalia. "The American people have allies," Khalil says. "We would stop the piracy if they will help us build a stable government in Somalia. Until that happens, don't expect much. We appeal to the U.S. to be serious about establishing a government." He and other Somalis are tired of the killing in their country. Piracy may have grown from the chaos, but it is not a long-term option for the future. "A majority of them die at sea," he says of the pirates. They go to sea because they're desperate for food and money. He says life in Somalia is a fight for survival and warns that Americans should not be surprised about "what is happening in Somalia" when so many people are desperate.

Piracy is a small part of a larger problem, Khalil says. "Forget about piracy. There is a lot of killing in Somalia on land. It should be considered a crime against humanity," he says of the destruction in Somalia. "There is no system [of government] there." The world should help put Somalia on its feet. "We want to help our kids. We want law and order. But we don't have that, so we have to do something we don't want to do," he says, which is piracy. "We only think negatively when we have difficulties."

6

NIGHTMARE ON THE DELTA

SOMALIA IS not the only African country enduring a plague of piracy. On the western coast of Africa, three thousand miles away, a more virulent form of piracy, hijacking, and hostage taking permeates Nigeria's sprawling and oil-rich delta region of the Niger River. As western Africa's largest river, it flows twenty-six hundred miles in an arc from the western African highlands of Guinea, through Mali and Niger, to the Gulf of Guinea in the Atlantic Ocean. The vast oil fields below the delta have made Nigeria the world's eighth-largest exporter of petroleum, supplying the United States with one of every five barrels of oil that it consumes. This brings billions of dollars annually into Nigeria's economy. Yet few of the 140 million people in Nigeria, Africa's most populous country, see the benefits of this oil wealth. Grinding poverty dominates the badly polluted Niger delta, where people live in vast mangrove swamps teeming with malaria. There are no schools, medical clinics, or social services in most delta villages, nor serviceable roads, clean drinking water, or electricity.

The situation has given rise to various violent antioil groups, most recently the Movement for the Emancipation of the Niger Delta (MEND). Attacks by MEND began in early 2006, damaging foreign oil company production facilities with the apparent aims of forcing the sharing of oil wealth with the delta residents and creating a pollution-free environment. MEND has succeeded in knocking out a significant percentage of Nigeria's oil output by sabotaging pipelines and abducting oil workers. More than two hundred foreigners have been kidnapped since MEND began, though most have been ransomed and released. The threat has forced major oil companies such as Royal Dutch Shell, ExxonMobil, and Chevron to remove nonessential staff from the region.

In addition to sabotaging and pilfering oil pipelines, one of the primary tactics used by rebels, and by what many say is a growing criminal element at work in the Niger delta, is to attack vessels that support the oil industry. Robbing, looting, and kidnapping for ransom are comparable to if not worse than what is occurring in Somalia but command far less attention. Piracy in both places is an outgrowth of weak or nonexistent government. In Somalia, piracy was spawned by war and chaos; in Nigeria, it is due to a badly corrupted government that has given rise to strong rebel and criminal elements. In Somalia, there has been overfishing and toxic waste dumping, and in the Niger delta, oil-polluted waters and decimated fisheries.

"In Nigeria, they shoot to kill. It is more dangerous in Nigeria," says Captain Pottengal Mukundan, director of the International Maritime Bureau (IMB), when I meet him one drizzly April morning in London. In Somalia, however, "they know it's a business, and they don't harm their hostages." Piracy in both Nigeria and Somalia features kidnapping, hostage taking, and ransoms, Mukundan says, but piracy in Nigeria has been more violent and politically motivated. The Niger delta pirates attack foreign oil companies, he says, who are blamed for the pollution and poverty in the delta despite the billions of dollars that Nigeria collects annually from the country's oil production.

Bad Day on the Delta

Someone who knows the dangers in the Niger delta is Donald Tyler, fifty-three, an oil supply boat captain who has worked on Africa's western coastal waters for years. Tyler explains how he survived a pirate attack just weeks earlier when we speak in June 2009. For the past thirty-five years, starting back in 1976 when he first went to the Louisiana oil fields, Tyler has worked the sea, between jobs alternating as an oil rig supply boat captain and a deep-sea fisherman. It was a good opportunity for someone without experience. "Most take the course [to become certified as a boat captain] now," he says from his home in Florida, still nursing an eye wounded in the attack. "I came through as a deckhand and climbed my way up the chain until I became a captain. I was just twenty years old when I was a captain."

Working in the oil business has been satisfying for Tyler. "The oil supply boats have come up such that you can make a decent living." And they've taken him to places like Nigeria, where he was ferrying anything that the offshore oil rigs needed. The supply ship he commanded was owned by Tide Water Marine Services, based in New Orleans, which contracts with ExxonMobil, he says.

Tyler's introduction to West Africa came when he took a job in Nigeria in 2002. He stayed for a year, then moved on to Angola, returning up the West Africa coast to work awhile in Equatorial Guinea. He has been in Nigeria for the past four years and likes it. "The nice thing about working in Africa is working in different countries," he says. "For a man who wants a little bit of adventure, this is the place to go. Every day is an adventure."

As much as he enthuses about Nigeria, he is quick to caution "Everyone is corrupt in Nigeria," which contributes significantly to the risks of living and working in the delta. After nearly seven years on the west coast of Africa, Tyler knows well what makes the Niger delta one of the most dangerous waterways in the world—second only to that off the Somali coast. "Most of the attacks take place in the river," he says, which is where he worked. But for the first few years, no one thought much of the danger. "We were running up and down the river on our own," he says. That changed in 2006 with the rapid rise in hijackings and attacks, and now the ships move only in convoys and with armed escorts provided by the Nigerian government.

It was Monday, April 27, 2009, and a fine mist hung over the river as Tyler began his day. As commander of the *Loving Tide*, a 250-foot oil rig supply vessel, he made regular round-trips from his port upriver in the delta to the oil rigs at sea. Tyler received an 8:00 A.M. call telling him to move the *Loving Tide* into convoy position in preparation for the run out to sea. The convoys typically left about 9:00 A.M. and were escorted by the Nigerian army river craft to land's end, he says, where they were then escorted by Nigerian navy craft out to the floating oil rigs they supplied. It is a trip of some twenty-seven miles and takes most of the day, with the ships arriving at their final destination by mid- or late afternoon. On this day, however, the convoy consisted of only five ships, fewer than half the normal number.

They made good time, and by about 10:45 A.M., Tyler remembers, the convoy was ready for the handoff to the Nigerian navy. Rather than head straight out to sea, *Loving Tide* and another ship were told to pull off to the side of the channel to clear the way for a large ship carrying liquefied natural gas. "In Nigeria, everybody has to get out of the channel" when encountering such a ship, he explains. But only his and one other ship stopped. Tyler watched helplessly as the other three ships disappeared into the distance followed by one Nigerian security boat. "There were two of us, then," he recalls. Unknown to Tyler was that one of the Nigerian naval vessels that was to escort his ship had engine trouble and hadn't reported for duty that morning.

Within minutes, the two ships were attacked. "The chief mate called me that there was a situation with the other boat," Tyler says. Pirates were attempting to board it. Tyler picked up his phone and put his ship into gear. "I called my office that we were witnessing an act of piracy. We went offshore as fast as our vessel would go," hoping not to fall victim to the pirates as well. Then things got confusing. "We heard that no, it was just a fishing boat," he remembers, not pirates. "We didn't believe it," he says, because he and his crew watched the pirates chase the ship as it took evasive action. "I had my binoculars, and I could see there was one man in the fast speedboat, and he was at the stern. I could see nobody on the bridge." He realized that the captain and crew already had locked themselves in a safe room. "We were fifteen hundred feet from them," he states. "Normally, you're going to see two or three people on [the] bridge at any time." Tyler decided not to stick around. "We went off at full speed," he says, and he fired off an e-mail to headquarters. He then was told what he most feared: "I heard one of the deckhands saying they're coming for us."

Tyler and his crew had little time to prepare, let alone figure out how to fight them off. "The pirate boat was coming but not directly at us. Then he turned right at us. At this time, I pressed the ship's security alarms that notified the coast guard." Tyler took other precautions. "I hid my documents behind the refrigerator and went back to the bridge," where he swallowed pills for his high blood pressure. The ship's Nigerian crew, meanwhile, seemed unruffled about the attack and lingered on deck to watch the attackers, Tyler recalls. To prevent their capture, he ordered the crew into hiding. "We were fishtailing back and forth," he says, but the ship's ability to evade was blocked as it entered a swarm of shrimp boats working the lucrative salt water just off the delta. Tyler navigated the ship as best he could, trying not to crush any of the shrimpers. The maneuvers did not slow the pirates, and soon, he says, "They were pulling up to the side of the boat." When he saw the pirates' weapons, he decided the chase was over.

"I told the first mate to stop the engines. I was at the back of the bridge when I saw them raise the gun. When he stopped the engines, I went to the wheelhouse to make sure the engines were out of gear." As Tyler turned to leave the bridge, the phone rang. "I was going to make my escape," he says, but he paused to answer the call. "It was my office," he recalls, and in a panic, he shouted, "They're on the boat! They're on the boat! They've made it on the boat!" Tyler turned to run, but a pirate already had him cornered. "I just dropped the phone, and there he was, at the window pointing the gun at me. He was dressed in sandals and army fatigues," Tyler recalls. "He had a red sash on his arm. It means they cannot be killed. Juju. They believe that as long as they have any red on their body, they cannot be killed."

The pirates had easily climbed aboard, Tyler says, because the ship was a low-slung affair with a deck only six feet off the water—a simple climb for a nimble pirate. "They're low because of the docks where we work all over the world. If they're high you can't see where to put the cargo," he explains. When pirates want to attack, "there is no doubt they're going to get on the boat." It was because of the ease in boarding that Tyler chose not to resist. "Either [you] make them angry [by running], or [you] stop and hope for the best. If you make them work to get on the boat, they'll be angry with you. It's a decision the captain has to make." If he had been farther out to sea, however, and if the ocean had not been blocked with shrimp boats, he would have made a run for it by continuing to maneuver, he says.

With pirates on board, Tyler had his personal safety to worry about. "He pointed the barrel and pointed to the door," Tyler says of the pirate. "I put my hands in the air and walked over to the door. When I opened the door, he started screaming, 'Get down on the floor! Get down on the floor!'" Tyler complied. "All I heard was the trampling of [feet]," he says. But the pirates needed him if they were going to loot the ship. "They snatched me to my feet right quick and had me silence the alarms. They had the gun right at my head. They were screaming, 'Where's the money, where's the money? Where's the crew?'" Tyler could only tell them, "We don't carry any money." The pirates didn't want to hear that. "They took me into my room and put me on my knees," and then repeated their demands and shouted, "Where is the money?" When Tyler insisted he had none, the pirates ripped his bed apart. "We did have a safe in my room," Tyler says, but, "I never kept it locked. There was nothing in it." Not only did the pirates see it, they also didn't believe that it was empty. Then Tyler realized he had accidentally locked it. With a gun on him, the pirates ordered him to open the safe. Nervous and fumbling, he tried the combination repeatedly. "I tried to open it twice, but it would not open. It was a cheap safe." Frustrated and frightened, he turned to the pirates and yelled, "Just take what you want. Just leave us alone!"

Again, it was not what the pirates wanted to hear. "One came up to me and asked me, 'Where's the money?' I kept telling them, 'There is no money,'" prompting a pirate to slug Tyler. "He came up to me, and he hit me in the left eye. 'You dog,' I said, and he hit me hard [again] in the same eye. He had a glazed look in his eyes. He might have been high on something." With his head ringing, Tyler realized his defiance could cost him his life. "Another man was telling me, 'Please, cooperate.' I insisted I was."

Tyler's attention was diverted when a couple of pirates came up the stairs with a deckhand they had captured, one who had not made it to the engine room. The pirates took both of them to the bridge and told Tyler, "Get on the floor." He complied, and one put a foot on his back to keep him down. At this point, "I was spread-eagle on the floor," he says. He remained where he was until "all went silent. I didn't see anything."

Suspecting that the pirates had left, "I slowly got up to my knees and didn't see or hear anyone." He looked over the ship's side, and he says, "I saw them all getting into their speedboat." Apparently frustrated at finding nothing to steal, "they left our boat, and they raced over to [a] shrimp boat. They threw them some fish. Everybody had their hands up."

The ordeal was over. Tyler called the crew back on deck. As he contacted the other convoy ships and pieced together the sequence of events, he suspected that the pirate attack may not have been an accident. Before Tyler could explain what had happened to his ship, the Nigerian navy asked if pirates had attacked him. Did the Nigerians already know? "The pirates were on board for thirty or thirty-five minutes," Tyler explains, which was just enough time to rob the ship while the escort ship slowed and turned around to retrieve the two ships left behind. Tyler then learned that the other ship that had stayed behind had, in fact, been boarded, but the pirates had abandoned it in favor of his ship. At this point, the Nigerian escort was notified of the pirate attack. Even though the Nigerians "knew we were being attacked," Tyler says, "it still took them thirty to forty minutes . . . to get to us. It's mighty funny that two boats can be attacked at the point they're supposed to be protected."

Tyler's suspicions grew stronger the next day when he learned that the attack had followed a familiar pattern. "It seems that every time there's an attack, the security boats are not around," he says. When the Nigerians were confronted about it, they said the escorts had simply lost track of the two rear ships. To solve the problem, "the [Nigerian] navy man said all the boats needed to have transponders" so the escorts could track them. But others angrily retorted that it was the Nigerians who need transponders so they can be tracked.

In retrospect, Tyler says, he didn't fear death as much as he thought he would. "I didn't think it was the end," he says. "It was a feeling of disbelief. My adrenaline. I wasn't scared at all, and I was surprised afterwards that I wasn't scared." He was mentally prepared for a pirate attack, he explains, because he knew an attack was always possible. "A lot of boats have been hit. The thought is there every time you go out: you could be boarded by pirates." He would have done nothing differently. "There's nothing we could do since we don't have any arms. It just happens so quick. I decided that I was going to cooperate. When I saw them coming, I knew it was going to happen. I turned the boat around then. The pirate boat had three times the speed of the navy boat. [The attack] went right by the book. I cooperated and told them I'd give them what they want."

Instead of continuing out to sea after the attack, Tyler turned his ship back upriver as his face began to ache. "The side of my face was red and swollen up," sending him to the local clinic where he was given anti-inflammatory pills. He went to bed hoping that sleep would speed his recovery. The next day he saw bright flashes, and the day after that, the pain increased, forcing him to visit a larger, better equipped clinic for X-rays. A few days later he was on his way home to Florida, arriving on May 4. Fortunately, a scan found no serious damage. His eye had hemorrhaged, but the effects went away, he says, although, "My left eye feels a little blurry now and then."

The attack did not force Tyler into another line of work or an early retirement. "I have a lot of friends in Nigeria. I've worked there a long time. There's a risk there, but there is always a risk walking the streets in New Orleans or New York City," he says. The continuing turmoil and violence in the Niger River delta has also not dissuaded him. He suspects that corrupt officials in the government and the military, as well as bandits, are using the political mayhem as a cover for crime. "The MEND and the pirates are two different organizations," Tyler explains. "The pirates are doing snatch and grab, just trying to get what they can. The pirates are out for the valuables." But, he admits, "There's a thin line between the two."

The harbor at Mombasa, Kenya, from Fort Jesus.

Shimo la Tewa prison, Mombasa, where suspected Somali pirates are held pending trial.

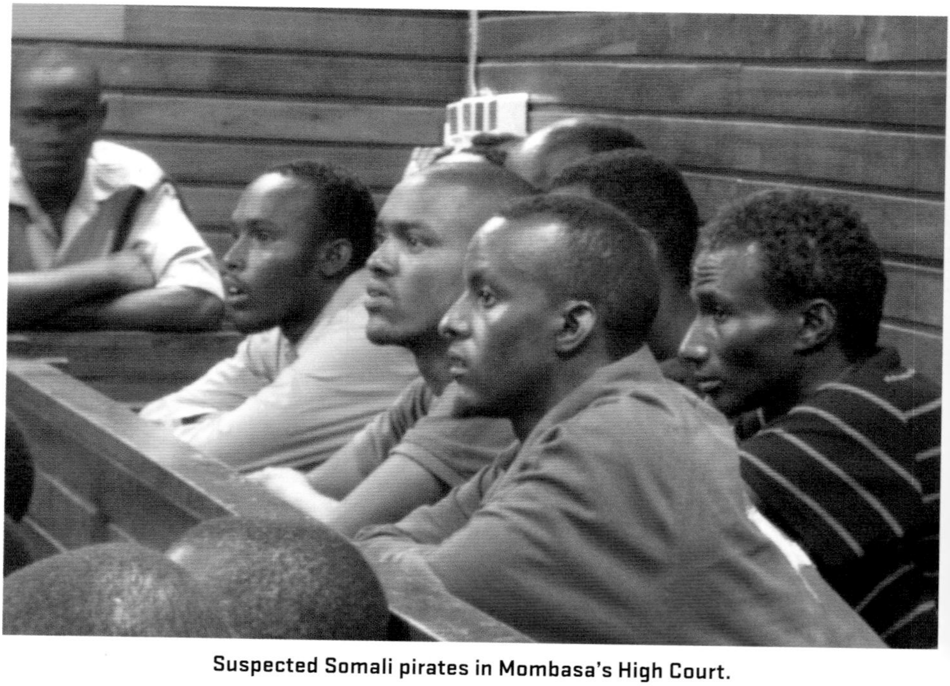

Suspected Somali pirates in Mombasa's High Court.

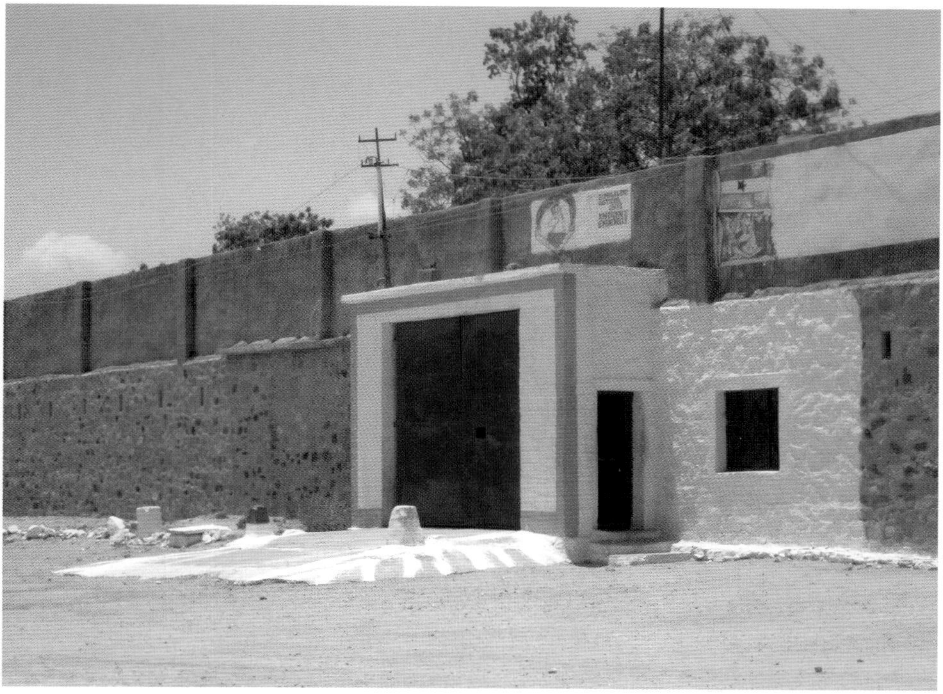

Somaliland prison at Madheera, where convicted pirates are jailed.

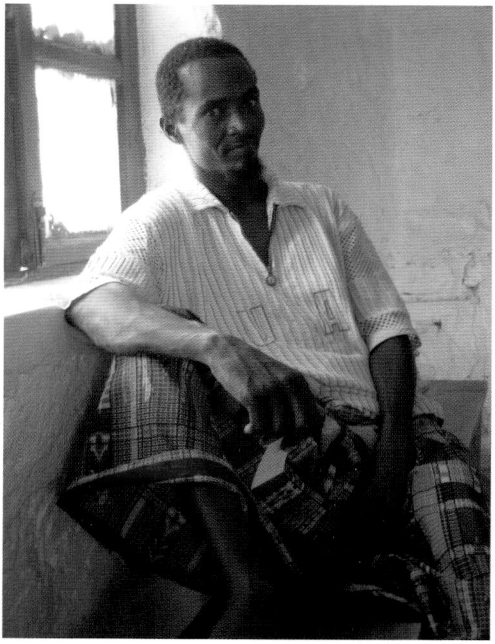

Convicted pirate Farah Ismail Eidle in Madheera prison, Somaliland.

Author, right, with Somaliland coast guard officer Isse Mahad Abdi.

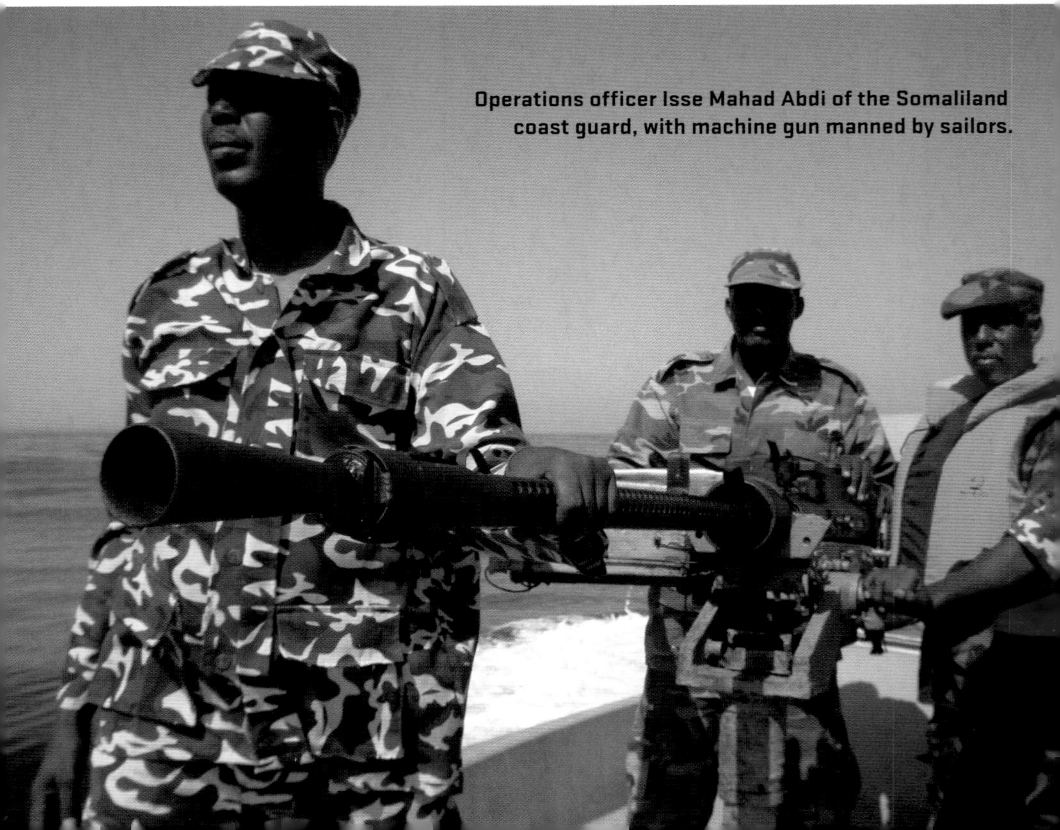

Operations officer Isse Mahad Abdi of the Somaliland coast guard, with machine gun manned by sailors.

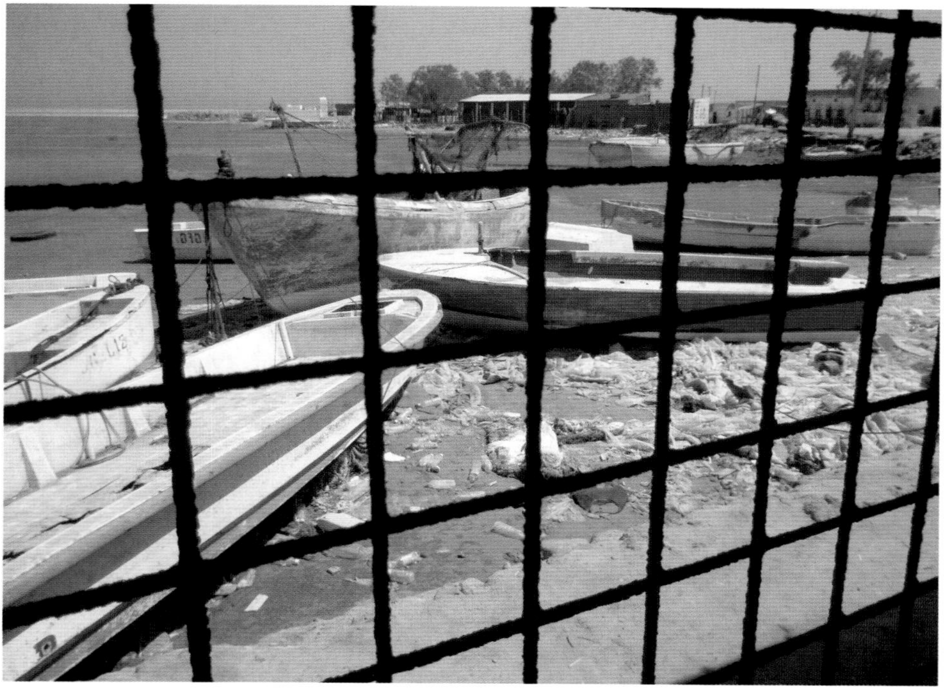

Fishing boats at Berbera, Somaliland, as seen from offices of fishing cooperative.

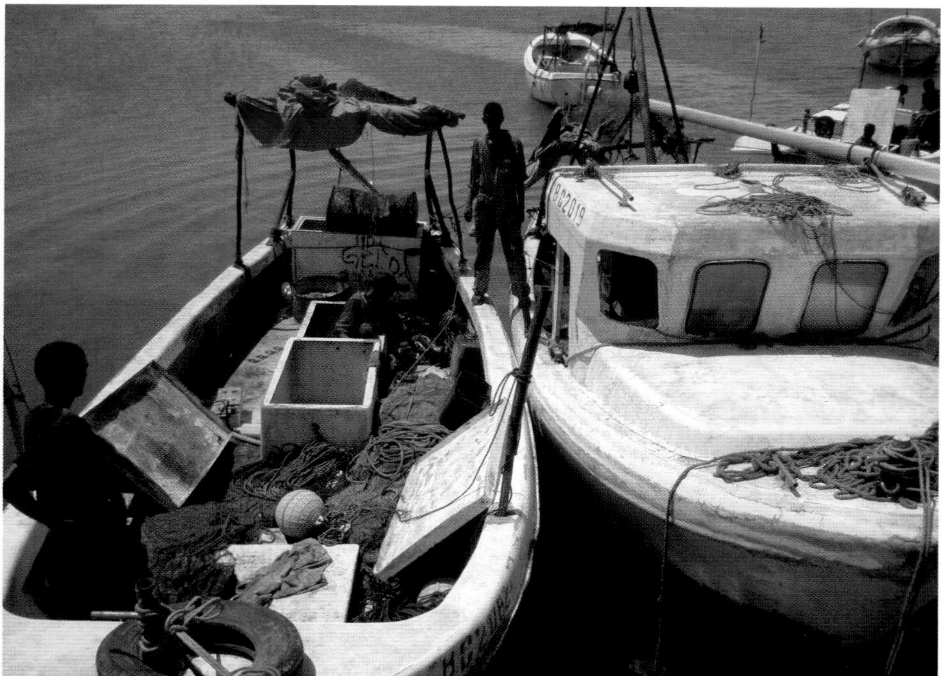

Fishermen in the Berbera harbor repairing boats.

Fishermen sitting in the shade on a dock in Berbera.

Driver and professed former pirate, Ismail Abdullahi Ibrihim, in Hargeisa, Somaliland.

Meandering camels on the road to the Dadaab refugee camp, Kenya.

Convoy paused on the road to the Dadaab refugee camp.

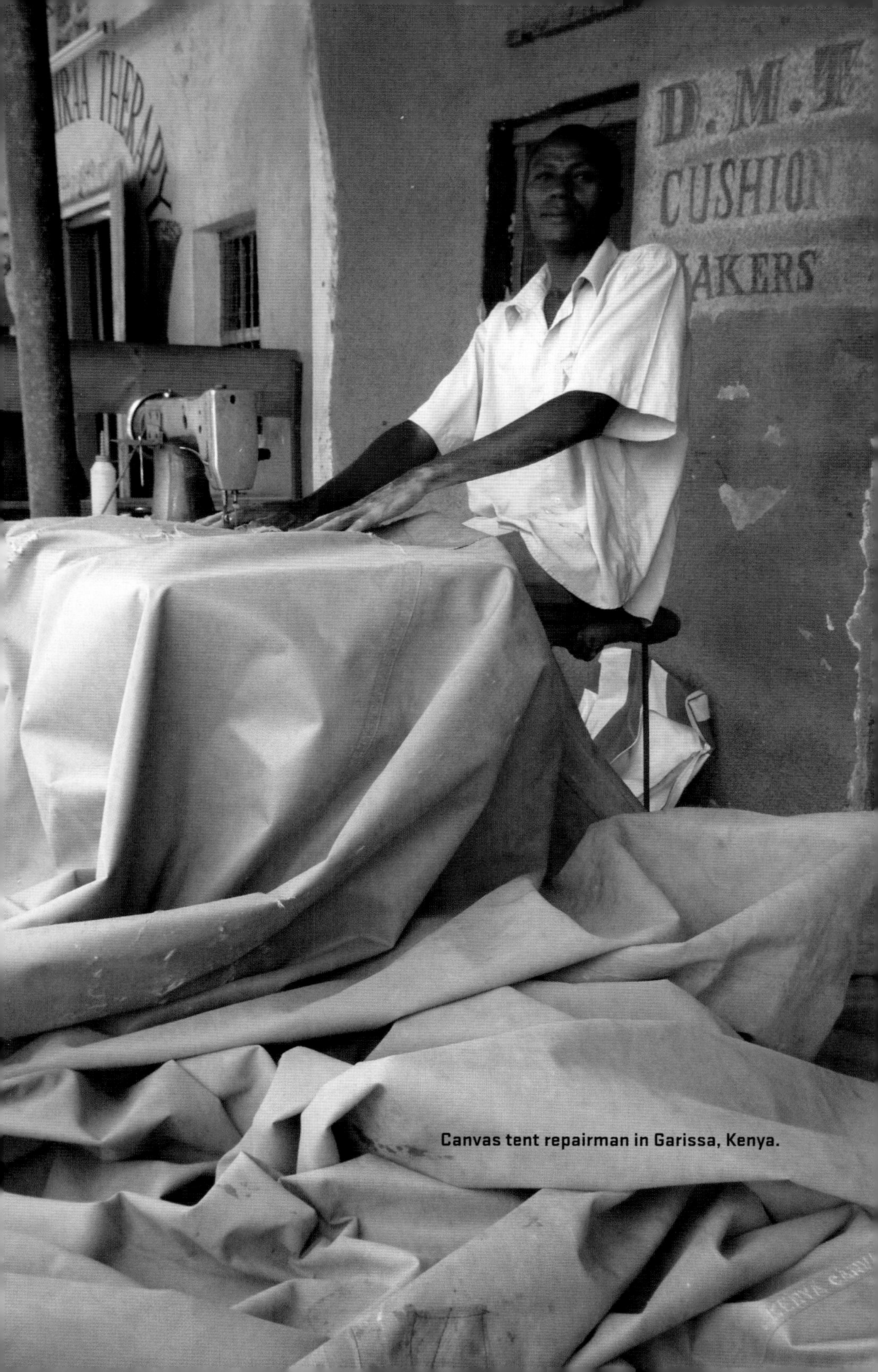

Canvas tent repairman in Garissa, Kenya.

People at the Dadaab center gate, waiting to get in.

Children at the Dadaab camp reception center.

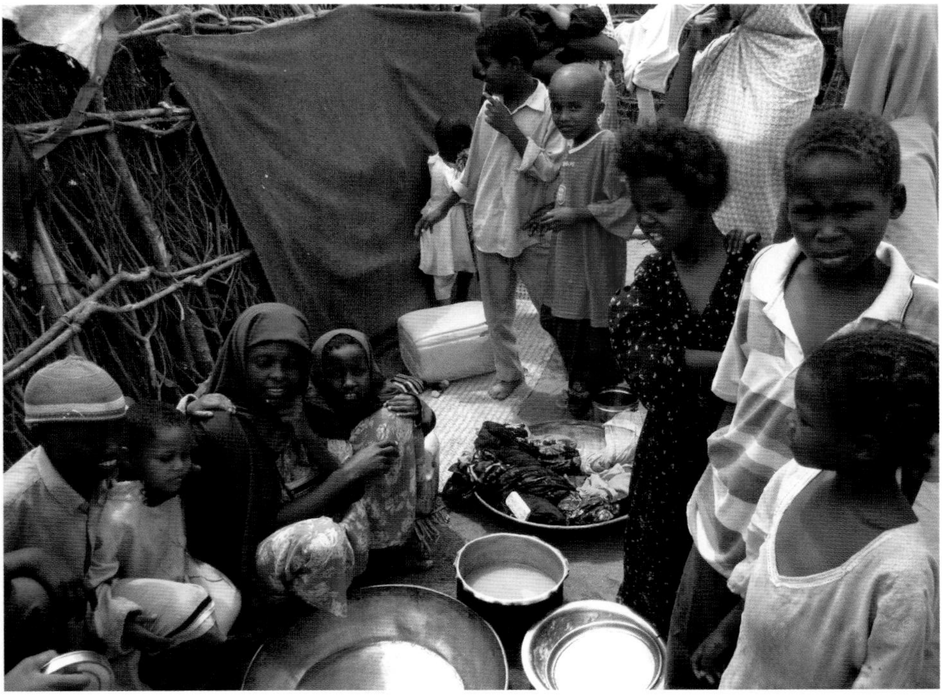

Fatima Gedi with her children in the Dadaab camp.

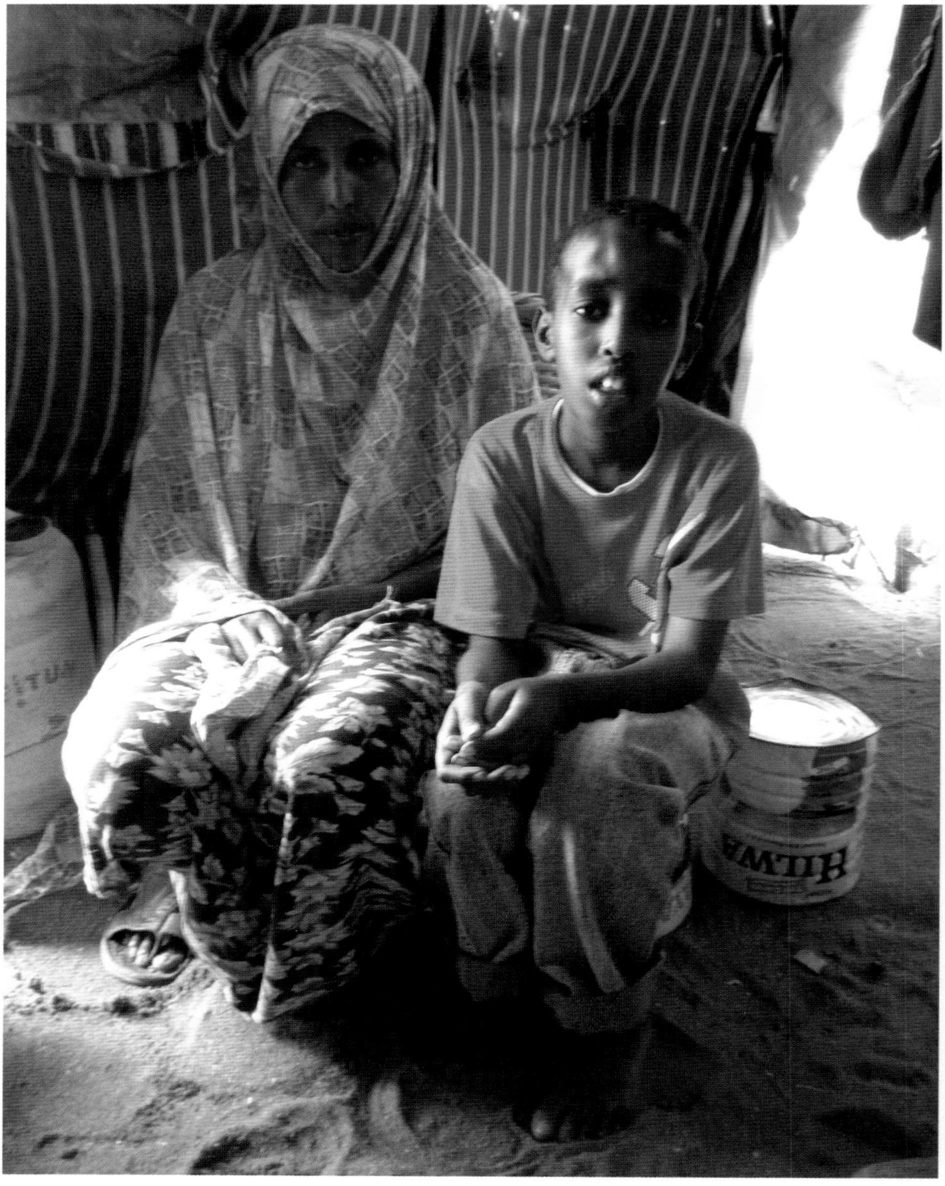

Dahbo Abdi in the Dadaab camp with her son, who was shot in the head in Mogadishu, Somalia.

Sahara Maalim with her son Abdirahman Khalif in the Dadaab camp.

Farah Hayd Ali, who was wounded in Somalia in 1991 and
has lived in the Dadaab camp for nearly twenty years.

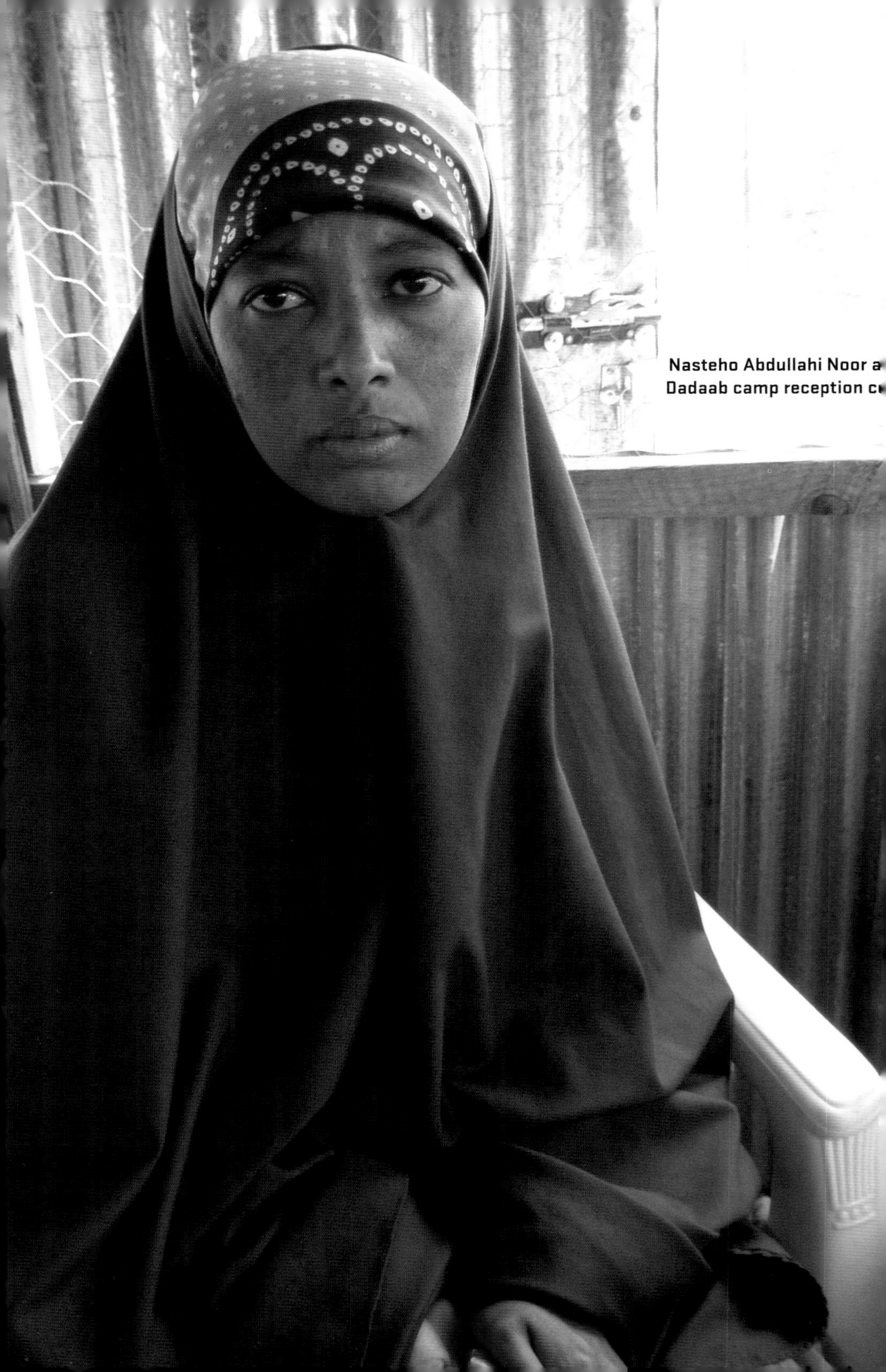

Nasteho Abdullahi Noor a
Dadaab camp reception c

A typical dirt road in the Dadaab camp.

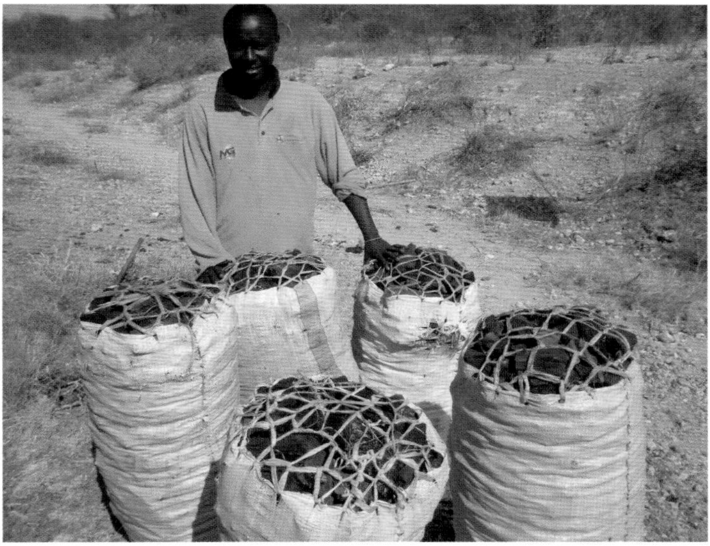

A charcoal seller on the road to the Dadaab camp.

Antipiracy command center on the Royal Dutch Navy frigate, the HNLMS *Evertsen*, off the coast of Tanzania.

Machine gunners firing from the deck of HNLMS *Evertsen*.

Simulated capture of Somali pirates by Dutch marine special forces.

Nigeria's Curse of Oil

THE BOUNTY of Nigeria's oil bypasses almost all of the country's population. Most of Nigeria's oil wealth is taken by a small percentage of the population, leaving the rest to live on dollars a day, making Nigeria one of the poorest countries in the world. A *Vanity Fair* article on the Niger River delta rebels said that during the past fifty years, "between $300 and $400 billion of oil revenue has been stolen or misspent by corrupt government officials," approximating Western aid received by Africa during those years.[1] While much of the blame for corruption is directed toward the country's leadership, corruption permeates society. The Nigerian constitution requires that nearly 50 percent of the country's oil revenues go to state and local governments, with the nine oil-producing states getting additional amounts. In 2006, these nine states should have gotten about six billion dollars. But once the money arrives at the state level, it tends to disappear. Not surprisingly, a financial crimes commission around that time found evidence that all but five of Nigeria's thirty-six governors were corrupt.[2]

A vast mangrove swamp, the Niger delta is one of the world's largest wetlands and has been producing oil for half a century. In most delta villages, however, the only evidence of oil production is the severely polluted water and land and the sporadic gas flares that can illuminate the night sky for miles. To get what many in the delta see as theirs, angry and poor Nigerians routinely tap pipelines and siphon off oil and fuel, exposing them to horrendous dangers like an explosion in 2006 that killed hundreds.

While MEND insists it is fighting so that all Nigerians can benefit from their country's resources, most in the delta remain impoverished and insecure, prompting some to suggest that the violence may be due in part to criminal groups unaffiliated with or loosely linked to MEND and its cause. In late May 2009, the Nigerian government launched a military campaign in the Niger delta to flush out the MEND rebels. By mid-June 2009, after a month of fighting, the government had freed about seventeen hostages taken by rebels, including Filipinos, Ukrainians, and Nigerians. But the overall results of the offensive were unclear. Human rights and aid workers said many people had been displaced, and civilian casualties were widespread. The military offensive did little to solve the situation in the delta, rights advocates complained. "A military response will not tackle the underlying issues of poverty and inequality, which continue to foment violence in the delta region," said Corinne Dufka, head of Human Rights Watch (HRW) for West Africa. "The government must address the causes of the political discontent in the delta, including the endemic corruption that sustains the shocking levels of poverty in the midst of tremendous oil wealth," said Eric Guttschuss, HRW's researcher in Nigeria.[3]

The Struggle Continues

WHILE BOMBS and bullets were flying in the Niger delta, a legal battle was being fought in New York on the same issue. In June 2009 an out-of-court settlement was announced between a corporate oil giant and families of victims of the Niger delta violence. The settlement came out of a lawsuit filed by the family of the late Nigerian poet and Nobel-prize nominee Ken Saro-Wiwa against Royal Dutch Shell in U.S. District Court in New York. It focused on Shell's work in Nigeria's Ogoni region, a densely populated area where the company first began operations in 1958. Shell has been accused of oil spills and gas leaks that have contaminated land and water. One claim in the lawsuit was that in June 1993, Shell allowed a pipeline to spew oil for forty days before fixing the problem. In the early 1990s, the people of Ogoni were organized by activists who included Saro-Wiwa and formed the Movement for the Survival of the Ogoni People (MOSOP). The group had bypassed the Nigerian government and complained directly to Shell and other oil companies, demanding ten billion dollars in lost royalties and compensation for environmental damage. The Nigerian army responded by reportedly razing thirty villages, arresting hundreds, and killing an estimated two thousand people. Saro-Wiwa was subjected to a sham trial and then hanged along with his alleged accomplices on November 10, 1995. Saro-Wiwa's last words were, "Lord take my soul, but the struggle continues."[4] That struggle resurfaced under the name of MEND.

Because the lawsuit involved Nigeria and the Shell operations there, the oil company had tried to keep the case out of New York. But in 2000, the Court of Appeals ruled that both the venue and suit were legitimate because one of the plaintiffs was a U.S. resident and because Shell had an office in the city, providing the necessary U.S. connections. The suit was based on an arcane law known as the Alien Tort Claims Act of 1789 that allowed U.S. federal courts to hear cases brought by foreigners for violations of international law by U.S. companies or companies doing business in the United States. The law was rarely used until the latter half of the twentieth century, when the U.S. Court of Appeals for the Second Circuit ruled that it could be used to address human rights abuses. While the law and the suits filed under it have drawn international attention, no foreign corporation has ever been found liable in a U.S. courtroom under the law because the corporations have settled out of court.

Because the case was settled on the eve of the trial in June 2009, an airing of the allegations against Shell and the company's responses were never heard in court.[5] Shell's filings in the suit, of course, present a far different view of the matter. Shell claimed it was victimized by violence and forced to abandon the Ogoni region in early 1993. The oil company lawyers claimed that the MOSOP activists had provoked the Nigerian military into attacking in hopes of generating international attention. "Shell has always maintained the allegations were false," said Shell executive Malcolm Brinded in an official statement, referring to claims that Shell conspired with the Nigerian government to eradicate the anti-oil movement. "While we were prepared to go to court to clear our name, we believe the right way forward is to focus on the future for [the] Ogoni people, which is important for peace and stability in the region."[6]

Royal Dutch Shell agreed to a $15.5 million settlement and the creation of a fund intended to change life for some of the millions of people who have not benefited from Nigeria's oil development. Shell continues to operate in Nigeria and said it hopes the settlement will prompt the "process of reconciliation." Shell admitted no wrongdoing regarding the 1995 hanging execution of Saro-Wiwa and the others. "This gesture also acknowledges that, even though Shell had no part in the violence that took place, the plaintiffs and others have suffered," Brinded said.[7]

Saro-Wiwa's fifty-year-old son, Ken Saro-Wiwa Jr., said he was glad to see the settlement because the suit had been tied up in court for thirteen years. "I think he would be happy with this," he said of his late father. "The fact that they would have to settle is a victory for us." Accordingly, the families of the deceased were to be compensated and their legal fees paid. About half of the $15.5 million goes into a trust fund to be invested in social programs such as educational endowments and adult literacy programs, agricultural projects, and support for small businesses. While $15.5 million seems a goodly amount, the cost to a company like Shell was negligible and was said to be comparable to the annual cost of renting one of the supertankers that delivers Nigerian oil to other countries.[8]

Perhaps the true value of the suit was not in the dollar amount but in the message that it sent to the corporations, especially global oil companies. "Is it enough to bring back the lives of our clients? Obviously not," said Jenny Green, a lawyer for the Center for Constitutional Rights in New York who helped file the lawsuit in 1996. The settlement signaled to multinationals operating in developing countries that "you can't commit human rights violations as a part of doing business," she said. "A corporation can't act with impunity. And we think there is accountability in this settlement."[9]

While it has been fourteen years since his father was hanged, Saro-Wiwa said companies like Shell are beginning to understand they need a "social license" to operate in foreign countries. Although Shell recently agreed to fund a study of environmental damage in the Ogoni region from oil drilling, "they have a long way to go," Saro-Wiwa said. "But at least they realize some of their actions can come back to haunt them, as we saw in New York."[10] Yet others argue that the lawsuit settlement has changed nothing about the way Shell and other oil giants do business in the Niger delta region. Steve Kretzmann, executive director of Oil Change International and a former adviser for the Saro-Wiwa lawsuit, said that although the suit has drawn attention to the region's problems, the situation remains the same. "You talk to the community activists, and they'll tell you there's not a substantial difference in the way Shell is operating now and the way they operated fifteen years ago."[11]

Extremely Bitter Men

Hope that some semblance of peace might eventually settle over the delta region faded in late 2009 after MEND declared an end to a cease-fire that had begun in mid-July. In mid-March 2010, the group underscored its threats with a car bombing that killed one person near where government officials were discussing amnesty for the rebels. MEND dismissed the government's amnesty proposal earlier in 2009 as a "charade" and warned that future attacks would not be as limited as in the past. "The Movement for the Emancipation of the Niger Delta (MEND) will resume with attacks against the oil industry at the expiration of our cease-fire."[12] The announcement went on to say, "MEND considers this next phase of our struggle as the most critical, as we intend to end fifty years of slavery of the people of the Niger delta by the Nigerian government, a few individuals, and the western oil companies once and for all." MEND then warned, "In this next phase, we will burn down all attacked installations and no longer limit our attacks to the destruction of pipelines."[13]

Although the government had claimed that the unconditional amnesty offered in 2009 for Niger delta militants was a success, MEND charged that those who reportedly had surrendered arms to the government were, in fact, people "rented by government in the hope that real militants would be persuaded to emerge." The rebels said the weapons claimed to have been recovered by the government were purchased for that purpose. The rebels also refused to participate in discussions on the Niger delta crisis, saying, "The government, in trying to further insult the people of the Niger delta, has selected to 'dialogue' with a class of individuals it can very easily manage." It also accused the government of trying to sell parcels of land belonging to Niger delta residents without their knowledge. "We will fight for our land with the last drop of our blood regardless of how many people the government of Nigeria and the oil companies are successful in bribing."[14] The struggle launched by Saro-Wiwa and others in the delta has continued but with a new generation that has inherited a problem that may take generations to resolve. "We are not communists or even revolutionaries," said a MEND spokesman to a journalist. "We're just extremely bitter men."[15]

7

TEN MONTHS IN HELL

On August 5, 2008, Somali pirates captured a tugboat off the Somali coast with ten Nigerian sailors aboard, launching one of the most agonizing episodes of Somali piracy. This Nigerian incident became noteworthy not because of the ransom paid or a dramatic rescue by swarming commandos, but because the Nigerians were among the longest-held hostages ever by Somali pirates. Ironically, these captives were fellow Africans, and the pirates never collected anything remotely close to the one million dollars they had demanded. Instead, the pirates reluctantly accepted piecemeal payments totaling a measly $130,000, a sum that possibly didn't cover the cost of keeping the crew alive. Much of the ransom came from the families of the captives themselves, not international shipping insurers or multinational shipping companies.

The crew's long-awaited release came one Friday evening, June 5, 2009, when their beleaguered tugboat, *MV Yenegoa Ocean*, left Cullula, the northernmost port town on the Puntland coast of Somalia, and chugged into the Gulf of Aden. Hours later the tug was intercepted as it limped toward the Yemeni coast in the predawn darkness by marines of the Dutch warship *De Zeven Provincien*. After ten months in captivity, the Nigerians could hardly grasp that they were free and had survived a torturous and harrowing ordeal. Once in the Yemeni port, the tug's Nigerian captain, Graham Egbegi, railed against his captors. "We were taken to a remote area off Somalia, and we were living like animals in that place." The crew was menaced by wild-eyed, armed, and edgy khat-chewing pirates, he said.[1]

A seafaring Nigerian familiar with the pirate-infested Niger River delta in West Africa, Egbegi never expected to be a victim of pirates from another African country. Yet he and his crew were caught in the confluence of two movements at opposite ends of the African continent. From the moment the Somali pirates boarded, Egbegi knew it was not going to be a picnic. The pirates carried AK-47s and rocket-propelled grenade launchers and confined the crew to their cabins. "They mounted an automatic machine gun on deck and pointed it at us," Egbegi recalled. "They became very hostile after that. They were always high on drugs. They were living like demons."[2]

The pirates' demand of one million dollars in ransom was probably less than the tug was worth, since it had been picked up just days earlier in Dubai and was on its maiden voyage through the Indian Ocean, tracking the Somali coastline, headed for the Cape of Good Hope, en route to Nigeria. When one of the crew suffered an apparent stroke, Egbegi directed the ship into port at Mogadishu, hoping to find medical care for the man. Instead, Somalis swarmed the tug and immediately commandeered it northward along the Somali coast to a protected pirate haven. The crew used mobile phones to contact friends and family, alerting everyone to their capture. The families in turn contacted the company. The tug's owner, George Onokpite, who was based in Malaysia, expressed alarm and assured the grief-stricken families that he would do all he could to secure the crew's release.[3]

Months later, the crew lingered in captivity as Onokpite confessed that he could not meet the ransom demands. He also balked at the appeals from Nigerian officials that he do more for the crew's release.[4] Rumors swirled that Onokpite was reluctant to fight for the crew and ship's release because the ship carried contraband, a charge that was never confirmed.[5] The pirates, meanwhile, did not let the new ship sit idle, and while negotiations dragged on, they used the *MV Yenagoa Ocean* as a mother ship to carry out other hijackings, moving it from Mogadishu to the port of Eyl and later Bosasso.

After months in captivity, the crew's condition deteriorated as the Somali captors turned the Nigerians' lives into a living hell. Egbegi said the crew saw little sunlight for the first three months and survived on a diet of rice, bits of bread, and an odd tomato or onion. The water was foul, he said. "People got sick. They didn't care about our lives. We were miserable for the first three months."[6] Weight loss was inevitable and universal. "My trousers are too big for me now, and I have no belt," Egbegi said after his rescue. "I can get a rope and tie it to my waist. . . . But this is not the time for fashion," he said, trying to make light of his condition. He then confessed what he and his crew wanted most: "I just want to go home."[7]

As the captive sailors clung to life, back in Nigeria the deputy majority leader in the Nigerian Senate, Victor Ndoma-Egba, appealed for public help. "Although the beleaguered crew members are still alive, they have had to contend with bouts of brutality, starvation, contaminated drinking water, and poor health conditions climaxed by the case of one crew member who once relapsed into a partial stroke in the absence of medication," Ndoma-Egba said, attempting to drum up support for the captives' release.[8]

Meanwhile, the pirates dismantled anything and everything they could, and what they didn't take, they destroyed. "The pirates were day by day stealing everything from us," the captain recalled, saying that the crew was powerless. "They pounced on our food and dry store. Everything in my ship is broken and looted . . . from electronics to personal TV sets." The crew's saving grace was its Christian faith, he said, which the sailors shared in the face of the smoldering, khat-chewing pirates. "We would pray and cry to God. He was our strength, and he did not abandon us."[9]

While the crew pondered and prayed, the families became increasingly desperate, realizing that neither the shipowner nor the Nigerian government—despite its sympathetic public comments—was going to do anything to secure the crew's release. Captain Egbegi's older brother in Nigeria began organizing efforts to gain the Nigerians' release. In addition, the captain's other brother, Geoffrey Egbide, who spells his name differently than his brother and who had been living in the United

States for nine years, was enlisted in the effort. Egbide lives in St. Paul, Minnesota, and contacted a leader in the city's large Somali population, Omar Jamal, director of the Somali Justice Advocacy Center.

"Three or four months ago, a family member came to our office," Jamal tells me in early June 2009, shortly after the Nigerians' release. "He did not know what to do," he says of Geoffrey Egbide. Jamal had dealt with some other cases like this, having become involved in contacting relatives of the Somali pirate captured by the United States after the attempted hijacking of *Maersk Alabama*. He was confident he could track down the pirates but knew the Nigerians' release would not be easy or come quickly. Jamal first contacted the FBI, not wanting to be accused of attempting to aid the pirates. "We brought it to the attention of the FBI," he says, but he was told that the FBI was not interested. "They said that the people were in Somalia," Jamal explains, and besides, they "weren't U.S. citizens."

Jamal called contacts in Somalia and soon found the pirate captors. "We started talking to the pirates. We asked them to free the crew and the ship." Jamal knew from Egbide that the Nigerians had already contacted the pirates because they knew of the pirates' demands. So Jamal asked the pirates to drop their ransom request and free the hostages. "The owner wasn't able to come up with the money," Jamal told the pirates, hoping they would realize that the Nigerians, like them, were impoverished. The crew was African, after all, he had argued, and not part of a large international corporation. The one million dollar ransom was out of the question. "We told them that that's not gonna happen," he says, and that "the Nigerian government is not interested in this."

Some money was collected, however, and transferred to the pirates. The first payment was eighty thousand dollars and apparently came from the ship's owner. "It was meant for the upkeep and maintenance of the hostages," Geoffrey Egbide explains to me in mid-June 2009. "It came from the boat owner. They sent it from Nigeria."

The money was necessary to keep the hostages alive, Jamal says. "They have to feed the hostages. They have to provide for them. Someone had to make sure they don't escape. A few guys with AK-47s, they have to do a lot of work to keep hostages." As talks languished, money continued to be collected in Nigeria and was periodically transferred to Somalia, Egbide recalls, with a second payment of forty thousand dollars followed by a third of ten thousand dollars.

The negotiations were tedious, Jamal adds, and forced him to change tactics. "I changed my position with them," and suggested something new: "Release the crew and keep the boat." That didn't work either, and it became increasingly clear the pirates were convinced that somehow the one million dollars would appear. When nothing happened, the pirates threaten to kill the crew. Having heard similar threats from other pirates before, Jamal remained calm and responded by asking the pirates to at least return the bodies to Nigeria. This threat, as well as all the other promises, turned out to be hollow, Jamal says. "They never lived up [to] their promises. When they got forty thousand dollars, they agreed to release both the ship and the men." But the pirates reneged on that promise, forcing Jamal to confront them. "Why are you doing this?" he asked. He received no reasonable answer, he says, and realized the pirates only wanted money. "They will say anything," he states. "Once they get the money, then it is their decision, not yours anymore [to release the crew and ship]."

Looking back, Jamal has little good to say about the Somali pirate who did most of the negotiating. "He was a crook. He would say anything. Once he gets the money, he asked for more." The pirate leader was a man named Mahad Ali Sarsed, Jamal says. "He was a big guy," unlike some pirates he has dealt with who were young and amateurish. "You have kids who try to get some money. You have another group that is little more organized. You have another group with links to England, and others to Kenya," Jamal said. "They come in different shapes and sizes. This was like the tenth ship he had attacked. He must be rich, though. He said at one point that [they hijacked ships] because they had nothing to do." Whenever Jamal criticized the pirates, he was repeatedly told, "Those ships we are attacking came to our coastline for fishing, and we used to rely on fishing, and we can't do it anymore." It was a familiar refrain.

Finally, after ten months of talk, thousands of dollars' worth of phone calls, and only $130,000 in cash paid, the pirates gave up. Without warning, the pirates told Captain Egbegi that he and his crew could leave. Fearing that the pirates might change their minds, the crew members started the ship's engines and called the International Maritime Bureau's piracy center, announcing that they'd been released. The message was relayed to European naval forces in the Gulf of Aden, and the Dutch warship steamed toward Bosasso to intercept the tug and its crew.

"Now I just want to speak to my wife and see my five children," Egbegi told a reporter shortly after he was freed. He had only bitter memories of his captivity. "From what I saw, the Somali guys are mean and can do anything. People should realize crews have families. Let the crews go home," he pleaded with the pirates, referring to the two hundred other sailors held hostage at the time.[10]

A Changed Man

WHEN I spoke at length with Geoffrey Egbide in June 2009, he had just gotten off the phone with his recently freed brother, Captain Egbegi, who was still in Yemen at the time. The captain had been calling everyone he could think of, filled with excitement and anxious to return home. Egbide had worked nonstop for the past ten months for his brother's release. "I called all my friends," he says, day after day, in hopes of finding a solution. The negotiations became a full-time job. "My phone bill for last month was six thousand dollars. I have been out of work for three months. I have not done anything else. A lot has gone into the process. The truth is they didn't get the one million dollars. Or the three hundred thousand dollars" that the pirates demanded.

The Somalis were tough negotiators, he says. "They didn't get tired of negotiating," but money spoke louder than words, he explains, because they only responded when money showed up. "It was money. I dangled money in front of them. It is not strange. It was enough to entice them. We sent 'x' amount of money," just as they had asked, but he became disheartened when the pirates "didn't get the job done."

Sometimes, Egbide used the pirates' unfulfilled promises to help him in the negotiations. "That became my advantage. Then we went to the second phase of the negotiations. One thing I believe is that you can get anything out of dialogue. We engaged them. We laughed. When they asked 'x,' we fulfilled it. We had access to the pirates directly. We knew their names and where they came from. And where they slept. Eighty percent of the Somalis are nomadic. If a Somali tells you his name, you know where he is from."

Egbide says he now has a much deeper understanding of both Somalia and his own country, Nigeria, as a result of the ordeal. "Every case is unique. It's not about the money. It's about what went into the release," he explains. "We used a lot of things" in the negotiations, which included "tracking down who these people are. Tracking down which community they came from. A lot went into it." Yet "there was never a time I was angry at the pirates."

Did he wish the Nigerians could have been rescued, much like the captain saved by the U.S. sharpshooters who had killed the Somali pirates about a month earlier? Egbide envies the United States' ability to use lethal power to solve problems. "If I was in their position, as the Americans were, I would have done the same thing. If I had the guns or the resources," he says, he probably would have used them. Rather than focusing on force, Egbide has developed sympathy for the Somalis. "When a man is destitute, he will do anything to survive. It is a desperate situation in Somalia. It is a place where might makes right. In Somalia, if they can hijack a ship and get one million dollars, then it is something right for them to do. Do I blame the pirates? Yes, for capturing my brother and doing what they're doing." But, he adds, "They were protecting their shores. The Somalis cannot fish the waters like the foreigners can. I don't know why they don't have a government that stands up for them. They were doing what they are doing because it is a desperate situation. It is bad, it is terrible, it is evil, but it does happen."

The negotiations changed him, Egbide says. "I got into this as an ordinary person, and I came out of this as an extraordinary person." He wants to become a negotiator and help Nigeria free itself of the violence that plagues the Niger River delta. "I want to focus on communities that are fighting each other. Oil has been taken from the region since 1937," he says of the delta, "but the people still don't have lights. The people can't fish their waters. When a man has no food, he will do anything. People who have prosperity do not carry guns. But violence will not bring any lasting solution." The violence, killing, kidnappings, and piracy in the Niger River delta can be explained simply, he says. "There is a basic, fundamental problem. There is no light. There is no food."

Egbide worried that the release of the Nigerians without payment of a ransom might prompt others to hold back ransom payments and abandon captured crews to a deadly fate. "There are fifteen vessels there," he says. "I don't want my victory to be detrimental to the other fifteen." When I ask if he harbors any resentment against the shipowner, who did little to free the crew, Egbide says, "The shipowner? I don't blame him." Does he resent the Nigerian government for failing to come up with any money despite the billions of dollars it collects from oil? "I don't blame the Nigerian government," he says but adds, "Could they have done more? Yes."

Within days of the release of the Nigerian crew, attention quickly turned to the government as people asked why, if Nigeria was awash in oil money, did the government not do something? The government response verged on the absurd, when Nigeria's Foreign Minister, Ojo Maduekwe, explained that the government was implementing a new policy called citizen diplomacy. "We did not pay any ransom," he said, offering that fact as evidence that the Nigerian government's policy had worked. Maduekwe then invited the released crew to his home, hoping the event might gloss over the government's failure. During the public portion of the visit, he insisted that the government had quietly used "development partners and friendly countries" to stay abreast of the negotiations. "We felt publicly, if we indicate[d] what we were doing, it [would] compromise your safety and security," he said to the crew. "We felt what will vindicate us was your safe return and not for us to go to the pages of newspapers to say this is what we are doing."[11]

What Nigeria did, if anything, was obscure at best, and Maduekwe continued a rambling defense of inaction, at one point confessing that the government couldn't respond to hostage situations. Nigeria "may not be a government that beats its chest every morning as to what it is doing," he said, but it should "be judged by the results and actions just like the release of the sailors." Nigeria was focused on other issues, he added. "It will be vindicated eventually whether in the area of power, infrastructure, fight against corruption, or sustenance of good governance at all levels." Good governance? Maduekwe concluded, "Those who are doubting whether citizen diplomacy makes any sense, if it's working or relevant, should look at the freed Nigerian sailors as the finest harvest of the policy."[12]

Captain Egbegi and his crew could only stand by and smile politely. Caught up in the moment, Egbegi called their release "the greatest miracle I have seen in modern times. Even if we are not 100 percent healthy, we thank God that we are alive." The captain was able, however, to subtly underscore the failures of the Nigerian government when he explained that their long captivity was not an issue of diplomacy or ideology but of hard, cold cash—the one thing that the Nigerian government could have provided but didn't. "[The pirates] made it clear to us that they were not into any religious struggle or political tussle. What they wanted was just money."[13]

Bunkering on the Delta

As the Nigerian government conveniently sidestepped the Nigerian captives' plight, it revealed an ability to ignore core issues, including the festering chaos in the nation's river delta. In October 2008, just a couple of months after the Nigerian crew had been hijacked in Somalia, Nigerian pirates attacked the country's private fishing fleet, capturing eight fishing trawlers and ninety-six crew members in what was possibly the largest Nigerian pirate attack on record. The president of the Nigerian Trawler Owners Association, Margaret Orakwusi, said the vessels were captured off the coast in the early morning hours and hauled to an unknown location. Orakwusi was outraged to learn that the Nigerian navy had turned down a request for help, saying the hijacking was outside its jurisdiction. "This is contrary to what we used to experience when distress reports are immediately and effectively handled without passing the buck. We appeal to the navy to allow the status quo to remain to enhance safety and marine activities to thrive," she said.[14] Piracy in Nigeria was much more violent than in Somalia, she complained, since her association had recorded more than sixty-four attacks in 2008 alone in which crew members were either killed or maimed. The fishing industry was a significant part of the Nigerian economy and employed half a million workers. "Where was the government?" she asked.

Indeed. One answer was in the status quo that Orakwusi referenced, the violent world of the Niger River delta where the dividing lines between pirates, criminals, rebels, and government officials were blurred. While militia groups such as MEND battled Nigerian armed forces and plagued foreign oil companies, they might not have been the righteous warriors they claimed. Some were said to be involved in the highly lucrative trade in illicit oil known as bunkering. In this thriving underground business, barges sidle up to oil docks throughout the delta under the cover of night as bunkerers work quickly to tap oil lines and fill the barges in a matter of hours. The barges then move downstream and are tied up to large ships that extract the illicit oil and convey it to oceangoing tankers that take the outlaw oil to world markets.[15]

In payment for the illicit oil, the oceangoing tankers arrive in Nigerian waters loaded with cash, weapons, drugs, or other contraband easily converted into cash by those stealing the oil. Falsified shipping documents legitimize the crude oil moving out to sea, which later disappears into markets in Europe or America. "This is an industry that makes sixty million dollars a day. They'd kill you, me, anyone, in order to protect it," a source said to the BBC. Billions of dollars are made every year by the oil-bunkering syndicates. The profits are huge for clandestine Nigerian and international traders who enjoy the benefits of the government's inability to curtail it or, quite possibly, the government's complicity. Consequently, the trade in contraband oil compounds the chaos and misery permeating the delta.[16]

The government's inability to control the delta and its oil had prompted Nigeria's president at the time, Umaru Yar'Adua, to label this lost revenue as "blood oil" in an attempt to tie oil theft to the blood diamond trade that has fed the civil wars in neighboring Liberia and Sierra Leone. While the top levels of government cry foul, allegations continue that this underground river of outlaw oil perhaps involves the highest levels of government. Consequently, any use of governmental force to curtail the underground oil might be for show. "If the president goes after them, they could destabilize the country, cause a coup, a civil war," a source told a BBC journalist. "They are that powerful, they could bring the state down."[17]

By not distributing the oil proceeds as a progressive regime might, the Nigerian government has created conditions that drive delta residents to take what they consider to be theirs. The chaos created by militants battling oil companies is a distraction, if not convenient cover for the oil-bunkering syndicates, which hire armed gangs from among the legions of the delta's impoverished and unemployed. This makes it difficult to differentiate between the militants and the armed gangs, which some say fight one another for lucrative bunkering turf.

Involving state and local authorities in bunkering is easy. "Most of the soldiers are paid fifteen thousand naira [around one hundred dollars] a month, so you go to the military man and say, 'I want to make you richer,'" a bunkering practitioner told a journalist. The man had just worked all night moving illegal oil that he estimated was worth one hundred thousand dollars. "You say, 'This pipe will bring money; every night you will work here.' Then they will guard you. We give them five months' salary in a single night. Every time they bring in new people, we make new friends."[18] The man said the government could stop the bunkering of oil, but local officials are making so much money off it that they would revolt if it was stopped. Bunkering is populated by well-trained but unemployed Nigerian oil workers. "They're offered positions by the bunkerers, so of course they take them."[19] With local officials compromised and the Nigerian authorities and military complicit, the circle is complete, leaving sabotaged oil operations not so much victims of rebellion but of a thoroughly corrupted system.

Legal channels can be used for the theft of oil, of course; stolen oil often moves right out of the same docks that pump legal oil into the oceangoing tankers, according to reports. Secret compartments apparently exist on some tanker ships and have capacities for tens of thousands of barrels of outlaw oil. Some sources describe the practice of partial fill-ups of legal crude topped off with pirated oil, the blending of which pushes up profit margins. Likewise, an entire tanker can be loaded with contraband oil that is then made to seem legitimate with fake papers. The International Maritime Organization claims that in 2007, some eighty thousand barrels of illegal crude were taken out of Nigeria each day. With oil valued at sixty to sixty-five dollars per barrel, that's about five million dollars a day. Over a year, that amounts to eighteen billion dollars.[20]

The potent mix of lucrative supplies of legal and illegal oil, with a host of ways to spirit it out of the country and an increasingly violent social and environmental movement, indicates that an end to Niger delta piracy is unlikely soon. With the government launching offensives and counteroffensives against delta militants and militant groups unwilling to work with the government, the resentment among the delta populace can only grow against the government and the international oil companies that look to the government for protection. When the Nigerian military reportedly demolishes communities and attacks and arrests civilians, it compels people to commit increasingly desperate acts. Among them are the dangerously escalating crimes of piracy and kidnapping on the Niger River delta.

8

MALAISE IN MOMBASA

THE OFFICE of Muslims for Human Rights, or MUHURI, is just steps away from the four-hundred-year-old Fort Jesus, a stone bastion built by the Portuguese on the craggy cliffs overlooking the natural harbor at Mombasa, Kenya. With four distinct winglike sections, said to resemble legs and arms, and a rectangle designated a head, the fort was deified with the name Jesus. That the angular defensive structure is a testament to western European colonialism, religion, and culture does not dampen the excitement of schoolchildren who swarm the fort on a warm day's outing or diminish the irony that this fort sits in the midst of a largely Muslim town and neighborhood.

I meander through the dusty passages of the fort in the company of my Muslim guide, who is dressed in an immaculate white flowing robe and cap. He grins broadly while pointing out the stone hole that Portuguese explorer Vasco da Gama supposedly used as his toilet. That landmark duly noted, we wander the narrow streets of Mombasa's old town. At one corner he points with pride to the renovations being done to a large apartment building, telling me the work is the result of Somali investors. It gives me pause, knowing that the building boom in Kenya is widely said to be the result of Somali pirate ransoms.

The MUHURI office is where I find director Khalid Hussein, who explains that the group was formed to advocate for the Muslim prisoners in the Kenyan jails. Of late, its focus has been the growing number of Somali pirates captured at sea by various naval forces and handed over to the Kenyan government. The Kenyans have an estimated 110 accused pirates in the Shimo la Tewa prison in Mombasa when Hussein and I meet in September 2009. The pirates arrive in groups ranging from four or five to twice that number, several times a month.

Jurisdictional issues swirl around the pirates, who are usually arrested in international, non-Kenyan waters and by non-Kenyan authorities. "So what are they doing here [in Kenya]?" Hussein asks. The pirates should be returned to Somalia for trial, he says, but Somalia has no functional government and is in a perpetual state of war, so common sense and human rights concerns prevent their return. As Somalia's pro-western neighbor, Kenya has been saddled with the task of putting the accused Somali pirates on trial. Although the problem of Somali piracy is international, Hussein says, "It's up to Kenya," which is backlogged with domestic cases and ill-equipped to prosecute and imprison the influx of Somali captives. "The UN is trying to see that the alleged pirates get what they need," he says, but "we fear they're not doing enough."

MUHURI's goal is quite simple: "We want to make sure justice is done." Kenyan law authorizes court-appointed attorneys for only specific crimes such as murder and violent robbery, Hussein explains. "Under Kenyan law they're not entitled to a lawyer because [piracy] is not a capital offense." However, the Kenyan courts have appointed defense attorneys for most of the accused pirates under an agreement signed March 6, 2009, with the European Union, which funds Kenya's prosecution of the seagoing Somalis. The agreement followed similar ones among the United States, Britain, and Kenya.[1] With pirates arriving every month, the Kenyan judicial process has shifted into high gear. Hussein explains that already a dozen or so pirates have been sentenced to seven-year terms in Kenyan prisons, the penalty for piracy under Kenyan law. Hussein complains that the EU pays only the expenses of the court and prosecutors, not the defense. "Will [pirates] be given lawyers to defend them?" he asks. "The EU is refusing to support [defense] lawyers' fees," claiming the fees are too high. The problem will hopefully be resolved, he says.

Most of the accused pirates are unhappy with their court-appointed lawyers and want international lawyers, Hussein says. “They don’t trust the Kenyan legal system or Kenyan lawyers.” Attempts by some of the accused pirates to secure their own legal representation have been thwarted by Kenyan authorities, causing the Somali prisoners to cry foul. Since they are prevented from contacting their families, the accused pirates are blocked from tapping into family money to hire their own lawyers. Kenya claims it cannot provide the translators necessary to monitor the face-to-face or telephone conversations that the accused Somalis may have with friends and family, I am told later, due to security concerns. Officials fear that the accused pirates could be plotting an escape or something more drastic, rather than discussing legal issues. Because of this, the pirates have remained isolated, filling their time by participating in prison work projects such as installing community water towers, painting cells, and general construction.

Hussein and his staff meet with the pirates almost daily, and by far the biggest complaint is medical care. One of the accused had a bullet wound and claimed the bullet was still inside of him. Another was a diabetic. One had a kidney infection. Two were underage: one twelve and another fourteen years old. Because of the prison policy, none “have contacted their families, and their families don’t know if they’re dead or alive.” Hussein is pushing for the better medical care since what care the prisoners receive is only what is required by law. For some of the accused pirates, this is not enough. While more health care can be purchased, the prisoners lack access to the cash necessary for that.

“They face discrimination,” Hussein says. “They say the other Kenyan inmates beat them.” Most of the pirates claim they’re innocent. “Some are saying they were fishing and were just picked up. Some are saying they were trying to get to Yemen.” Hussein tries to keep an open mind but suspects many of the accused could be pirates. “How else can you get a bullet wound?” he asks.

The pirates complain that they’re hindered from practicing their religion. When I meet with Hussein, it is the time of Ramadan, which carries strict Islamic rules for fasting from sunup to sundown. The prison's normal dinner hour is at 3:00 P.M., when the Muslim prisoners can't eat. The prisoners have a choice of either violating the rule of fasting, letting their food sit for several hours, or not eating. In addition, the prison reportedly lacks washing facilities, so the Islamic prisoners cannot wash before their daily prayers. Such issues should have been resolved long ago, Hussein says, because Mombasa is 65 percent Muslim, and many communities along the Kenyan coast are as high as 85 percent Muslim.

On top of everything else, Shimo la Tewa is overcrowded, having been built for eight hundred but holding more than two thousand prisoners at the time, Hussein says. "It's a sorry situation. They're not getting much support from the [Kenyan] government."

Hussein invites me to see the prison and talk to the prisoners myself, and I readily accept. During the thirty-minute ride to the prison with the MUHURI staff counselors, I talk with Yusef Lule Mwatsefu, the group's program coordinator, as we navigate Mombasa traffic, a chaotic mix of cars and taxi vans called *matatus*, most of which are highly decorated with metallic-flecked paint and strings of blinking lights. Some have small video screens mounted inside to entertain passengers. On the way we follow a *matatu* painted with the phrase "Silence Is Defeat" in flowing script. I suspect that maybe what motivates MUHURI is giving voice to the accused pirates in Kenya's prisons. Mwatsefu tells me that his group is supported by the Muslim community because "it's important for [the] Muslim community to participate in the human rights agenda." The organization "gives Muslims a human rights face."

My thoughts sour, however, when Mwatsefu points out that while prosecuting the accused pirates in Kenya may be a convenient solution for the international community, it puts Kenya in the crosshairs of a retaliatory attack by militant Islamists. Such an attack would not be new to Kenya. I recall the 1998 al-Qaeda bombings of the U.S. embassies in Nairobi and Dar es Salaam, Tanzania, that killed hundreds. More recently was the November 2002 attack on the Israeli-owned Paradise Hotel on the beach in Mombasa, not far from where I am staying, that killed thirteen people, including two Israeli children. Most of the dead were members of a traditional Kenyan dance group hired to entertain the arriving and departing guests.

We pull into the neatly swept grounds surrounding the painted headquarters of Shimo la Tewa prison. After a half hour, we're ushered into the offices of Provincial Prison Commander James K'odieny, a bear of a man who smiles as he explains that a meeting with prisoners is only possible with permission from prison authorities in Nairobi. He obligingly makes repeated calls to his boss in Nairobi, who is locked in a meeting that his secretary says could go on for hours.

I end up in the group's van staring at the front door to the prison as the MUHURI counselors disappear inside to meet with the accused Somalis. I'm left with Fredrick Okado, twenty-four, a human rights officer with MUHURI who has worked in the prison for nearly two years, mostly with accused pirates. They're mixed with other prisoners, Okado says, and in this English-speaking country, the biggest barrier is the language. The Somalis must rely on other jailed Kenyans who are from northeastern Kenya, predominately ethnic Somali, who speak both Somali and English. The Somalis each have their own foam mattress and blanket, and all make court appearances every other week. For many of the accused pirates, it comes as a shock that "there are some things that they cannot do," the effect of living in a society governed by laws, he says. While this may be unremarkable to most people, it is a problem for the Somalis. But they're adapting. "When in Rome . . . " Okado says with a smile. "They're coming along quickly." It has taken about six to eight months, which is how long most have been in prison, for their new realities to settle in. They're not used to the fact that if you hit someone, there will be consequences, Okado says. "In Somalia, you can hit someone or even kill them, and no more steps will be taken."

Calamity in the Courts

Just a block from the Mombasa High Court, the Lotus Hotel has an open, tiled courtyard enlivened with leafy potted plants, giving the place an air of quiet refuge. It is here where I meet Mombasa attorney Paul Munyao moments after one of the many brief court hearings in the ongoing trials of accused Somali pirates. Munyao represents two groups of accused pirates: seven Somalis captured by the U.S. Navy and eleven captured by French naval forces. "They have a lot of challenges," Munyao concedes. "There's a language barrier and a cultural barrier. They need translators," who explain not only the evolving legal process but the prison's dos and don'ts as well.

How are they coping? "They're taking the situation individually," Munyao says. Most of the Somali prisoners are unfamiliar with judicial procedure and decorum. "They become arrogant at trials. They have to be silenced." Reflecting a disdain for the trials, he says, the pirates are impatient. "There's a sense of urgency. They want the case over quickly." I would have thought that the pirates would want the process drawn out to delay their prison time, I say, but he shakes his head in disagreement. "Some are resigned to their fate." Most view the judicial process as a "means to an end," with the end being their conviction and jail sentence. "This is just a way to convict them," Munyao says of the Somalis' view. That perception is cultivated because "the court has refused to let the prisoners communicate with family and friends because the court cannot know what they're saying."

But that hasn't stopped a few Somalis from trying to retain their own attorneys, he says, and already one of his assigned clients had taken steps to do that. Although the pirates are being tried under agreements among Kenya, the United States, the United Kingdom, and the European Union, "it's unfavorable to the pirates because it doesn't fund their defense. Most [defense] lawyers are working pro bono," and as a result, the Somalis suspect that the defense is doing only the minimum. The designated lawyers are waiting for the European Union agreement to include money for the defense, Munyao says. Because the EU is funding the prosecution and paying court costs, the prosecution can present expert witnesses. Since the defense attorneys have no money, they are unable to present their own experts to counter the prosecution. As a result, the pirates are easily convicted. "It's not easy for the defense and the pirates. The EU . . . should be funding the defense so that the playing field is fair. They are very one-sided."

While defense funding is a problem, so are the jurisdictional issues with the pirates. "It's not Kenya territory in any way," Munyao says of the locations of the pirates' arrest. "That's a very obvious discrepancy." Another constitutional problem is that the accused pirates have been imprisoned without formal charges beyond the limitation specified in the Kenyan constitution, he says. Under Kenyan law, a detainee must be charged within twenty-four hours of his arrest or be released. Even though the Somalis have not been arrested by Kenyan authorities, they are being held and tried under Kenyan law. Each time Munyao or other defense attorneys raise these issues with the court, they are overruled, he says, leaving the defense lawyers helpless. If the pirates admit their guilt, then the legal questions are somewhat moot, I suggest. But that's not the case, Munyao says. "They usually say they were fishing, and the U.S. [or French forces] just picked them up." He urges me to attend a court session for myself and puts me in contact with the court-appointed Somali translator, Dekow Mohamed.

When I call Mohamed the next morning, he tells me that if I want to see the captured Somalis, I need to be in court at 9:00 A.M. It is already 8:30, and that gives me thirty minutes. I swallow hard, knowing that terrible traffic jams are daily events between the beach communities and downtown Mombasa. I toss my camera and notebook in my bag and run to the hotel lobby, waving at one of the hotel's taxi drivers. I climb into an aging Toyota Corolla and tell the driver, Simon, that I need to be at the Mombasa High Court in thirty minutes. He looks at me like I'm crazy. "No, I have to be there!" I tell him. Simon shrugs, puts the car in gear, and it promptly stalls. He looks at me with a sheepish grin, grinds the starter, then revs the engine four or five times before slamming the car into gear, making it lurch. Not only does Simon's car not idle, it has a bad clutch. I am tempted to jump out and run for it, but I have no idea where I am going.

Moments later we encounter the inevitable traffic jam, but Simon swerves sharply, bypassing a clogged intersection, only to bounce onto the main road, where we're engulfed by diesel-belching trucks and glittering candy-colored *matatus* muscling their way down the road. Simon's battered Toyota warms up to the task, however, and runs reasonably well as we creep along. Simon is middle-aged with graying hair, a Mombasa native, and stomps on the gas after we nudge past a large truck that has crumpled the rear of a small car. We navigate a roundabout, swerve down a muddy alley, then slide to a halt behind a man pushing a large two-wheeled donkey cart. Simon leans on his horn. My phone rings. It's Mohamed telling me that the court room had been changed. I thank him as we dart across one of the city's main streets, then veer down another alley, and angle along a couple more streets. The courthouse suddenly looms. Simon points to where he will be waiting when I'm finished and deposits me at the court steps. It is exactly 9:00 A.M. A man at the information desk points me down the hall to the courtroom.

The court is crowded. The public gallery benches are set amphitheater style, rising from floor level to high against a back wall that faces the judge's bench. To one side are the defendants, and immediately I recognize the Somalis, nine accused pirates in the back row behind Kenyan criminal defendants. I also spot Mohamed, a studious-looking young man with glasses and a tie, who slips from behind his desk, assuring me that I can take photos, "no problem." I shuffle between crowded benches, clumsily banging knees, before taking a seat just a few feet from the accused pirates. It's not long before the Somalis notice me taking pictures, pointing and shaking their heads, irritated at the attention. After about twenty minutes, I realize I didn't need to rush to court. It will be another hour and a half before the judge appears.

When the judge finally arrives, he fiddles with the air-conditioning unit on the wall above him, then orders the Somali defendants to stand and be counted. Moments later the court clerk announces that the trial for the Somalis will begin the following Monday, in just four days' time. The statement is translated by Mohamed. The Somalis nod and promptly file out. It's over.

In the hallway outside the courtroom, Mohamed introduces me to Jared Magobo, one of two Kenyan attorneys representing this group of nine Somalis. Given the long delays in bringing them to trial, I ask Magobo how the Somalis are holding up. "They're not confident," Magobo confesses, and they don't trust the Kenyan courts. "They believe their fate has been decided. They believe they're being discriminated against." They believe their rights are "not being taken seriously." Does he agree? He nods his head, admitting that there is a "certain degree of bias" against the pirates and that their complaints of discrimination are "not without foundation." Most of his defendants "claim they are fishermen," he says, and the rest say they're smugglers caught ferrying human cargo to Yemen. "They insist they are innocent." The accused pirates, like many in the legal community, are frustrated by the jurisdictional issues. Like others, Magobo asks, "Why are they bringing them to Kenya?" But he only shrugs when I ask if he thinks the Somalis are guilty as charged. The truth most likely never will be known, he says.

The Pirate Whisperer

One of the most important players in the evolving world of Somali pirates is Andrew Mwangura. For many years Mwangura has been the go-to man when it comes to negotiating the ransoms and freedom for ships hijacked by the Somali pirates. When Mwangura's phone rings, it could be a billionaire owner of a global shipping line, the relative of a pirate hostage, or the brother of a recently captured Somali pirate. Each would be seeking his help.

For the past dozen years, Mwangura, forty-five, has headed the East African Seafarer's Assistance Program, based in Mombasa. His wealth of experience and myriad contacts are routinely tapped to track down hijacked vessels, investigate deaths at sea, and negotiate with pirates. This has earned him the nickname of the Pirate Whisperer. He survives on donations for his services and works as a freelance writer. Most recently, Hollywood has come calling, and reports are that his life story may become a feature film.

At one point, Mwangura had forty volunteers working for him, but most were dismissed after he suspected some were informers for the government. He has moved from his home in Mombasa to a more discreet location up the coast to protect his wife and child. His security concerns are well founded. He was arrested in October 2008 and put in the Shimo la Tewa prison for nine days by Kenyan authorities. Mwangura had rankled the Kenyan government during the seizure of the weapons ship the MV *Faina*. He was involved in the negotiations for its release and was the first person to report that the weapons on the hijacked ship were headed for South Sudan, not Kenya, as the Kenyan government had been saying.

We meet at the China Town restaurant in downtown Mombasa, a very public place, rather than his office, "for our security reasons," he says. When I chuckle at the remark, he says, "Why do you laugh?" Is it his or my security that he's worried about? I ask. He says both. His response does little to put me at ease.

"Are you in danger?" I ask.

"I'm always in danger," he says, explaining that he's been accused of dealing with criminals, a reference to the Somali pirates he must negotiate with in order to obtain the release of ships and hostages.

"Am I in danger?" I ask.

"This is Africa," he says. "Someone could break into your hotel room and take your computer to see what I told you." His paranoia concerns me and dominates our conversation. Though I hardly think that either of us is in danger, Mwangura explains that his arrest was on charges that he made "alarming statements" during the hijacking of the MV *Faina*, which implied that he was a threat to the state. He was also charged with possession of marijuana. He rejects both accusations, saying, "I don't even smoke cigarettes," and would never consider smoking marijuana.

The Kenyan government's claim that the weaponry aboard the MV *Faina* was bound for Kenya was easily unmasked. Many of South Sudan's supporters, including Kenya, wanted to hide the fact that South Sudan was arming itself in the run-up to South Sudan's independence vote in 2011. The cover blown, Kenya was irritated. But the information that Mwangura had was correct. The weaponry has since been tracked to South Sudan's capital of Juba. The intrigue surrounding the MV *Faina* offers an insight into the murky world of Somali piracy, Mwangura says. "Not all ships are taken blindly. There's a story behind the story." The charges against Mwangura were dropped but have not been removed from his record, he says, so he fears that now he's a marked man. Anything that he might do to contradict Kenyan policy could be used against him.

Mwangura shows up at the restaurant wearing a baseball cap with a leather visor and monogrammed with the words "Born Free" in gold letters. His eyes remain hidden behind large sunglasses that he only occasionally lowers and looks over. "I'm a seaman. I don't work with criminals," he says, answering the complaint of Kenyan authorities. "I work for a [nongovernmental organization]." He pauses to scan the restaurant, which is empty except for a table of Chinese men sitting nearby, their suitcases beside them. "In this world, everybody is a criminal; everybody is a terrorist. There is no honest man in the world. This is Africa. Our crime is just to help," he says of the hijackings. The objective of the Seafarer's Assistance Program is "safety and security at sea and at port." It is "free of charge." Their goal is to help stranded or, in this case, hijacked seamen and their families, he says. "Seafarers' welfare is everything. We do personal visits to hospitals, ships."

When seamen anywhere in the world encounter problems, his group tries to help. "They are in the foreign land without relatives. We are their relatives. Seamen are forgotten people," yet are vital to the world's economy, he says, and because of this, seamen are not appreciated. "Ninety percent of the world's cargo moves on ships. Without ships, it would be the end of the world." Though his group provides a vital service, it is persecuted. "What we are doing is supposed to be done by governments, but the [Kenyan] government does not seem to care about that." That may be changing, however, since Mwangura has been helping craft policy for the European Union regarding the Somali pirates.

Only recently, after the *Maersk Alabama* was attacked, have the Somali pirates been recognized as a global problem. "It took an attack on a U.S. ship for people to start paying attention. When an American is attacked, then people wake up," he says. Yet Somali piracy has been going on for years. The first well-publicized assault by Somali pirates was on November 5, 2005, when the *Spirit*, a Seabourn Cruise Line ship with about 150 passengers and an equal number of crew, was attacked by four or five pirate skiffs loaded with armed pirates who fired rocket-propelled grenades that damaged the ship and injured one person. The cruise ship eluded the pirates, however, and continued on to the Seychelles islands.

The attack on the *Spirit* catapulted Mwangura into the international spotlight. "I didn't sleep for two days," he says, as he was flooded with calls largely from the U.S. embassy officials wanting to know the status of the passengers. But the attack on the *Spirit* was nothing new. "Somali pirates have been [in the Gulf of Aden] for a long time," he states. The first contemporary Somali pirate attack he has on record was in 1989 when the pirates hijacked a Greek-owned cargo ship and took the crew hostage. After a week, the crew overpowered their Somali captors and escaped.

Mwangura scoffs at the impression that the crew of the *Maersk Alabama* was the first to successfully resist a pirate attack. There have been five earlier such incidents in which crews overpowered their Somali captors and escaped, he says. The *Maersk Alabama* was the sixth such case, and none of the prior crews were American. In fact, the vast majority of those still held by the Somali pirates are from Asian countries such as India, Bangladesh, Indonesia, and Malaysia, or Africans. Yet few people pay much attention to their plight. "It's nonsense" that no one cares, he says.

Given his years of experience with the Somali pirates, does Mwangura think Somali piracy can be brought to an end? "You cannot fight poverty using the gun," he says. "You need to fight the root cause, then you will find a solution to [piracy]." The situation in Somalia is hard to solve from the outside, which is why the international community has been reluctant, I say. Does he agree that the Somali pirates have been forced into piracy? "They're right to think that," Mwangura says. "We say the root cause of Somalia piracy is poverty." Contributing to that poverty is illegal fishing in Somali waters, toxic dumping, and drought. For nearly two decades, foreign ships have been fishing

Somali waters, so he asks, "Where are [Somali fishermen] going to fish?"

The plunder of Somali fisheries was made possible by Somalia's chaos. "It is one way of killing the fishing community" if the seas are fished so heavily that nothing is left for the locals. While the Somalis themselves "may not be consuming fish, they do business with fish. Most of the fish in Mombasa is from Somalia," he says, which keeps the Somali fishing industry viable. Somalia was once known not only for its fish but also for banana and cattle exports. The loss of these businesses converged, giving rise to piracy, he says. "Because of [drought] and instability, the community is very poor. The only way out [for a Somali] is to take a gun and go take a car, a ship, kidnap a journalist or an [aid] worker, and get some money." The Somali problems on land must be solved, he says. "The only way out is to tackle those issues."

Mwangura fears that even if the international community is willing to tackle the larger Somali problem, some people don't want solutions in Somalia. "Profiteers are making money out of instability in Somalia, the Congo, and elsewhere." These profiteers "create conflict and make money out of the resources. It's a very complex situation. Warlords are making money." He suggests the international community may be complicit because each time it tries to solve a Somali problem, it gets worse, not better. "They always come to Africa talking to the wrong people or giving aid to the wrong people," he says. "After many years, the aid is gone and you are still poor. Where did the aid go?" An example of exploitation is that valuable minerals are exported from Africa each day, though Africans rarely benefit, he says. Kenya licenses diamond exporters even though Kenya does not produce diamonds. The diamonds come from the Democratic Republic of the Congo, one of the most fought-over regions in the world. "Conflicts in Africa [are] connected to minerals and to the sea," he says.

When Mwangura was in prison, he talked at length with the Somali prisoners and came away more convinced than ever that the Somali pirates were the hapless victims of a much larger problem. "They're arresting the wrong people," he says flatly of the U.S. and EU naval patrols. "Those are not the pirates. Those are just the foot soldiers.

The real pirates are making a lot of money, but it is very hard to arrest them because it is hard to link them to the pirates. Very rich people finance this. It's very big business." Look at how the pirates are equipped, he says. "How does a young pirate have a satellite phone if the average Kenyan cannot afford a simple cell phone?" Funding hijackings requires weapons and equipment, then supplies to keep hostages and pirates alive for months at a time. "It's like an industry," says Mwangura, and it takes a lot of people. Piracy has some wealthy backers who have the means to support the hijackers until the ransom money arrives.

Does the loss of fishing in Somalia warrant the scope of piracy that has developed? Mwangura says that the extent and value of illegal fishing has been underplayed. "Illegal fishing is more money, [generating] $450 million a year," he says. "If [piracy] ransoms are thirty to eighty million dollars a year, which is the bigger crime? Illegal fishing or piracy?"

The real criminals are not being identified, Mwangura insists. While the world is "calling the Somalis criminals," it is "not listening closely to what they say. Somalia could be stable if people listened." The unheard message has been that Somali waters are plundered and polluted. When no one took action, the Somalis did. "Desperate people take desperate measures," and the depth of that desperation has been ignored, Mwangura argues. "Most [pirates] don't know how to swim, yet they go two hundred miles out to sea" to attack ships. "It means he's ready to die and to kill you."

Mwangura offers a chilling prediction. If action isn't taken to solve the problems in Somalia, "something worse will happen in Somalia than what is happening now, worse than Nagasaki and Hiroshima." At that remark, Mwangura falls silent as I try to discern what that would be. I think of the many ominous warnings and fears that have surfaced over the years, should militant Islamists or even a small but dedicated group of terrorists come to possess a nuclear weapon or, worse still, a nuclear arsenal. Iran's steady progress toward construction of a nuclear weapon and the country's belligerent remarks about Israel suddenly come to mind. Somali piracy pales in comparison with such an eventuality. His warning, however, makes me want to keep digging. The roots of piracy reach deep into Somalia, and to get as close as I can to Somalia, I go to the Dadaab refugee camp in northeastern Kenya, the world's largest refugee camp and home to some three hundred thousand Somalis.

9

DESPERATION AT DADAAB

THE DADAAB refugee camp is about three hundred miles northeast of Nairobi in Kenya's desert lands, which are dominated by scrub brush and populated by camels, antelopes, and occasional giraffes. Herds of goats scamper across the rock and dirt, nibbling on whatever they can find. Dadaab also is just fifty miles from Kenya's porous four-hundred-mile border with Somalia and consists of three separate camps called Hagadera, Ifo, and Dagahaley. Combined they make up the world's largest refugee center. It takes an hour or so to travel from one camp to another since it must be done in regularly scheduled and escorted convoys. About 5,000 Somalis arrive at Dadaab every month, more than 150 a day. Although the camp poses a security risk for Kenya, there is little control over who arrives and leaves the camp or when and how they do it. Somalis show up, stay as long as they like—some for years—then leave.

These Somalis have fled what some are calling the world's most failed state, which has given rise to a flourishing trade in piracy. The United States has taken a jaundiced view of Somalia since the 1994 withdrawal of U.S. forces there yet conducts highly targeted strikes against terrorist leaders and their cells in Somalia. While foreign governments attempt to carefully exert pressure, it is apparent that the ultimate solutions must emerge from the Somali people themselves. Is this even possible? I wonder. Only if it is, as I have been told, can piracy be curtailed. What do the Somalis themselves have to say about their country's demise and a way out of the morass that is Somalia?

While the camp is run by the UN, the real work of providing for refugees is done by dozens of aid groups. The Kenyan government provides a small security force at the camp and escorts convoys between the camp and the nearest town, Garissa. I am able to visit the Dadaab camp as a guest of the International Rescue Committee, a New York–based organization providing health care to thousands of desperate refugees in Dadaab and other locales across Africa. After being initially denied a travel permit by Kenya's Refugee Affairs office, I secure one and the next morning head to the camp with several African IRC employees. The IRC staff at Dadaab lives in a complex of tents just steps away from the hospital compound the organization runs for the nearly one hundred thousand Somalis who live in Hagadera, the oldest of the three Dadaab camps. The IRC staff here is almost exclusively African, a change from much aid work I have found elsewhere in Africa, giving it a refreshing twist: Africans helping Africans. It is a simple existence with baths taken from buckets. Since we're in the midst of the Ramadan period of fasting, days begin well before dawn when the calls to prayer echo across the gritty landscape. Following the evening meal to break the fast, the camp is noisy as chatter mingles with the evening prayers blaring from many corners.

After a simple dinner of roasted goat, rice, and greens, the staff gazes at a television to watch the Kenyan parliament haggle over the controversial reappointment of the government's ineffective corruption commission chairman. The controversy followed U.S. secretary of state Hillary Clinton's visit to Kenya weeks earlier, when she chided Kenya for endemic corruption. As the debate drones on, I ruminate on Clinton's August 6, 2009, meeting with Sharif Sheikh Ahmed, the former leader of Somalia's fundamentalist Islamic Courts Union (ICU) who now heads Somalia's troubled Transitional Federal Government (TFG). Overwhelmingly, the greatest threat to the TFG is the militant Islamist group al-Shabaab, formerly the armed wing of the ICU, which was singled out by Clinton for its "disregard for human rights, for women's rights, for education and health care."[1]

From my meetings with Somali pirates and others, I am well aware that militants of al-Shabaab use the Dadaab camp as a transition point to move between Somalia and Kenya. And while the presence of militants in Kenya is largely an accepted fact, it is rarely discussed, despite the enormous security threat that easy movement poses for Kenya, one of Africa's most stable and secure countries. This threat was briefly highlighted only after Clinton had left Africa, when reports surfaced of a bomb plot against her. Five alleged terrorists were arrested by Kenyan authorities, who claimed to have foiled a plot to detonate three bombs simultaneously in Nairobi during Clinton's visit. One was to have been at the Hotel InterContinental, where Clinton stayed; the second at the Kencom Bus Stage, a sprawling bus terminal in downtown Nairobi; and the third at the city's Hilton Hotel. According to an unnamed, high-ranking security official quoted in the *Daily Nation* newspaper, the plan was hatched in Somalia but was uncovered when Kenyan security officials intercepted the plotters' communications in Nairobi.

The plot was attributed to al-Shabaab militants in Somalia who were "neutralized" by military and "other security agencies," said a source. "The operation in Nairobi netted five crucial suspects, one of whom carries Danish identification documents but is believed to be a Somali national. The other four, one of whom is a woman, hold Kenyan identification documents believed to be fake. Investigations into their identity and plan are on." The official added: "While in the past the real target of the attacks has been Western interests, the al-Qaeda leadership has since made Kenya a new target. So serious is the threat that during the [African Growth and Opportunity Act] meeting, the al-Qaeda intended to strike at the heart of Nairobi during the rush hours."[2]

The suspected plot was virtually unreported outside of Kenya. While the story could be dismissed as after-the-fact self-aggrandizement by Kenyan officials, the plot was apparently taken seriously by the United States. In the September 5, 2009, edition of the *Daily*

Nation, a senior Kenyan security official said the mastermind of the attack was a man named Anas, a close associate of Saleh Ali Saleh Nabhan. Nabhan, as I wrote earlier, was on the FBI's terrorism most-wanted list for his role in the 2002 Mombasa hotel bombing and the attempted attack on an airliner as well as for his role in the 1998 bombings of the U.S. embassies in Kenya and Tanzania. On November 28, 2002, the Israeli-owned Paradise Hotel on the beach in Mombasa was attacked by a suicide bomber reportedly riding an all-terrain vehicle that crashed through the gates and exploded in the hotel lobby, killing thirteen people. Almost simultaneously, two surface-to-air missiles were fired at an Israeli charter jet taking off from Mombasa's Moi airport. The missiles missed the target.

Less than ten days after the *Daily Nation* story on the terrorist arrest was published, U.S. helicopter gunships attacked a convoy in southern Somalia, killing Nabhan and others, whose bodies were taken away to be identified. Was the swift strike against Nabhan, reputed to be the region's main link to the al-Qaeda network, a response to the bomb plot apparently directed at Clinton? While the attack on Nabhan was widely reported, it was not done in the context of the Clinton visit but rather as America's new and more targeted approach to the war on terror.

THE MORNING after my arrival at Dadaab, I meet two longtime residents of the camp, Hassan Sheikh Ali, twenty-four, who grew up in the Hagadera camp, and Abdirazak Muhumad Ibrahim, twenty-eight, who works with the IRC's hospital counseling staff. Hagadera was established when the regime of Siad Barre collapsed in 1991. As Barre and his army fled Mogadishu, so did thousands of Somalis who settled in what became the Dadaab camps. For both of these young men raised and educated in the camp, it is their home. Fluent in Somali and English, they both agree to be my guides and translators in the camp.

Family and clan compounds in Hagadera and throughout Dadaab are marked by fences made of thorny brambles and sticks and accessed by simple gates that open into a swept-dirt area dotted with huts made of plastic tarps, scraps of cloth, leaves, and branches—anything readily available and serviceable. Stories of dead friends and relatives hover in the camp like the lingering effects of a recurring nightmare. But the physical damage caused by the fighting in southern Somalia is equally evident.

Fatima Gedi

FATIMA GEDI, an engaging thirty-six-year-old woman, is surrounded by a dozen children as she scours aluminum pots and pans. Originally from Mogadishu, Gedi came to the camp two years ago with her eight children crammed in a car, she says. She made the trip just days after giving birth. "In our country there is a problem," she explains, "excessive fighting." She fled Mogadishu seeking safety from the endless war but found that "life is very hard" in the camp, consumed as she is by a daily struggle to feed her children. When I ask about her future, she says she would like to move to the Kakuma refugee camp in north central Kenya, where her sister went as part of an effort to move thousands of refugees out of Dadaab due to the ongoing influx of new arrivals. Would she ever return to Somalia? She nods her head. "When I am sure there is peace, I will go back." When I ask her how peace might come to Somalia, she shrugs, saying it depends on the warlords and militia leaders who refuse to make peace. She expects the fighting to continue, she says.

Sahara Maalim

GEDI'S NEIGHBOR is Sahara Maalim, a woman in her early forties and the mother of seven, who fled Somalia in September 2008 after her husband, a ranking official with the UN Development Program in Mogadishu, was killed by al-Shabaab fighters. Maalim lives in a spacious hut with her sixteen-year-old son, Abdirahman Khalif, and invites me inside, where I sit on a clean vinyl ground cloth. The al-Shabaab militia shot her husband in 2007 when he was on his way to prayers at the local mosque because he worked for the United Nations, considered the enemy. "They had told him, 'We will kill you,' so many times," she explains. "He was a very devout Muslim. He was afraid every day he would be killed." She heard the shots on the day he died and wants to get her revenge against al-Shabaab. "If I had the ability, I would kill those men," she says bitterly, because once her husband was dead, al-Shabaab "threatened to kill the children."

Following the killing, Maalim shuttered herself in her home with her children and planned their escape. Borrowing the eight hundred dollars she needed for the trip from Somalia from her family and friends, she and her children left Mogadishu and reached the border. From there, they got a ride to Dadaab. Would she go back? "No," she says adamantly. "If I can find a peaceful place, I will go," she says, which would be any place far away from Somalia. I ask if peace is possible in Somalia, and she nods yes, "It is possible," but only "if the warlords come together and negotiate. That is the only way we can have peace."

Her son Abdirahman shares his mother's anger at the death of his father. He "does not want to go back ever," he says, even though he misses his friends and relatives. He expects never to see them again. He prefers to focus on his studies, he says, which he resumed after arriving at Hagadera. "I'd like to be an educated man and reach the position of my father," he says. When I ask him what he thinks of al-Shabaab, he says, "I don't want to hear the name." Even though her family has been in Dadaab camp for a year, Maalim tells me she still fears for her life. "I am still afraid because they can cross the border," she says of al-Shabaab, a fear I hear often in the camp.

Dahbo Abdi

IN ANOTHER hut I find Dahbo Abdi, thirty-six, the mother of five, who came to Hagadera just nine months earlier. "There was violence in Mogadishu," she says, explaining her presence in this camp. Her family survived a hail of bullets and bombs that destroyed her house and killed two relatives, she says. As fighting raged around her, she lost her husband, who she presumes was killed. During one of the battles, her ten-year-old son was shot in the head just outside the family's house. She took him to the Ugandan army hospital in Mogadishu, staffed by army medical personnel as part of the African Union Mission in

Somalia, AMISOM. After the severe head wound was treated, she collected what she needed and secured a ride to the Kenyan border. Just a month after her son was shot, she arrived at the Dadaab camp. Her son is her constant companion and for the most part seems to have recovered from the horrific injury. Would she go back? Abdi nods reluctantly. "If peace comes, I will go back." When I ask how she explains the violence in Somalia, she volunteers, "They are using religion for the fighting. They are saying, [the enemy] are nonbelievers." The militants "are using religion in their struggle for power."

Farah Hayd Ali

WHILE INCREASING numbers of Somalis arrive at the camp each day as fighting continues in southern Somalia, many at the camp left Mogadishu and southern Somalia nearly two decades ago. Among them is Farah Hayd Ali, sixty-three, who fled Somalia with the initial Somali exodus in 1991. Farah and his son, who is twenty-four and also goes by the name Farah, went to Kenya when the warlords overran southern Somalia. "Armed militias came and killed my brothers. That's why we fled," young Farah tells me. His father was shot in the head during the fighting, he says. The bullet lodged in his skull, causing partial paralysis. Farah's older brother was traumatized "when he saw the bloodshed of my father and brothers." Although the situation in Somalia was bad when the family left, it is "worse there than before," the young Farah says. "The killing is still the same. They kill you for no reason."

The young Farah considers Hagadera his home. "We have grown up here in Kenya. We can't go back now because [Somalis] don't know us." If the family returned, they'd be accused of being spies and killed, he says, by the militants. "The religion is the same, but they're making it another thing," he says of the Islamist extremists. "We don't wish to go back because the [violence] there is still existing." Peace in Somalia will come only with "reconciliation" of warring factions, he says. Is that possible? "I can't foretell," Farah says. He is less interested in Somalia than in a future in a different country. "I want to get further education," he says, and to live in a country with a functional government.

Farah's father, who walks quite well for a man suffering from partial paralysis, appears from one of the small houses in his family compound and settles on the ground in front of me. His beard is tinged with red dye, a common practice of elderly men. When I ask the father about Somalia, he strokes his reddened beard and says, "We came here because of war. It is still persisting. The problem of Somalia is still there." But, he adds, "if we can get international support, we can have peace in Somalia. Now we have no hope." The appeal for more international help is one that I hear often and makes the United States' longstanding hands-off policy in Somalia, mimicked by much of the world, look like the cause of more problems than it has solved. "War was based on tribal issues," the elder Farah explains. "Now it has become a matter of religion. If the international community can join together and help," the Somali people would join as well, he says. Can Somalia ever be peaceful? "I don't expect it will happen in Somalia," he says with a shrug. "I'm so frustrated about the problems in Somalia. I can't do anything about it."

Hassan Sheik Ali

Having spent most of his life in Hagadera, my translator, Hassan Sheik Ali, fondly remembers his former home in the Lower Shabelle region south of Mogadishu. He describes it as an abundant land of bananas, maize, rice, and mangoes. Having left at the age of seven, he is comforted by these memories, which help him confront the harsh realities of camp life. His father died in 1997, and later two of his brothers and one sister also died. His losses have motivated him to study hard and helped him graduate from the camp's secondary school. The fighting in Somalia began when clans fought over land, Ali says, but now the fight has shifted to religious factions. The Islamist militias kill any and all who resist them, he says. "They say [Somalis who resist them] are nonbelievers." He does not intend to return to Lower Shabelle. "I've grown up here. Why would I go back? This is permanent," Ali says of Hagadera. It is very hard to get the permanent residence status that would allow him to live in Nairobi, he says, and a return to Somalia is virtually impossible. Ali's brother, twenty-seven, has a family and runs a small shop, but Ali shakes his head when I ask if that's what he'd like to do as well. "It is not my profession." Most of the camp's long-term residents dream of a visa to another country, he says. "Many are expecting to go to foreign countries." But it is only possible "if you are very lucky."

Abdirazak Muhumed Ibrahim

HAVING LIVED in the Hagadera camp since 1992, Abdirazak Muhumed Ibrahim fled Juba, a province in southern Somalia immediately across the border with Kenya, with his family. His homeland was fertile and had many farms, but his memories are of violence. "The fighting was all over Somalia" when his family fled, Ibrahim says. Although no one in his immediate family died in the fighting, many of his friends and extended family did. "We left because of fear," he says. Ibrahim's father passed away in the camp in 2006, and his mother is now ill, but he takes heart in his own family of four boys and a girl. "I love all my children, but my girl is the brightest. Each time she sees me she has to kiss me," he says with a beaming smile.

Would he ever return to Somalia? "Somalia is the place I like most, but the problem is the fighting there." His family once owned farms and was prosperous, but "the ones who made us leave have taken our property. I can't go back until there is peace. There is no law and order in Somalia. Everybody is fighting for power," Ibrahim says, despite the fact that "we are all part of the same religion." His earnest hope for the future is that Somalia would once again be united. "We want Somalia to be one. That is our wish, and with one president."

Mohamed Hussein Ali

IBRAHIM'S FRIEND, Mohamed Hussein Ali, is in his mid-thirties and a longtime camp resident. The warlords are Somalia's impediment to peace, Hussein Ali says. Each has his own established territory, which may include a port or an airport, and they're equipped to fight for it.

They control all the land and houses within their territories and send their children and relatives to schools overseas, he tells me. With each leading his own security force, the only way to break the warlords' stranglehold on the country is for the international community to present a united front. "If the international community got together and had one goal, then it would happen," Hussein Ali says. It is essential that outside support for the militia fighting in Somalia, especially the influx of weapons, be stopped, which could be done if the UN's arms embargo was enforced, he tells me. "Where would they get bullets and guns if they did not have an outside source?"

The Somali pirates, Hussein Ali argues, are an example of outside manipulation of the situation in Somalia. "Somebody has to be directing them from outside," otherwise they would not know which ships to attack, he says. "Someone is guiding them. There're a lot of hands in Somalia." The international community can be blamed for the rise in piracy, he says, because it did not help rebuild the country after the defeat of the Barre regime and instead withdrew from the country in the mid-1990s. "The international community that created [Somalia] is also making it fail."

Faisal Mahamud Hashi

ALI'S FRIEND, Faisal Mahamud Hashi, twenty-seven, returned to his family home in southern Somalia in 2000 from the Dadaab camp but left again because of the fighting. "I have no hope," he tells me. "Al-Shabaab is cutting off hands" to intimidate people and to control the country. Most of al-Shabaab are foreigners who claim allegiance to Osama bin Laden and al-Qaeda, Hashi says, and are from countries such as Yemen and Tunisia. One way al-Shabaab has battled the transitional government is by telling people that Somali leader Sharif Sheikh Ahmed, president of the transitional government, is no longer a Muslim because he shook the hand of Secretary of State Clinton. Hashi explains that al-Shabaab asserted, "If he greeted a woman, he cannot be a Muslim. You should not follow this man."

Despite al-Shabaab's growing control over the country, the group will not last, Hashi believes. "Al-Shabaab cannot survive," because the foreigners who control and lead it are from urban areas and lack the stamina for the rugged rural life in Somalia. "Al-Qaeda cannot survive the country and the climate. It is very fragile. They survive in big cities."

Hashi supports the Somali pirates, however, saying they are fighting foreign encroachment on Somali fishing grounds. "The difficult life they have, that situation makes them do piracy." Instead of helping Somalia get on its feet, Hashi says, the European Union and the United States have sent warships. "They send their navies while Somalia burns," he complains. Yet fishing trawlers from foreign countries prompted the piracy. "They are the people who forced them to do it," Hashi says. Fortunately, piracy has generated an influx of cash that is good for Somalia. "Puntland is growing."

Ismalil Abdulla Mohamed

ORIGINALLY FROM the coastal town of Kismayo, Ismalil Abdulla Mohamed has lived in Hagadera for eighteen years and was among the first to arrive when the camp was opened. As the community's health committee chairman, Mohamed works as a liaison between the community and IRC staff and doctors at the camp hospital. "In terms of security, it is good here," he says, and he has no desire to return to Somalia. "If there is peace, I will go back." When I ask if peace is possible, he shakes his head no. He prefers to go to another country, and America is his goal. "I would be very happy if the U.S. could take all of the refugees," because "everyone is happy with what America is doing for the refugees."

Mohamed is willing to fight for that chance, it seems, and shows me his swollen and severely bloodshot left eye. It was hurt while protecting a fourteen-year-old American Somali boy who had come to the camp after traveling from the United States to visit his father. Divorced long ago, the boy's mother had gone to the United States and let the boy travel to Hagadera to reunite briefly with his father. In the camp, however, the boy was attacked by someone angry at the United States, so Mohamed stepped in and took a blow to his eye. He shrugs it off.

Like others, Mohamed is convinced the fighting in Somalia is not about religion. "Everybody is looking for power," he says, and wistfully he thinks about a more peaceful past. "Before the time of the warlords, it was not like this." If he returned to Somalia, he says, "they would force me to fight." Even now, children and young men are conscripted into the militias. "They force young children to go to the front lines," Mohamed says. "The youth are being forced to go fight. If the parents refuse, then they may kill the parents. They came in the name of religion, but they are not religious." The current fight is not part of Islam, Mohamed says, because Islam forbids the killing of another person.

Zainab Shine Farah

THE DADAAB camp's main registration center is supposed to be the refugees' first stop and is where they receive a ration card. The building is in a dusty corner of the camp and surrounded by a massive chain-link fence. We pass through about one hundred people gathered at the gate and waiting to get inside, where knots of men, women, and children, many with hardened yet expectant stares, bide their time to meet officials. In a shaded cluster of tables and chairs beside the main waiting area, I meet Zainab Shine Farah, a middle-aged woman from Mogadishu who has been in the camp already for two weeks with her family of nine. She is only now registering because she has been staying with relatives in the camp. The trip from Mogadishu took seven days, she says, most of which was spent sitting on top of a large cargo truck. It was very hot, but she and her family survived. Militants attacked her house and "looted all my property," she says, forcing her to leave. Four of her relatives were killed, all of whom had been targeted by al-Shabaab. "I don't know why they were being killed," she tells me. "People were shot without being asked anything." Many in her family were traumatized by the killing, and she hopes to find treatment in the camp. Peace for Somalia is elusive, she says, and can only come when warlords settle their differences. She doubts it will happen. "I don't expect to go back. The problem is still there."

Nasteho Abdullahi Noor

FLEEING WHAT she calls "a merciless war" in Somalia, Nasteho Abdullahi Noor, twenty-four, arrived in the camp just five days ago. She has been staying with her father, who had left Somalia a couple years earlier. Noor fled the fighting accompanied by her mother after two of her younger brothers died when their house was bombed. "Every day the war is going," she says. With the selection of Sharif Sheikh Ahmed as the new president, she says, the militants have targeted government forces, especially the AMISOM troops.

"The civilians are in the middle" and suffer the most. In Mogadishu, she says, "if you go to the market, you may never come back. I've seen so many dead. The country has few natural resources, but there is fighting. Everybody has a gun. Even the children. Only women don't have guns." Children are drawn into the conflict by militants who give them money and a gun. The militants "tell the children to go shoot," and the children comply, unaware of whom they're shooting or why. "They're exploiting young children," she says of the al-Shabaab militia. The country will not have peace for many years, she says, which is why she came to Dadaab. "In Kenya, there is peace and security." Noor was living in Mogadishu with her mother and, as the eldest in the family, had been helping take care of her siblings. Since she was without a job or a husband, her mother said she was a burden and told her to leave. Noor has no idea what the future holds for her and, though happy to be out of Somalia, seems lost.

Hussein Mohamed Isaak

HUSSEIN MOHAMED Isaak is a teenager from the southern Somali mountain town of Baidoa and has been in the camp for nearly eighteen months. He is at the center this day because he wants to go to Kakuma, the refugee camp in north central Kenya. When I ask why, Isaak is at a loss to explain, telling me with vacant eyes and slow speech, "I want to be a teacher." When he describes his background, I begin to understand. A victim of polio, he's been left physically weak and was traumatized when his family of nine died during the bombing of their home in 1997. "All my family was massacred," he says. He had been at school that day and was on his way home when the bomb hit. "When I came back [to the house], that is when I discovered what had happened." He was taken in by relatives and stayed with them in Baidoa until June 2008, when he crossed the border to Dadaab. Isaak remains angry about his loss but tells me he is certain that if he can get to the Kakuma camp, his chances of going to another country for his education are much better than staying in Dadaab.

Keyro Hussien Ahmed

"I CAME here because of hunger," says Keyro Hussien Ahmed, a woman in her early forties who has been in the camp for just four days. She was caring for two girls and a son in Somalia but struggled because she had no goats to help her survive. Militants and clan gangs stole the food aid provided by the UN by threatening the aid workers who distributed it, she says, and sold it to the people to whom it was to be given. Her subclan was targeted. "I love my country," she says, but "it was difficult for me to cultivate land without [my] husband," who had died five years earlier. She was left with two daughters, now eleven and fifteen, and a son by a different man. "I don't want to go back," she says. "I have already tasted life in Somalia."

10

HAVEN FOR TERROR

JUST DAYS after the release of *Maersk Alabama* Captain Richard Phillips in April 2009, the Russian navy arrested a group of twenty-nine suspected Somali pirates that included Iranians and Pakistanis. Like other navies, the Russians were patrolling the Gulf of Aden to protect Russian cargo ships. That Iranians and Pakistanis were among the group of pirates drew little attention. Yet it meant that piracy had leapfrogged from Somalia to other countries in the region, attracting pirates and possibly Islamist militants who perhaps hoped to share the big ransoms.

According to a report by the Reuters news agency, the pirate vessel was seized by a Russian warship just fifteen miles off the coast of Somalia shortly after noon on Tuesday, April 28, 2009.[1] The pirates had attacked the *NS Commander*, an oil tanker manned by a Russian crew, twice the day before, armed with AK-47 assault rifles and grenade launchers, opening fire as they approached in three small vessels. "The captain quickly notified the coalition of naval forces in the region of the attack," said one report. "Direct communication was opened with Russian naval ship the *Admiral Panteyev*, which was 120 miles from the site of the incident." Each time the pirates had drawn close, however, the twenty-three-member crew drove off the pirates by spraying them with the ship's high-powered fire hoses. After the pirates retreated, the ship and its cargo of eighty-three thousand tons of fuel oil continued to Singapore, unharmed.[2] The Russian navy didn't catch up to the fleeing pirates until they were nearly at the Somali coast.[3] Seven AK-47 rifles, various pistols, and an aluminum ladder were seized, along with a variety of satellite navigation equipment and a large amount of ammunition. "This allows us to assume that this group of pirates undertook two unsuccessful attempts to seize the *NS Commander* tanker with a Russian crew that was traveling through this region yesterday," a Russian news agency quoted a source as saying.[4]

A month later, however, the Pakistanis and the Iranians were turned over to their respective governments after Russian officials decided they couldn't be convicted in Russian courts. "We have to admit that not all the legal and practical issues have been resolved," official Russian Foreign Ministry spokesman Andrei Nesterenko explained. "We have come up against difficulties in bringing the suspects to justice."[5] Like all other countries, Moscow was entitled under a United Nations Security Council resolution to take pirate suspects to Russia for trial, where piracy is punishable by a prison term of up to fifteen years and a fine of fifteen thousand dollars. Though the crew was Russian, the ship was Liberian-flagged, which meant it was registered in Liberia, not Russia, and technically not a Russian ship. Therefore, the suspected pirates could not be prosecuted in Russia.

The capture of the arms and ammunition, as well as the aluminum ladder, supported the notion that the attackers were in fact pirates. Yet enough questions surrounded the capture that speculation arose that the pirates may have been involved in something else. In early June 2009, that possibility was voiced by London-based piracy expert Roger Middleton, a Somalia analyst with the Chatham House foreign affairs think tank, who noted, "It is the first time there has been any suggestion of foreign nationals being involved in Somali piracy. In the past, people thought there may have been some Yemenis involved, but in most cases when Yemenis have been found, they have actually been hostages."[6]

The suspected pirates may have been smuggling arms, he said, and as such may have had links or dealings with Islamist militants in

Somalia. "If they were engaged in piracy, it would be as criminals, I would have thought," Middleton said. "If they were engaged in arms running—the most likely probability—that is criminality, obviously."[7] The capture of the Iranians and Pakistanis suggested a very real but murky world in which the Somali pirates worked with various links to militant or criminal groups operating in the region. But the details may never be known. The Iranian and Pakistani captives were released, fading back into their respective worlds.

Because of such incidents as this and what the UN arms embargo monitors reported back in 2008 of the growing ties to Islamist militants, I am anxious to learn more about the militants who control much of south Somalia. I discuss al-Shabaab extensively with Aziz, my Kenyan journalist acquaintance. An ethnic Somali, age thirty-one, and the father of two children, he also supports his sister's nine children. Aziz had traveled to Somalia just a month earlier on a personal reporting trip where he learned more about the militants of al-Shabaab. I am aware that he maintains extensive ties into the Somali community in Nairobi and is absorbed in the ongoing conflict in Somalia and its connections to piracy.

Aziz is convinced that the capture of the weapons ship MV *Faina* was due to the Sudan government's intelligence and links with pirate groups in Puntland. "There were a lot of interested external forces talking to the pirates," he tells me. The Sudan government wanted not only to prevent the weapons delivery to South Sudan but to have the pirates off-load the weapons, which Sudan had apparently offered to buy from the pirates. Once that was done, the Sudanese wanted the ship sunk, Aziz says. Sudan's president, Omar al-Bashir, was involved in these dealings, he says. While I can verify none of this, it seems plausible. The deal also soured Sudan's relations with Russia, he says, because the weaponry was apparently Russian-made, though carried on a Ukrainian ship. The weapons deal also strained relations between Kenya and Sudan, of course, which share a remote and troubled border region. The weapons were unloaded in the Kenyan port of Mombasa under a permit owned by a Kenyan firm controlled by ranking Kenyan officials who facilitated the deal, Aziz says. While the intrigue is fascinating, I lack the time or wherewithal to verify it. Yet, like pieces of a jigsaw puzzle, it all seems to fit together.

During one of our many meetings in Nairobi, I press Aziz for details of his trip into Somalia, one I could never attempt because of the extreme danger to foreigners found there. He had crossed into Somalia in July 2009 and traveled to the town of Afmadow, about ninety miles into the heart of al-Shabaab territory. "Dealing with insurgents and with an extremist group is very difficult," he confides. "The threat from those people is very high." If any of the al-Shabaab soldiers are caught talking to foreigners, they put themselves in danger. "I was very afraid." He survived, he says, because he met with a childhood friend, Fahim (not his real name), a Kenyan-born Somali who had joined al-Shabaab and was fighting against the transitional government in Somalia. Fahim had greeted him in Somalia while wearing a face mask, Aziz says, to hide his identity. He escorted Aziz into a tea shop where Fahim told him, "To save you, I took you" off the street.

Aziz spent about a week with Fahim and during this time learned how al-Shabaab operates. Fahim had received extensive training in the notorious militant stronghold of Ras Kamboni, a town on the Somalia–Kenya border where the Islamic Courts Union fought its final battle on January 16, 2007. Ras Kamboni is a small coastal community with a peninsula jutting into the sea and has long been a radicals training center.

Aziz tells me that Fahim had been struggling financially and became drawn to his local mosque, where he was contacted by an underground network of Islamist recruiters. Fahim was told, "We want youth who are ready to sacrifice their lives for God. If you die for jihad, you will go to heaven." Fahim was attracted to this message because it gave his life a higher cause and meaning, Aziz says. The recruiters don't work for free. "They're given money and told to recruit young."

Once recruited, Fahim was given a new name so that "relatives don't come trying to find you." The militants also told him if ever he was traced, "we will be very hard on you." Throughout his training, Fahim was shown photos of Osama bin Laden, Aziz says, and told, "You should be like this man." Most of the leaders and trainers of al-

Shabaab are foreigners, Fahim told him, and are Muslim extremists from Pakistan and Eritrea, and include Afghan Taliban commanders. Discipline is rigidly enforced, and recruits are expected to listen and obey. "Those guys cannot question anything," Aziz says of the fighters-in-training. This includes "no points of clarification." After rigorous physical training, the trainees are taught how to use light weapons and rocket-propelled grenades, including how to shoot down aircraft. They learn how to make roadside bombs and become suicide bombers. Fahim was among about three hundred recruits, who were divided into specialties. After about six months of training, they were sent to Mogadishu to fight the transitional government. Others were sent to help al-Shabaab control towns throughout southern Somalia, where al-Shabaab enforced its harsh Islamist ideology, which included compelling people to go to the mosques.

While the foreign leaders of al-Shabaab were driven by what Aziz calls "misguided ideology," the Somali youth who were doing the fighting were "attracted by the money only." As soldiers, the young Somalis are given about one hundred dollars a month. The money comes from outside sources, Aziz says, who want to create a militant Islamist haven by exploiting the chaos and poverty in Somalia. "They're holding the local leaders hostage. They came with money, and they went directly to the youth. They create a warlord. He is told, 'We want to put in sharia law, make one Somalia, and protect our land from foreigners.'"

"This is not a conventional force," Aziz says of al-Shabaab. It "was created out of a vacuum in leadership, out of a lack of a stable government." Because Somalia has been in the midst of chaos for the past eighteen years, Somali youth are highly susceptible to religious dogma, he says, despite the many contradictions between reality and what is preached. "No one thinks about it because there is no education. They can't question these guys. They've never seen a school." Al-Shabaab recruits are easily taught to kill because a typical young Somali "doesn't know the viability of peace or the love and happiness of life. At nine or ten, he is given a gun. He values nothing. He does not value life because he does not know the value of life. He has never known peace," Aziz says.

Aziz is adamant that if given an alternative to al-Shabaab, most of the fighters would abandon the Islamist militia, just as Fahim ultimately did. Most are afraid to leave because "they'll be hunted" and killed by al-Shabaab agents. "They have the power and the means" to track down deserters, Aziz says.

The heart of the Somalia problem is political, not military, according to Aziz. "The political crisis created the military crisis." For the past eighteen years, whatever form of government has existed in Somalia has been imposed from the outside. This has made it easy for al-Shabaab to say it is driving the foreigners out. The irony is that al-Shabaab itself is largely composed of foreigners, Aziz says. If the current transitional government led by Sharif Sheikh Ahmed would call for Somali youth to join his government, they would, Aziz believes. "All the Somali families I spoke to would do so," he states. The appeal would be great. Joining the government would mean employment but also "support [for] your mother, your father, and your country" and would be a big step toward a better future for Somalia, Aziz says. If youth begin as fighters for their country, Aziz says, then "why not as a shopkeeper or teacher" when peace comes?

Unfortunately, most Somalis are crippled by an overwhelming sense of hopelessness. "Courage is not there," Aziz says. "Hope is not there. Most youth are very pessimistic about life. After eighteen years of chaos, they will do any kind of activity that comes along." This is true for the pirates as well as for those who join al-Shabaab, he says. Sadly, "the youth [have] never [been] involved in the system. They are required only as an object of fighting" for Islamist militants. When people have no prospects or hope for the future, Aziz explains, they think only of the short term. "'We shall get money if we hijack these people.' They don't care about the risks. They only think about the money. It shows how easily the youth can be misled."

A Former Fighter Speaks

WHEN AZIZ tells me that his friend Fahim recently returned to Kenya, I ask if we can meet. Fahim had walked away from al-Shabaab after two years with the group, having grown disgusted with the killing. Granting an interview would be risky, but Aziz assures me he will try to arrange the meeting.

Nearly two weeks later, after I return to Nairobi from Somaliland, Aziz informs me that a meeting with Fahim is possible. I am nervous about it. I have no way of verifying that Fahim is a "former" fighter with al-Shabaab or that what he may tell me is accurate. He could still be active with the group. Since kidnappings are a common tactic among Islamist militants, this is a concern as I think of the late *Wall Street Journal* journalist Daniel Pearl and the *New York Times* reporters who were kidnapped in Afghanistan despite promises of security and the host of other kidnapped journalists, including two being held at the time in Somalia, who were eventually ransomed. The kidnapping of an American writer working in Nairobi would be a coup for a militant group and would highlight Kenya's extreme vulnerability due to the country's swollen Somali population.

While Fahim is a concern, I also don't know much about Aziz. Although he has been recommended by other foreign journalists in Nairobi and has come through for me so far, he might also be used by militants and be unaware of it. Despite my concerns, it is an interview I can't pass up.

We agree to meet in the quiet bar adjacent to my hotel, a public and open place. But even as I hang up with Aziz, I worry about other scenarios, such as a suicide bombing. I dismiss this as paranoia, since neither I nor my drab hotel, which is not known as a haven for American tourists, is a high-profile target. Aziz tells me that Fahim is far more anxious about the meeting than I am, suspecting that I might be an agent setting him up for an arrest. I insist that is not the case, and my only desire is get his story.

The day we're to meet, I get several calls from Aziz telling me that he and Fahim have been delayed. This only increases my unease. Fahim lives about forty miles outside of Nairobi and is taking a variety of transports to get here: bus, taxi, and minivan. In addition, Fahim wants first to meet with his sister. I have no choice but to agree, though each delay heightens my fears. Even though we're meeting in a quiet, public place, no one is going to stop a couple of armed men who might want to drag me out of the hotel and shove me into one of the taxis parked out front.

Finally, the call comes in the early afternoon. Aziz and Fahim are downstairs and waiting. I join them in the bar. Both are nervous, and Aziz talks quickly. I look around. The coast is clear. There is no one else in the bar except a waiter and the bartender.

Fahim is a solid but slim man of thirty-one who reiterates much of what Aziz has already told me. An ethnic Somali, born in Kenya, Fahim left Kenya to join al-Shabaab early in 2007, returning just a month ago. "I was encouraged by friends [to join al-Shabaab]," he says, who told him, "You are going to fight for the Islamic religion. Whoever dies here [on earth] will be rewarded [in heaven]. If you live, you will be successful. You will be taken care of. You should be ready to sacrifice your life." Fahim explains that he was contacted through a mosque by a person who acted as a broker, finding new recruits, providing them with money, and arranging their passage into Somalia.

Fahim dropped out of school in the second grade because his family was poor and could not afford his school fees. "My parents had no job," he says, and he didn't want to be a burden. He began to work in a small shop and was making about fifty cents per day. He never liked it, because he "was working for others, getting nowhere." He gravitated to the local mosque, where he was convinced that "a secular education could not take me anywhere." He was told, "You're on the wrong side of religion," and if he became more involved with Islam, "You will see your life change dramatically." Fahim believed it and convinced himself, "It is better that you die than live in this situation of poverty." Recruiters for al-Shabaab arrived, telling the young men, "You're going to sacrifice your life for the sake of God and against the foreign occupation." Convinced, he went to Somalia. "I joined [al-Shabaab] and I never feared it."

His expectations were soon fulfilled. He was given a salary of $150 per month and told that the money would increase if he proved to be a good fighter. He spent three months in training in Ras Kamboni. The training was rigorous and included a lot of running and physical exercise, followed by training in rifles and small arms. He learned to make roadside bombs and put booby traps in buildings and cars. "I was trained by a Pakistani and a Yemeni," he says, and another trainer from Afghanistan. As a new al-Shabaab soldier, he was sent to fight in Mogadishu. "We were *mujaheddin*" fighting "against a foreign government," which is what al-Shabaab called the Somali transitional government. Any humanitarian organization or foreigner was a target. "The [transitional government] was the mouthpiece of the foreigners," he was told, and Somali president Sharif Sheikh Ahmed had "betrayed us. Whoever kills him will go to heaven. He's a traitor to Islam" who had "succumbed to power and money."

Fahim fought in Mogadishu, and though the fighters were young and inexperienced, they learned quickly. Occasionally they would fake an attack to draw out the AMISOM forces to determine their strengths and weaknesses. Often, he says, they were "playing a trick with them . . . to gauge their strength . . . to see what kind of weapons they have." In Mogadishu, however, the realities of war settled on him. When many in his unit were killed in a firefight that went badly, he began to have doubts about his life as a fighter.

He then was sent to Baidoa, a regional capital in south-central Somalia in the highlands, not far from Ethiopia. Baidoa had been controlled by Ethiopian forces and had functioned as an alternative seat of government when the Islamist militants controlled Mogadishu. Militants attacked Baidoa in an attempt to drive the "foreign occupiers" out, Fahim explains, and there he became a commander of a small unit of fighters.

Fahim, however, grew increasingly disenchanted with his life. "I was fighting [for a] misled ideology. They said we're fighting for our religion. They came to mobilize the Somalis, the Muslims in Somalia." He realized, however, that the militant Islamist movement had purposes that extended far beyond Somalia when he was told, "We came here for the implementation of sharia law, not only in Somalia but every nation we see." Somalia was a testing ground for a movement that wanted to encompass the world, he says.

After two years of fighting for al-Shabaab, he concluded "We were only killing our own brothers." One night when he was in the south

Somali port town of Kismayo, he was overwhelmed with a desire to return home. "Sitting alone, I thought of my wife," he says, and he remembered that he wanted to have a child, something that could never happen in his situation. "I was in the wrong place. We are fighting the wrong people. We are killing our own brothers." Wracked with doubt, he confided to one of his comrades, "I have been thinking about my friends and family." His comrade asked, "Why are you thinking this way? Do you want out?" Fahim knew that if he told the truth, it would mean his death. He kept silent, telling himself, "I have to save myself and see my parents and wife and have a child. I'm too young to die."

Not long after, when he and his unit were at the Somali border with Kenya, he decided to act. "In the middle of the night, I just left. I didn't take anything." He walked across the desert for three days, being careful to avoid detection, and wandered into the Hagadera camp—the same camp where I had stayed.

There was no particular incident that drove him to leave al-Shabaab, Fahim tells me. Instead, it was "just something that God made me realize. I looked at it from every angle. I saw a lot of children and mothers dying. It affected me a lot." Though thankful to be back in Kenya, which he repeatedly calls "my country," he is despondent, fearing for his life and that of his family. "I came back to my country, but I can't inform my country because I will be arrested. I have no money. I have nothing. It is only God who can save me from these guys."

Kenya is very much at risk from an attack by militants due to the large number of Somalis in the country and the probability of plants and moles throughout Kenya. "There's a lot of laxity in Kenyan security," Fahim says, and "a lot of gaps to be covered." Kenya remains vulnerable because of the continuing political turmoil from the 2008 election in Kenya that resulted in a power-sharing government. "Political instability means people can take advantage of the situation. It is very easy for penetration. You cannot identify them," Fahim says of the militant underground. Kenya is not the only risk. "They've planted a lot of moles in different countries. I expect an explosion in this country. At the moment they are very powerful, and the threat is imminent."

Radical and militant Islamist elements have targeted Somalia, Fahim says. "I see Somalia as a haven for these people. The Somalis don't know what the real agenda is." However, he says, 80 or 90 percent of the Somalis would support the transitional government if it presented them with an alternative to al-Shabaab. "Now the people feel they're being held hostage," he says. "Now they see no option," even though most Somalis know that at least 40 percent of the al-Shabaab fighters are from foreign countries. Fahim would like to see more international support and involvement, including military action, on behalf of the transitional government. "Hope is coming," he says.

While Fahim agonizes over the future of Somalia, he has his own future to worry about. "It will take a long time for me to forget what I saw and did in Somalia," he says. "I will pray a lot." He will probably leave Kenya, he says, and seek a job somewhere else in Africa, perhaps in the oil fields of Angola. "I heard there are jobs there." He must leave, he says, for the safety of his family as well as his own. His relatives have already been approached, he says, but have denied that they've seen him. They tell the suspected al-Shabaab operatives that Fahim left for Somalia two years ago and that they were told he was dead. Fahim says that his sister told some people asking about him, "How can I remove a body from the grave?" His friends have advised him to "get out" because "those guys [al-Shabaab] have come to Kenya. I am a threat now. So I can't stay with my wife. I've distressed my mother," he says. He also mourns the loss of his father, who died during his absence. Al-Shabaab spies are everywhere, he says. "I am one of the few they're looking for," he says, because "I know what they are planning. I will never think of going back to Somalia."

View from Outside

It's a "marriage of convenience" between al-Shabaab and the Somali pirate networks, says Bruno Schiemsky, the former chief monitor for the United Nations group of experts keeping track of the myriad violations of the UN's arms embargo on Somalia. Now an independent consultant, Schiemsky meets me at a popular coffee shop in downtown

Nairobi where I hope that he can shed some light on the terrorism links between Somalia's pirates and the Islamist militants trying to control the country. For al-Shabaab to fight, it needs weapons, he explains, which is why it needs the pirates to import them. "They know how to evade" the naval forces trying to disrupt the pirates, he says. However, "they don't do it for free." While pirates have collected pay in weapons and cash, they have also traded their services for training, Schiemsky says. "Al-Shabaab trains the pirates in conventional use of weapons." A couple of years ago, the "pirates realized they were no match for outsiders," such as the special forces that have occasionally gone after the pirates on sea and land. The most dramatic case, Schiemsky says, was when French forces attacked the pirates on land, killing some and recovering part of the ransom money after the pirates had hijacked the French luxury ship *Le Ponant* in April 2008. Pirates, meanwhile, are cooperating with al-Shabaab in what is believed to be the creation of al-Shabaab's own maritime component. Additional links have been developed between pirates and arms traders in the region, he says, easing the movement of weapons into the country.

The Somali pirates are not one monolithic group but comprise loosely organized, localized bands based on tribal and land ties, Schiemsky explains. These groups intermittently seize the most vulnerable ships on the Gulf of Aden and Indian Ocean. Alternatively, some pirates groups are well organized and supported by foreigners and members of the Somali diaspora. In these cases, the Yemenis and Pakistanis "are the brains and organizers of it." As evidence of the wide network involved in piracy, Schiemsky tells me that pirate money has been traced to property purchases in Europe. In addition, "some money is being invested here," he says of Nairobi, although he is skeptical that pirate money is responsible for the mild building boom taking place in Nairobi.

Control of the coastline in a lawless country like Somalia has some advantages because it allows for a wide range of illegal activity, Schiemsky says. Somali pirates are suspected of providing protection for drug smugglers and drug shipments of opium and heroin that flow from Afghanistan and Pakistan, either to or through Africa. With

Afghanistan producing nearly 90 percent of the world's heroin, the drug flows through Pakistan where it can be loaded onto dhows that skirt the Arabian Peninsula and land on the Somali shore to be forwarded on. This method is also used for the weapons trade, he says, which involves suppliers for al-Shabaab from as far away as Kazakhstan and Turkmenistan. "They have contacts all over the world," Schiemsky says of the pirates and the Islamist militants.

More must be done to tackle the piracy problem, Schiemsky says, adding, "It's more of a land problem than a sea problem. You need to have a government and one with a capacity and willingness to do something about [piracy]." That capacity needs to be built from the ground up, he says. It begins with a judicial system that includes police, investigators, prosecutors, judges, jails, and prisons.

There's a lot that the international community can do that is not being done. Freezing of assets is one in particular, Schiemsky says, because large amounts of money move in and out of Somalia. Many of the pirate attacks are financed by wealthy businessmen. "The international community can do something about these men who live in Dubai, et cetera. Freeze the money flowing out of piracy and into Europe." Following who is financing the pirates, and how, is well within the scope of international authorities, he says. "If I can get the information, then the police can. When the international community starts looking into bank accounts, that will have a real big impact."

Shutting down the international financing of piracy must be done in conjunction with nation building in Somalia, Schiemsky says. Otherwise, "I don't think we'll soon have a solution." The navies of the European countries patrolling the gulf may have an effect, but "they're only using the stick. If we don't deal with the problem on land, we'll never be able to stop piracy."

But the problem on land is more than just the lack of a viable government, I suggest. It is now militant Islam. Schiemsky agrees, adding that the problem "is wider than controlling Somalia," which he says "is a first step, part of a larger game." Once Somalia is under the control of militant fundamentalist Islamist groups, they will use Somalia as a base to export their jihad. They plan to take over Yemen, then all countries on the Arabian peninsula, expanding throughout the Muslim world and beyond, he says. Schiemsky advocates a low-key but firm approach to stopping the spread of militant Islamist groups. He's opposed to such high-profile moves as putting al-Shabaab on the United States' terrorist group list. That kind of designation only enhances the group's standing in the militant Islamist world and helps it raise more money from backers of jihad. "What did they achieve by doing that?" Schiemsky asks of the United States' terrorist group designation. "Now they're taken seriously."

11

FIGHTING BACK

I GRIP THE rusted barrel of a large-caliber machine gun for balance as the sleek, gray gunboat rumbles out of the harbor in Berbera, Puntland. Beside me is Isse Mahad Abdi, the operations officer for the Somaliland coast guard, dressed in camouflaged fatigues. He gazes out to sea, occasionally signaling to a second gunboat at our side. The Somaliland coast guard largely consists of these two low-slung craft, each equipped with a radio and bow-mounted machine gun rusted by the salty air. Manned by a few dozen sailors, these gunboats are supposed to control piracy along 850 miles of remote Somaliland coastline stretching from Djibouti on the west to neighboring Puntland on the east.

This has to be some kind of joke, I think, when I'm told that the coast guard has no money for fuel and this "sea tour" will cost me money. Despite the obvious lack of resources, Abdi tells me that they've been able to capture five groups of pirates in the past year or so—almost all of them on land, not the sea—and lock them away in prison. "We depend on the fishing community," he explains, most of whose members support the fight against piracy. The people of Berbera and Somaliland depend on food and other goods to be brought into the country by sea. Piracy drives up the cost of everything and means "people cannot buy." A couple of times the coast guard chased pirates from water onto shore, he says, where they were easily captured. The coast guard has had better luck on land than at sea because the pirates' "small boats are hard to find."

Across the Berbera harbor, not far from the coast guard docks, I find Yusuf Mohamoud Mohamed in the dusty and dark offices of the Berbera Fishing Cooperative. As chairman of the group, he confesses sympathies for the Somali pirates. "Fishing trawlers destroyed the fishing and forced [fishermen] to be pirates," Mohamed says. Still, what these former fishermen are doing is "illegal, and it's a problem" because "it prevents ships from importing goods to here." In addition, "our religion prohibits sea pirates." I am skeptical that piracy prevents the importing of goods to Somaliland, but a look out at the virtually empty Berbera harbor confirms it. The harbor is marked by a couple of half-sunk hulks and little else.

The fishing cooperative has about six hundred members who live and work along the Somaliland coast, and lately fishing has been profitable. "It's good now," Mohamed says, and local fishermen have been hauling in tuna, typical for this time of the year. The cooperative's biggest troubles are not from pirates, he says, but from the Yemeni fishermen who cross the Gulf of Aden and drop their nets in Somaliland waters. "They are thieves," he says. Despite the cooperative's professed abhorrence of piracy, Mohamed tells me the angry locals have taken to kidnapping Yemeni fishing boats and collecting ransoms.

Commander Abdi, who has joined me in the interview, shrugs at the Berbera fishermen's tactics, explaining that the coast guard would protect Somaliland fishing rights if it had more boats, weapons, radios, equipment, training, and presumably fuel. These things have been promised by the international community, but so far, they've seen none of it, Abdi says.

Frustration at the lack of international support for the Somaliland military is shared by people like Abdirahman Yusuf Duale, the program coordinator for the Somaliland Academy for Peace and Development, based in Hargeisa. Duale is a veteran of Somaliland's civil war, fought from 1981 to 1991, that ended with the defeat of former Somali president Siad Barre. The two regions went their separate ways.

Somaliland leaders prepared for independence while the southern warlords turned on one another, reducing the capital of Mogadishu to a wasteland. "We knew the damage of the war, but it was new to them," Duale says of the southern leaders. Each had his own so-called liberation movement, yet collectively they had "no organization to take power." More than a decade after the Black Hawk Down debacle, the United States backed the same warlords it had once fought, supporting the defeat of the Islamic Courts Union that had taken control of the south. The Americans' tactic has backfired, Duale tells me. "This gave rise to the Islamist movement like al-Shabaab, who are fighting in Somalia now."

Somaliland has been peaceful and stable because after Barre's defeat, Somaliland dismantled its military and set up a two-year transitional government that ended in a democratic election in 1993. Duale is frustrated because Somaliland has been praised as a model for all of Somalia but has been denied recognition as an independent republic. "We are not from Mars," says Duale, suggesting that Somaliland has been treated unfairly, as if it is inhabited by aliens from outer space. Somaliland also evolved much more democratically than its nearest neighbor, Puntland, which is also a semiautonomous entity but where piracy has flourished. When illegal fishing and toxic dumping peaked off the coast of Puntland, the Puntland fishermen became pirates, capturing foreign vessels and holding them for ransom. "From there . . . the Somalis organized themselves and went into business. Now it's a mafia. It's a combination of Somalis and expatriates," he says.

While piracy has generated multimillion-dollar ransoms, only part of that money stays in Somalia, while much of it lands in foreign banks. "The intelligence organizations all know this," Duale claims. "They know what is going on and who is doing it. They are watching it all." But instead of doing something about that, "they are now sending warships," he complains. "The amount of money that is spent on these ships is high, but nothing is done on land." Duale wonders why. "Are they safeguarding those who are dumping waste here? If they really want to do something about piracy, why don't they do something about people transferring the money? Instead, they are attacking the small pirates."

If capturing pirates is the preferred tactic, Duale suggests, western nations should support those closest to the situation, such as the Somaliland coast guard. Without some international support, "we cannot defend our coast," Duale says. "Why can't they provide us with some boats and training? You have to attack the root, not the branches," he says of the piracy problem. "Why can't they help us build a navy? They can do that with just 2 percent of the expense of running a warship in the gulf. This is not a local issue. It is an international issue. It's a big business that involves all of us. We don't see the solution as sending [war]ships to our coast."

On an Antipiracy Frigate

A WEEK after I meet with Duale, I travel to Dar es Salaam, the coastal capital of Tanzania, where I board the Royal Dutch Navy destroyer the HNLMS *Evertsen*, a rare chance to get on board a naval ship in the thick of the fight against piracy in the Gulf of Aden. I join the *Evertsen*'s crew and commanders for a day before it heads back to troubled waters. Like most similar ships, the *Evertsen* is staffed with a crew of 220 and spends about five weeks at sea before being resupplied. The *Evertsen*'s equipment typified most ships working in the gulf: machine guns mounted around the deck, a massive bow-mounted cannon, a helicopter that can be airborne quickly, and various high-speed inflatable craft manned by heavily armed special forces who can be on the water and chasing pirate skiffs in minutes.

The *Evertsen* is part of the multinational fleet assigned to Operation Atalanta, the European Union's naval force known as EUNAVFOR. At the time of my visit, the EU's antipiracy mission is commanded from this ship by the Dutch Commodore Pieter Bindt. Operation Atalanta was launched to protect the World Food Program ships carrying food supplies to refugees in Somalia and the most vulnerable vessels in the Gulf of Aden and off the Somali coasts, extending to Seychelles. In addition to the EU force there are the NATO Maritime Group 1, the

United States–led Combined Task Force 151, and Russian, Indian, Japanese, and Chinese naval forces with specific missions to protect their nation's merchant fleets.

While the number of pirate attacks has increased from 2008 to 2009, the number of successful hijackings has dropped, the Dutch tell me. Instead of chasing individual pirates, a protected shipping lane had been established with entry and exit points at either end of the gulf. Merchant ships are asked to "concentrate at a certain area that has been cleared of pirates," Dutch Lieutenant Commander Mark Corveleyn explains. Merchant mariners are escorted by navies from Holland, Germany, France, Italy, Belgium, Greece, and Sweden through the corridor at speeds between ten and eighteen knots per hour, he says. Ships that move at less than ten knots per hour and have a deck, or freeboard, that is close to the water, Corveleyn says, are extremely vulnerable to pirate attacks. Merchant ships traveling faster than eighteen knots per hour are usually not attacked, because at that speed "you're not really a target." Ships are free to not use the convoys, but then they leave themselves open to pirate attacks.

The *Evertsen*'s control room for Operation Atalanta is a high-tech wonderland. The desks are cluttered with laptops, and the walls are covered with large digital screens that depict traffic in and around the protected shipping lane. As merchant ships approach the protected corridor, each contacts the Maritime Safety Center, Horn of Africa, providing the ship's details so that naval escorts "know which are slow and which are not," Corvelyen says. In addition, the command center charts and tracks every pirate attack. "We try to get the best picture of where pirates operate . . . and try to find pirates before they attack."

The fight against piracy is critical because at least 80 percent of the world's goods travel this region by sea, Commodore Bindt tells me. Europe gets about 90 percent of its trade via the gulf, including vast amounts of natural gas and oil. If piracy continues to fester, it will lead to greater crimes and perpetuate the instability in Somalia. "It is serious, and it is disruptive," Bindt says. The force he commands consists of up to fourteen ships, five patrol aircraft, and eleven helicopters. He says the area that the navies are trying to protect "is enormous" and equates their task to safeguarding a section of sea equal to the landmass of Europe.

Because the justification for Somali piracy has been the exploitation of Somali fishing grounds, the EU navies inspect fishing vessels in the gulf. Ironically, they had yet to find any illegal fishing activity, Bindt says. "We don't see fishing ships without licenses from Puntland," he says, which counters the Somali pirates' mantralike justification for their actions. The EU forces have recognized the designated "exclusive economic zone" for Somali fishing water that extends two hundred nautical miles out to sea, far beyond twelve-mile limit for what is considered territorial waters. "There is still fish" to be caught, Bindt says, noting that the trawlers they stop "have plenty of fish."

Operation Atalanta has blunted piracy by reducing the successful attack rate from 43 percent down to nearly zero during August and September 2009, Bindt says. A big factor, however, is that August, September, and October are the windiest months of the year, forcing pirates to stay on shore. At the time of my visit, the EU navies had detained 143 alleged pirates and turned 68 of them over to Kenya for prosecution since it began operations in 2008.

The EU force has broad authority to stop ships in the gulf, Bindt says, "when there is a suspicion of piracy or slavery." Many suspected pirate skiffs are engaged in human trafficking. "Daily we see skiffs filled with these people," he says. One skiff had apparently been drifting for five days with ten people aboard. They were treated by the ship's doctor and given food, water, and fuel, he says. The human smugglers are profiting from the many people fleeing Somalia for better opportunities in Yemen. Traffickers get $150 per person and prefer these lower-risk trips over piracy, Bindt says. When suspected pirate skiffs are stopped, the occupants claim to be fishermen, even when they're caught with Kalashnikovs and grenade launchers. "You don't need an RPG or an AK-47 to fish," Bindt says. "Typically, suspected pirates try to flee."

Bindt admits that piracy cannot be resolved by a dozen or so warships from the world's navies. "Obviously, the solution is not at sea. The solution is on land. What we do is suppress the activity." The EU "recognizes that we're fighting a symptom" of a larger problem of

Somalia. "Piracy is one of the oldest problems in the world. To think we can stamp it out is unrealistic. The situation on land drives people to the sea," he says, which is why the EU is working in Puntland and Somalia to "help them fight the problem." But it will take time, Bindt says. "You don't invent a coast guard out of nothing."

Think Like a Pirate

SHORTLY AFTER the *Maersk Alabama* attack in April 2009, the U.S. coast guard issued a "Port Security Advisory" authorizing U.S. merchant ships to bring private security guards on board if the ships were operating in the Gulf of Aden and the Indian Ocean. The directive recommends antipiracy actions but "does not preclude the employment of increased security measures by vessel masters above and beyond those recommended or required." The directive was part of the coast guard's "Guidelines for U.S. Vessels Operating in High Risk Waters," known in the industry as Maritime Security Directive 104-6. It requires U.S.-flagged ships to have extensive security plans that include the use of "soaps, foams, netting, barbed wire, electric fencing, et cetera" to deter pirates from boarding ships. It also requires that shipowners equip their vessels with "nonlethal means to disrupt, disorient, and deter boarders; e.g. loud acoustic devices, high energy light beams, or other equipment to repulse attackers." The directive then recommends that shipmasters "consider supplementing [the] ship's crew with professional armed or unarmed security." However, the directive then states that "if transiting the Horn of Africa region, all vessels shall supplement ship's crew with armed or unarmed security based on a piracy specific vessel threat assessment conducted by the operator."[1] By issuing these requirements, the United States made it clear that the use of force to repel and deter pirates and piracy was not only acceptable, it was largely required for all but the most impregnable ships plying the pirate-infested waters. The U.S. shipowners would take the requirement to heart.

In part because of the U.S. coast guard requirement for U.S. ships in the Gulf of Aden and the Indian Ocean, and in part because of basic business sense, piracy has generated a booming business for private security companies. Most of these companies grew out of the wars in Afghanistan and Iraq as the U.S. government and other countries hired thousands of combat veterans and ex–special forces to supplement and support military operations. As piracy has mushroomed, many of these companies have expanded into maritime security.

The leader of one such firm, Michael Murrell of ISSG Holdings, Ltd., talked with me in early August 2009 from his home in the Philippines. His company works in the Gulf of Aden, providing security for merchant ships. A retired army paratrooper and military policeman with a degree in forensic science, Murrell has worked with boarding teams in the U.S. Coast Guard. Based in Seychelles, an archipelago in the Indian Ocean, his company has ready access to the Gulf of Aden. When we talk in the late summer of 2009, he explains that most shipping companies were using the seasonal high winds to protect their fleets transiting the gulf. "Right now the weather is so bad. The shipping companies bank on that . . . to save money."

A key consideration is that most shipping companies and their insurers would prefer not to have to deal with either pirates or security companies, Murrell says. "Shipping companies don't want you on board." But "you're a necessary evil" if shipping companies want to protect their crews and cargo.

The high cost of security has become an issue, he says, so he tries to keep the cost "less than one hundred thousand dollars" per transit. He has achieved this in part by employing trained commandos from India rather than the higher-priced former U.S. or British special forces. "They want one thousand dollars per day. It's so horrendously expensive. I can't justify that to insurance companies." Although private security firms that have worked in Iraq expect to collect huge fees, "the global recession has hit the shipping companies just like everyone else," Murrell says.

Yet successful security operations require "people who are familiar with vessels. We use all former navy commandos. They've been on ships, and they're trained right. They have discipline. Maritime security is very unique." His team members have a minimum of fifteen years' service, with specialties in bomb disposal, deep sea diving, and combat medicine. "They get paid well."

Unlike some companies, his personnel are unarmed, Murrell says. "We don't use firearms. We're not armed. We don't want to kill anyone. We've never had to do that." He prefers to "maintain the pulse of what is happening" and to understand the mind of the pirates, so they can be outsmarted. "There's a difference between criminals and terrorists," Murrell says. "Right now [piracy] is a financially motivated crime. They're not out there to sink a ship or blow you out of the water. They're going to fire a few rounds but rarely hit the ship with an RPG. They're doing it to scare the crew and get the ship to stop. If you have the plan, you have the advantage. The only advantage they have is . . . the firearms, and [they] have more speed with their little boats."

An example of what can go wrong when security forces are overly anxious to shoot at suspected pirates occurred in November 2008, when pirates hijacked a Thai fishing trawler and reportedly fired weapons at an Indian warship. The Indians returned fire, destroying the Thai ship and killing fourteen of the fifteen crew along with the pirates. A sole surviving sailor spent six days adrift in the shark-infested waters before another ship picked him up.[2]

Look at a ship from the pirate's point of view, Murrell suggests. "Forget about guns. Think like a pirate. Put yourself in his shoes. Play the criminal mind. What will determine or delay me?" The answer requires thinking and preparation, he says, and it involves more than a few hired guards. "You just can't get a bunch of bodies and put them on a ship. There's a lot that you have to go through. We always want the pirate to think he has [an] advantage, until at a certain point . . . the ship needs to take evasive measures," Murrell says. "If you get up there and [fire] a couple of shots, you may open yourself into a gunfight. You have to give them an opportunity to spot you and go away."

It is a lot easier for a pirate firing a grenade launcher to hit a ship than for security personnel to hit a small skiff in the distance. "Their range is three hundred meters, and you're a really big target. Your ability to hit them at three hundred meters is a lot harder than their ability to hit you. You don't want to get into a firefight. You want to get into a [situation] so that weapons are a last resort. If you show your hand too soon, you have a problem. If you engage too soon, you have a liability issue. You just can't start shooting people. No pirates have just come up there and just started shooting people."

A practical and nonlethal deterrent is to "wrap the entire ship in razor wire," Murrell says, which prevents the easy boarding that has made piracy an attractive business. "You expand it out and attach it to the rail. Each ship is different. . . . We sandbag positions on the deck. You've got to create some of these things for yourself." When pirates see protective measures, they back off, he says, and wonder what else might be there that they can't see. "When [the pirate] gets close enough to see that, he's going to [think], 'Oh, they're prepared.' He's got to weigh, is it worth the risk? Those are the kinds of things we do, but we go a lot more in-depth."

Another key is having the right-sized security team on the ship, Murrell says. A "transit risk assessment" is conducted for each ship and route, "then we build what we need to do." For most cargo ships and certainly oil supertankers, "Three guys [are] not going to do it," because there are "a lot of square meters and perimeter to cover." Typically Murrell assigns a team of eight men to a ship, although it can be as few as five or as many as twenty. "You've got to be flexible."

The reason shipowners take protective measures is that "pirates look for the easier target. If your [ship] is hardened, they will look for another target," Murrell says. Pirates have communication systems that allow them to find and attack the most vulnerable ships. "They're just watching you. If you're not prepared and you're not the right type of vessel . . . pirates will call ahead." Shipping companies "need to show [pirates] you're very aware of what's going on."

Murrell suggests that piracy in the Gulf of Aden has been bigger in the past than shipping companies have wanted to admit and, as a result, has been obscured. "Fifty percent of the attacks are never reported," he claims. Shipping companies face escalating insurance costs due to piracy, so if the number of attacks is statistically low, the statistical risk is reduced and ultimately the insurance costs remain low.

Despite the clear need for better maritime security, Murrell says, "The majority of shipping companies are doing nothing. They're rolling the dice." Shipping companies read reports and assessments that say that any given ship transiting the gulf has a 2 percent chance of being attacked. "That's not accurate," he argues. Even the presence of security personnel on ships may not improve reporting, however. "We have confidentiality agreements with these carriers," he says, so reporting is determined by shipping companies that "don't want to be out there talking about this stuff," he says. "They're reluctant to do it."

Determining shipping risks in the Gulf of Aden is not a function of statistics, Murrell argues, but a function of the ship itself. "It's vessel-type specific. If you're a tug . . . or a ship with a low freeboard, then you're in a different category" than "giant ships with high shipsides" that travel at eighteen to twenty knots per hour. Fully loaded oil tankers, he says, travel at a maximum of only fourteen knots per hour. In addition, "western flags are more attractive," because the pirates "want to maximize their payday." The most vulnerable ship is the "tug and tow," which is a tugboat pulling a barge, because it can only travel at speeds of up to five knots. In such cases, both the tug and the barge need to be protected.

One of the most unique and useful tools against piracy is the unmanned aerial vehicle (UAV), which functions like the aerial drones employed by the U.S. military. "They're pretty small," Murrell says, and they can fly out about twenty miles and stay aloft for eight hours. Each one has a GPS tracking system and streaming video and comes with a control station. They're handy for spotting and tracking suspected pirate skiffs. "It also gives you identification capabilities. If you see a small boat," he says, you can quickly determine if it is a threat or a fisherman and whether the suspected pirate skiff has weapons. With digital technology, the UAV also allows the operator to send a photo to naval ships in the region, so "your help can arrive much faster." The UAVs have about a six-foot wingspan, are gasoline-powered, and are launched from a catapult. They land in the water and can be retrieved by a net, he explains.

The legalities surrounding the use of security personnel on merchant ships can be a problem, especially if it involves weapons. When shots are fired at a suspected pirate in or near a country's territorial waters and the shooting is challenged, questions arise over the prosecution of the allegations and can damage a ship or shipping company's right to conduct maritime trade. According to Kenneth C. Randall, the dean of the University of Alabama School of Law, "Commercial vessels have the right of innocent passage through most coastal waters. Some nations might say once you're armed, you're no longer innocent."[3]

As part of their efforts to control arms smuggling and terrorism, Egypt, Yemen, and Oman do not allow firearms on board merchant ships harbored in their ports, Murrell explains. However, if the ship owns the weapons, they're permitted in most circumstances. "Otherwise, you're involved in gunrunning," Murrell says. "You don't want to be involved in that." The weapons ban includes night vision goggles, which are considered military equipment. "You've got to be creative on how to get around all of this. There are ways to do that."

On the Bandwagon

As THE problem of Somali piracy has grown, so have the proposed antidotes. Just a month after the *Maersk Alabama* incident in April 2009, the head of Interpol, American Ron Noble, called for an international alliance to track and stop the flow of money around the world from the million-dollar ransoms paid to pirates.[4] At a Group of Eight meeting of justice ministers in Rome, Noble said, "We've got organized criminals targeting victims, taking them hostage, and using extortion to get money. And what's happening now is that the world has focused on a military response." While he supports the use of naval forces, Noble suggested that international investigators create a database of photos, DNA, and fingerprint records to keep track of pirate suspects. In addition, the problem may be deeper than just the pirates on the water. "There is the whole question of corruption on shipping lines," he said. "How do you think these pirates are able to find the ships to attack? Obviously they have inside information. Obviously there are conversations that are going on or e-mails that are being exchanged. And you find their modus operandi by debriefing people you arrest."[5]

About the same time, officials from the Netherlands suggested that a special tribunal be established to try accused pirates.[6] The proposal, however, was shelved when the European Union signed an agreement with Kenya to conduct the trials. But that could change if the Kenyan trials prove to be unviable or are successfully challenged on the basis of jurisdiction or inadequate defense. While the Dutch support the Kenyan prosecution, "the Netherlands also wants effective prosecution, trial, and punishment," the Dutch foreign ministry has stated. The idea of a special pirate tribunal surfaced after the Netherlands had to release nine suspected pirates because no legal framework existed to prosecute them in Europe at the time. The proposal was made because the Netherlands has extensive experience in international tribunals and would be an ideal location for a special piracy court.[7]

In June 2009, the U.S. Congress got into the act as well when New Jersey representative Frank A. LoBiondo introduced a bill to grant immunity to U.S. merchant mariners who might wound or kill pirates attacking their ship. The U.S. Mariner and Vessel Protection Act also called for mariners to be trained in how to handle weapons and authorized the U.S. coast guard's Maritime Safety and Security Teams to ride on U.S.-flagged ships transiting the gulf. As of late 2009, the bill languished in committee.

Countries such as the United States are leaning toward a more muscular approach rather than a judicial one when it comes to Somali pirates. Perhaps the most dramatic development surfaced in late October 2009 when the U.S. Navy unveiled a new, high-speed ship ideally suited to chase pirates in the Gulf of Aden and beyond.[8] Two such ships were commissioned. One was the *Independence*, a 418-foot warship built in Alabama, capable of forty-five knots per hour, or about fifty-two miles per hour, in tests conducted in the Gulf of Mexico. A second ship, the 378-foot *Freedom*, built in Wisconsin, had similar speeds. Propelled by diesel engines boosted with gas turbines, the ships use steerable water jets instead of propellers and rudders and have shallower drafts than conventional warships, which allow them to race close to shore. Due for deployment in 2010, the ships are promising but costly. Final bills were expected to be at $460 million per ship. While some other naval vessels are capable of faster speeds, few have the same combat capabilities and sustained speeds, according to Loren Thompson, a defense analyst at the Lexington Institute. He noted that these new ships hit high speeds despite headwinds and six- to eight-foot seas. "For a ship of this size, it's simply unheard of to sustain that rate of speed for four hours," he said.[9] Whether or not these ships will help in the fight against piracy remains to be seen. Many around the world will be watching.

12

SAILORS TAKE WARNING

IT SEEMED impossible, but it happened. On Wednesday, November 18, 2009, Somali pirates again attacked the *Maersk Alabama*, the same U.S.-flagged cargo ship that was nearly captured seven months earlier. Though fraught with irony, the second attack received little notice, revealing what had changed in the intervening months on the pirate-infested waters of the Gulf of Aden—and what had not. Gone were pronouncements from the White House to pummel piracy into submission. Instead, President Barack Obama was occupied by global economics, global warming, reverberations after ordering a troop buildup in Afghanistan following President Hamid Karzai's dubious reelection, and the need to push through health care reform, which languished in Congress.

Although shoved into the dark corners of international affairs, piracy surged toward the end of 2009 as Somali pirates spread their operations deep into the Indian Ocean. No one, it seemed, was immune. Just nine days before the second *Maersk Alabama* attack, a Hong Kong–flagged crude-oil tanker, the *BW Lion,* was attacked by pirates in two skiffs far into the Indian Ocean, some four hundred nautical miles northeast of Seychelles and nearly one thousand nautical miles due east of Mogadishu. It was the longest range of a pirate attack off the Somali coast on record at the time.[1] Suspected Somali pirates fired automatic weapons and rocket-propelled grenades, but the ship was able to evade capture.

Although the European Union's limited naval forces were stretched to the breaking point, EU ships intercepted the suspected attackers a week later near the midpoint between the Indian subcontinent and Africa. Spotted by an EU maritime patrol aircraft based in Seychelles, the suspected pirate skiffs were known to be three hundred nautical miles north of the Seychelles islands, with two additional suspected pirate craft spotted further to the east. On the morning of November 18, 2009, the same day the *Maersk Alabama* was attacked, the Greek warship HS *Adrias* intercepted and boarded the first group of suspected pirates and their mother ship, arresting ten men and seizing their weapons, paraphernalia, and skiffs. The *Adrias* then chased down the second group, seizing another two skiffs and a mother ship and arresting five men, for a total of fifteen.[2]

As the EU chased suspected pirates ever deeper into the Indian Ocean, another drama was unfolding in the Gulf of Aden. Shipping companies, particularly those from the United States, had taken to heart the U.S. coast guard guidelines discussed in the previous chapter and put armed guards on U.S. ships transiting the gulf. Private security guards on board the deck of the *Maersk Alabama* returned fire when Somali pirates attacked, driving them off. The attack had come at 6:30 A.M., which was the same time the ship had been attacked previously. Four suspected pirates in a skiff came within three hundred yards of the ship, which this time was nearly six hundred miles off the northeast coast of Somalia, more than twice as far at sea as it had been the first time it was attacked and in presumably safer water. Like the first attack, the ship was on its way to the Kenyan port of Mombasa. According to news reports, the security team fired small arms and cranked up an acoustical device that generated an ear-splitting, painful sound. Evasive maneuvers were taken, and the pirates retreated. "This is a great example of how merchant mariners can take proactive action to prevent being attacked," remarked Vice Admiral Bill Gortney of the U.S. Central Command.[3]

Though the U.S. Navy reported no injuries or damage to the merchant ship, the Somali pirates' fate was likely different. A self-proclaimed pirate in the Somali pirate haven of Harardheere told the Associated Press that colleagues out at sea had called friends around 9:00 A.M. the day of the attack, some two and a half hours after it had happened. "They told us that they got in trouble with an American ship, then we lost them. We have been trying to locate them since."[4] Another reputed Somali pirate said at least four of his colleagues were dead, although it was impossible to verify either the deaths or their connection to the incident. A Somali pirate boss known as Red Teeth told a reporter, "We have been told over the phone today that four of our colleagues were killed and two were injured." Red Teeth then vowed, "We will keep attacking on foreign vessels until illegal fishing and toxic dump is stopped."[5]

Red Teeth's threat rang hollow, since few except the pirates themselves still claimed that fishing and dumping had anything to do with Somali piracy. About the same time, witnesses in Harardheere reported that scores of luxury automobiles were crowded onto the shore in this coastal town as pirates, their families, and friends scrambled to claim their share of a reported $3.5 million in ransom that just had been paid to free a Spanish fishing trawler. "I came here to get some money from my friend, who is receiving his share today," said Harardheere resident Mohamoud Elmi.[6] The ransom payment had brought the release of thirty-six crew members and their Spanish fishing vessel, the *Alakrana*. Spanish Prime Minister José Luis Rodríguez Zapatero refused to comment on the ransom except to say, "The government did what it had to do."[7] Despite the apparent bounty of luxury vehicles bought by the ransoming of the Spanish ship, the realities of the Somali pirates were revealed as the Spanish hostages recounted their ordeal. They painted a grim and desperate portrait of the pirates. The Somali captors were emaciated men in their twenties and thirties. "The Kalashnikovs were so heavy they bent the men over backward," Spanish trawler crew member Iker Galbarriatu told the Spanish newspaper *El Pais*. "They would not have been able to shoot without falling down."[8]

Even as the pirates in Harardheere were dividing their spoils, yet another hijacked ship sat offshore. Just two days before the second attack on the *Maersk Alabama*, pirates had hijacked the *Theresa*, a ship that operated out of Singapore, taking twenty-eight Korean crew members hostage. It too had been headed for Mombasa when pirates captured it about two hundred miles northwest of Seychelles. Two days later, the pirates said the ship captain's body was in the ship's refrigerator after he had died from gunshot wounds. A pirate named Omar said the captain had fired a flare gun during the attack, and, thinking they were being shot at, the pirates had fired back, killing the captain.[9] The ship was eventually released, in March 2010, after a reported ransom of about $3.5 million was paid.

In all, some fourteen commercial vessels and their crews were being held by Somali pirates at the time, including a British couple, Paul and Rachel Chandler, who had been grabbed at gunpoint from their thirty-eight-foot yacht sailing off Seychelles in October.

The aggressive armed response from the *Maersk Alabama* to the broadening threat of piracy was greeted by cheers from many quarters. Among those in support of it was Captain Joseph Murphy, the father of Shane Murphy, the former first mate of the *Maersk Alabama*. Although the United States asked all merchant ships to protect themselves against pirates off East Africa, Murphy, who teaches maritime security at the Massachusetts Maritime Academy, estimated that only about 20 percent of the ships there were armed. After the April hijacking, the owners of the *Maersk Alabama* made the ship pirate-proof, Murphy said. Some changes were structural and involved safety equipment, but the most dramatic was the addition of "highly trained" ex-military personnel. "Somali pirates understand one thing and only one thing, and that's force," Murphy said. "They analyze risk very carefully, and when the risk is too high, they are going to step back. They are not going to jeopardize themselves."[10] Meanwhile, the wife of Paul Rochford, the new captain of the *Maersk Alabama*, told a Boston radio station that she was "really happy" there were weapons on board at the time of the second attack. "It probably surprised the pirates. They were probably shocked," said Kimberly Rochford. "I'm really happy at least it didn't turn out like the last time."[11]

Despite the effectiveness of arming merchant ships, the practice also drew some criticism. The international maritime community was still "solidly against" armed guards aboard vessels at sea, said Roger Middleton, the piracy expert at the London-based think tank Chatham House. "Shipping companies are still pretty much overwhelmingly opposed to the idea of armed guards," Middleton said. "Lots of private security companies employ people who don't have maritime experience. Also, there's the idea that it's the responsibility of states and navies to provide security. I would think it's a step backward if we start privatizing security of the shipping trade."[12] Reflecting the preference to rely on naval forces rather than private security forces, the EU in November 2009 extended for another year the mission of the EU naval operations in the waters off East Africa as commander British Rear Admiral Peter Hudson claimed that no ships operating under the EU escort arrangements had been hijacked by pirates. Richard Scurrell, an analyst for the global insurance broker Willis Group, explained that although many security companies offered armed protection personnel for ships, companies feared that crew members could be killed or injured. Incidents involving injured crew could raise insurance issues, and most countries have very different rules about weapons aboard ships.[13]

Even as more ships used armed security to repel the pirates, pirate groups were flexing their muscles on land. In mid-November, gunmen in the Puntland port city of Bosasso killed one of the region's most active antipiracy judges. In addition to jailing suspected pirates, the victim, High Court Judge Mohamed Abdi Aware, reportedly had also jailed four members of Somalia's Islamist insurgency just days before he died. According to eyewitnesses, armed men wearing masks killed the judge as he left a Bosasso mosque. "These gangs hate him for his justice," said Aware's cousin Abdulahi Jama. "We suspect one of them may have something to do with his assassination."[14] Since targeted killings in Puntland were rare, unlike southern Somalia, the killing of a top judge in public set an alarming precedent, prompting speculation that pirate groups were tightening their grip on the Puntland government, which was already thought to be complicit with piracy. Furthermore, fears grew that Islamist militants had infiltrated the region and pirates' ranks, making the pirates a threat on land as well as at sea. The emerging pirate threat posed grim possibilities for the region and the world at large.

By the end of November, it was clear the pirates were just getting warmed up. Like they had done more than a year earlier when the oil tanker *Sirius Star* was seized, pirates captured the Greek-owned oil tanker *Maran Centaurus*, said to be headed for New Orleans from Jidda, Saudi Arabia. According to reports, nine pirates hijacked the tanker and its thirty-member crew deep in the Indian Ocean, nearly eight hundred miles off the Somali shore. The pirates diverted the oil tanker toward central Somalia, presumably to the coastal town of Eyl or Harardheere. "They have definitely increased their capacity and their ability to stay out at sea for longer," said Cyrus Mody, manager of the International Maritime Bureau (IMB) in London. That the pirates had fully resumed their attacks was no longer in doubt, having attacked ships at a rate of one every other day since the beginning of October and having successfully hijacked ten in the span of two months, according to IMB statistics. "It's 2.5 million square miles we're dealing with," explained Lieutenant Matt Allen, a spokesman for the U.S. navy's Fifth Fleet, based in Bahrain. "It's a very large area. It's a daunting task."[15]

Shattered Hopes

Reflecting the growing menace on the Somali seas was the creeping chaos across the Somali landscape as the militant Islamists of al-Shabaab steadily extended control over southern Somalia. On November 21, al-Shabaab took over the town of Afmadow, some four hundred miles south of Mogadishu and close to the Kenyan border, after its rival Islamist militia, Hizbul Islam, abandoned the town. The fall of Afmadow left al-Shabaab in control of most of southern Somalia and most sections of the capital of Mogadishu.[16]

The group's grip over Somalia became horrifyingly evident when a suicide bomber dressed as a woman killed himself and twenty-two others attending a university graduation in Mogadishu on December 3. Among the dead were three Somali cabinet members and several journalists. The attack lent sad credence to the assertion that the Islamists, not the transitional government or the 3,500 or so soldiers of the African Union mission, were in control of the country. The attack took place as several hundred people gathered in the decorated ballroom of the Shamo Hotel to celebrate the diplomas being granted to forty-three medical, computer science, and engineering students from Benadir University. Established in 2002 by Somali doctors, the school advances higher education in a country where physicians and other professionals have become the victims of the country's endless violence and the people are in sore want of health care. Medical degrees are obtained after six years of study, and the group was only the second class to receive diplomas from the medical school in nearly twenty years of war. Attendees were sitting on plastic chairs facing a small stage when the bomb went off. Instead of waving their diplomas in the air, as the school's first graduates had a year before, some of the 2009 graduates and their admirers died gruesome deaths. "What happened today is a national disaster," said Somali Information Minister Dahir Mohamud Gelle. "A man who disguised himself as a woman, complete with a veil and a female's shoes, is behind the explosion," Gelle said. "We even have his picture."[17]

The Somali government quickly blamed al-Shabaab because of its ties to al-Qaeda and prior readiness to claim credit for such attacks on high-profile targets. "The investigation is still underway to uncover evidence of who might have been behind the attack, but we already know that this is the work of al-Qaeda through its affiliated group al-Shabaab, because of the nature of the attack and the tactics used," said Security Minister Abdullahi Muhammad Ali.[18] Due to the huge public outrage that was generated by the blast, however, al-Shabaab denied involvement with the killings.

"We are very sad about it," said al-Shabaab spokesman Sheik Ali Mohamud Rage, who pointed a finger at the Somali government. Somali Information Minister Gelle scoffed at the accusation, saying, "Mogadishu residents are angry, and al-Shabaab doesn't want to earn the wrath of the angry population. The people here are on the verge of revolt against them." Gelle accused outside forces of conducting the attack, explaining that Somalis would never do such a thing, even in an act of clan revenge, and that the attack was done "because of twisted religious beliefs."[19] Somali president Sharif Sheikh Ahmed also weighed in on the issue, saying, "This is not Somali work. It is a newly imported idea to destroy Somalia and prevent its people from having stability, peace, and their own government. We are committed to making the dreams of our people a reality, and such terrorist acts will never deter us."

The depth of the sorrow and anger in the Somali community was hard to miss. One of the surviving medical graduates at the event, Sakhaudin Ahmed, twenty-three, described the drama of the day's events. "I was extremely happy that after six years I was finally getting my degree; it was the happiest day of my life. I was one of the first graduates to get to the venue for the ceremony," he said. "You have no idea how hard we worked to get our degrees. There were days we could not go [to] class because of the security situation. I had to cross roadblocks to get to the university and brave gunfire many times; therefore graduation day was an emotional day for all of us.

"But then, just as we were about to receive our diplomas, a huge explosion ripped through the place," he continued. "For a minute I was so dazed I could not understand what was happening. Then I realized my leg was bleeding, and when I looked at where my colleagues had been sitting, there was nothing but death and destruction. Six students who were to receive their degrees [in computer science] were killed instantly. One of my favorite professors was also killed.

"What was supposed to have been the happiest day of my life turned into a nightmare; it is a day I will not forget for the rest of my life. I guess I am one of the lucky ones, I survived," Ahmed said. "We were there to celebrate our accomplishments, and someone turned it into a dreadful thing. We are not into politics; we simply want to help our people and ourselves.

"Thursday's bombing was meant to kill any hope for a better future for us, but those behind it will not succeed. I am reporting to work at a hospital [in Mogadishu] today. I will not be deterred by anyone in fulfilling my ambition of being a doctor and helping others. Every day I go to the hospital my friends and professor will be in my thoughts," Ahmed said.[20]

The graduation bombing stunned many Somalis and provoked a reaction that few had anticipated. Some suggested that this unprecedented attack on civilians who were the country's only glimmer of hope for the future might finally launch a rejection of the militant Islamist tactics and al-Shabaab itself. "They are killing our best and brightest. They are the enemy," said Abdi Mahad, a civil society activist who organized anti–al-Shabaab demonstrations just four days after the bombing. He said that the attack was "a wake-up call for all. Up to that point, everybody assumed they were fighting foreigners and the government, but we realized . . . that they are at war with us; it was the last straw. We will do whatever it takes to stand up to them."[21]

The antimilitant sentiment was voiced by one Mogadishu mother, Ibado Abdi Mohamed, who said, "I used to be afraid, but no more. We have watched for far too long our children being killed senselessly." Mohamed criticized the core concept that al-Shabaab has used to recruit fighters and accused it of being anti-Islamic. "Islam teaches us compassion and kindness," she said. "What they did . . . and are doing is cruel and inhuman." Another woman, who lost a son in the bombing, was justifiably bitter. Hawa Siyaad had attended the graduation with her eldest son, Mohamed, who was in his fifth year of medical school. "He was there to help with the ceremony," she explained. "One minute, he was there, the next minute he was gone. He did not do anything wrong. Why would anyone kill innocent students?" She accused the bombers of being "people who do not want to see anything good in Somalia; that day they shattered many dreams and hopes, including mine."[22]

Had al-Shabaab finally gone too far? Would such an event be enough to turn the tide in Somalia and put it on the road to functioning statehood? "I think they overreached," said Paula Roque, a Horn of Africa analyst with the South Africa–based Institute of Security Studies. "It was a big mistake on their part. It is one thing to target AMISOM [African Union Mission in Somalia] and government structures; it is quite another to target innocent civilians." The bombing, she said, meant that al-Shabaab was no longer seen as "uniting Somali nationalism and Islam."[23]

While the smoldering outrage could signal a reversal for Somalia, that reversal could only come from the people themselves. As I had been told by the former al-Shabaab fighters and others, the Somalis viewed most of the militant group as foreigners and "occupiers" rather than leaders of a movement to unite the country or to bring about peace. It was a moment for the government to step up and take the initiative to launch a drive against the group. With popular backing, a Somali-led government could bring about much needed law and order to the chaos that has gripped Somalia. A functioning government in Somalia would spell an end to, or at least difficulties for, the surging Somali pirates.

As of this writing, however, there were few, if any, indications that the government would move beyond the confines of Villa Somalia, the presidential compound in Mogadishu. An example of the deeply rooted corruption and complex web of relationships embedded in Somalia surfaced in mid-December when members of the UN's group of experts tracking violations of the Somalia arms embargo revealed they had been receiving death threats. The source of the threats was thought to be some Somali businessmen suspected of diverting aid to terrorist groups, including al-Shabaab. At stake were millions of dollars in contracts held by these businessmen, who had long-term working relationships with the UN World Food Program. These same concerns also had prompted U.S. officials to delay food shipments to Somalia.[24]

If agencies of the UN had difficulties working with seemingly trusted Somalis and delivering badly needed food aid to the estimated three million starving Somalis, how could a shell government assert control over a country deep in the grasp of Islamist militants in the south and pervasive pirate networks that control not only the lengthy coastline of Somalia but vast portions of the Gulf of Aden and the Indian Ocean? The answers were elusive at best.

EPILOGUE

A MODEST PROPOSAL

For Somali pirates, 2009 was a good year. Business was up. They had attacked 217 merchant and fishing vessels in the Gulf of Aden and the Indian Ocean, according to the International Maritime Bureau, nearly doubling their attacks of 2008. But although the pirates had attacked more ships and successfully hijacked 47 of them in 2009, their success rate was actually down from the previous year, when 111 vessels were attacked by Somali pirates resulting in 42 hijackings. The pirates were taking about one in every five ships they attacked in 2009, compared to one in every three attacked in 2008, and clearly they had to work much harder in 2009 to achieve previous results. Still, the hijackings generated a total ransom purse pegged at $82 million for the year, an increase from about $1.25 million per captured ship in 2008 to $1.75 million in 2009.[1]

The lower success rate was attributed to aggressive enforcement by NATO warships in the Gulf of Aden coupled with increasingly belligerent responses to attacks by private security guards. Pirates had been pushed away from the NATO-protected shipping corridor in the Gulf of Aden and had been forced to go up to one thousand nautical miles deep in the Indian Ocean, a trend I noted earlier. The pirates consequently depended more on mother ships, often taking highly prized fishing vessels, not for ransom, but for their use. From a well-stocked mother ship, pirates could survive for weeks in remote waters while sending out multiple pirate crews to attack often defenseless and unsuspecting ships.

The increased pressure led to the Somali pirates fighting among themselves. In January 2010, rival pirate gangs began blasting each other over a hijacked oil supertanker just as a reported ransom of $5.5 million was to be delivered. In a bizarre turn of events, the pirates on board begged for help from the European Union naval forces to drive off the attackers. Fearing that the tanker might explode, NATO helicopters were sent, helping to end the gunfight that could have ignited two million barrels of crude oil on board, potentially killing the twenty-eight-member crew and their pirate captors and creating a major environmental disaster. Crude oil is so flammable that smoking was forbidden on deck. The supertanker was a Greek ship, the *Maran Centaurus*, destined for the United States, and had been taken about eight hundred miles from the Somali coast. The oil was valued at $150 million. NATO chased away the two attacking pirate skiffs, allowing the pirates on board to collect a ransom dropped from a couple of delivery planes. A source close to the negotiations said the second group of pirates wanted to scare the pirates on board into handing over some of the money, despite the clear dangers involved.[2]

The increased attacks by Somali pirates did not come without a price, however, illustrating yet another trend set in motion by the end of 2009. In late March 2010 private security guards shot and killed a suspected Somali pirate. Although other pirates had been killed in earlier incidents, such as the three who were shot by U.S. snipers in April 2009, this pirate death became the first confirmed killing by onboard private security.[3] International navies were thought to have killed about a dozen pirates throughout 2009, according to NATO sources, and hundreds likely died at sea, either by drowning or through dehydration after their water and fuel ran out.

The shooting came during an attack on the MV *Almezaan*, a Panamanian-flagged ship reportedly owned by an entity in the United Arab Emirates. European Union Naval Force spokesman Commander John Harbour explained that the *Almezaan* had been approached twice by the pirates, prompting a gun battle between the guards and the pirates. A Spanish warship was sent, and a helicopter descended on seven pirates, including the one who apparently had been shot, and intercepted two skiffs and a mother ship. Spanish forces arrested six pirates, secured the dead pirate's body, and then sank the mother ship. The forces reported that the two skiffs had been riddled with bullets. Formal charges of piracy were pending, and the suspected pirates were to be handed over to the Seychelles or Kenya for trial.[4]

Facing deadly fire from guards on merchant ships was just part of the mounting troubles for the pirates. In early March 2010, aggressive French naval forces claimed to have captured thirty-five Somali pirates in just three days, putting the French at the top of the antipiracy struggle. Four mother ships and six smaller boats were seized in four separate operations, the French military said.[5] About ten pirates were awaiting trial in French jails at the time. The French reportedly had captured nearly one hundred pirates and killed half a dozen others since a luxury French yacht was hijacked by pirates in April 2008.

In yet another bizarre incident indicating increasing desperation among the Somali pirates, a small group of them attacked a U.S. warship at the end of March 2010, not far from the island nation of Seychelles, deep in the Indian Ocean. The USS *Nicholas* had been tracking a suspected pirate mother ship when it came under attack around midnight. U.S. Navy personnel returned fire, then boarded the skiff, capturing three pirates. The naval forces then boarded a nearby mother ship and captured another two pirates, all of whom were taken on board the U.S. naval vessel after the pirate skiff was sunk. While it was not the first time a U.S. ship or an EU naval vessel had been attacked, this bold move indicated these young pirates were likely distraught and frustrated after fruitless weeks at sea and out of desperation would attack any large ship they encountered, regardless of the consequences. Such an act could only come from people convinced, perhaps, of their own invincibility, or anxious to be captured. As of this writing, it was unclear where the captured pirates might be taken, although it was possible for them to be taken to the United States to stand trial. If so, they would join the pirate Musi, the sole survivor of the attack nearly a year earlier on the *Maersk Alabama*. It would bring to six, then, the number of suspected pirates facing trial on U.S. soil.[6]

Despite these successes, a report released by the United Nations in March 2010 revealed that little had been accomplished in 2009 to end Somali piracy. NATO and other national naval forces simply had put a lid on a boiling pot, and piracy continued to spill ever deeper into the Indian Ocean. Likewise, little had changed on the ground in Somalia to improve the chaos that allowed piracy to flourish. The experts of the UN Security Council's Monitoring Group on the Somalia arms embargo reported that, "southern Somalia remains a patchwork of fiefdoms controlled by rival armed groups—a political and security vacuum in which no side is strong enough to impose its will on the others. Meanwhile, the relatively stable northern regions of Puntland and Somaliland have suffered increasing spillover from the conflict to the south in the form of targeted killings and bombings."[7]

The experts revealed that corruption permeated the Somalia Transitional Federal Government and that officials at the highest levels of the autonomous Puntland government were alleged to be complicit in piracy. In the war-torn south, the corruption involved hundreds of millions of dollars in UN food aid pouring into southern Somalia each year. A small clique of wealthy Somali businessmen, some of whom had their own militias, controlled the flow of food aid into Somalia. These same men also controlled Somali "affiliate" organizations that were to distribute the food but were accused of diverting and selling it instead, sometimes to Islamist militants. In some cases, the hijacking of food shipments was thought to have been staged so that the food could be sold later.

In addition to food corruption, the sale of foreign travel visas by Somali officials had allowed some pirates to travel back and forth from Somalia to Europe. Officials in the Italian Embassy in Somalia also had been implicated in visa fraud. The UN experts said they knew "of several members of a Puntland-based pirate militia who obtained asylum and travel documents in Europe during the course of 2009. One obtained asylum in Sweden, one travelled via Italy to the Netherlands and one reportedly obtained entry into the United Kingdom.

All three subsequently returned to the region to resume their involvement with pirate militias."[8] It meant that pirates and their leaders were able to travel abroad at will, enabling them to conduct business, find investors, or, better yet, spend their ill-gotten gains in capitals across Europe.

But that was just the beginning. The experts were convinced the reach of the Somali criminal networks had expanded. "These [visa fraud] cases represent just a glimpse of a far larger phenomenon," the experts reported. "Information obtained by the Monitoring Group indicates that a large number of countries beyond Western Europe, including Turkey, the Russian Federation, South Africa and Ukraine are also affected by this phenomenon. The scope for exploitation by members of Somali armed opposition groups and criminal networks is equally vast."[9]

While the UN experts noted that piracy was "the most obvious symptom of the war economy," prompting a dramatic doubling of ship attacks due to piracy's "high profitability and relatively low risks," there were other causes. "[The increase] is also a reflection of the complicity of senior figures in the Puntland administration," the experts found, confirming what I had been told during my time in northern Somalia. "Several notorious pirate leaders remain at liberty in Puntland," the experts explained, "and senior officials have at times intervened to secure the liberty of kinsmen detained during the course of counter-piracy operations."[10]

As prior UN reports had detailed, the names and locations of pirate clan leaders were known. In central Somalia, Mohamed Abdi Hassan "Afweyne" (Big Mouth) continued to operate in Harardhere and Hobyo, along with his son, Abdiqaadir, and together they apparently had hijacked at least seven ships in 2009. The experts noted that Afweyne had established ties with Libyan leader Moammar Kadafi, who had hosted Afweyne for four days in September 2009 and later proclaimed his sympathy for Somali pirates.[11]

There were other big-time pirates also operating in Puntland, the experts said. One was Abshir Abdillahi Boyah, thought to be forty-four years old, who claimed to head a network of five hundred pirates. He had been a leading figure in Somali piracy since the early 1990s and was among those who claimed that Puntland officials got 30 percent of most ransom payments.

The UN experts again identified Mohammed Abdi Garaad, who previously had been noted by the UN as a top pirate leader and who bragged that he controlled eight hundred pirates organized into thirteen separate maritime militias. Garaad's pirates had attacked the *Maersk Alabama* in April 2009. After the pirates were killed by U.S. snipers, Garaad vowed revenge against the United States, and five days after the attack on the *Maersk Alabama*, his pirates attacked but failed to hijack the *Liberty Sun*, another U.S.-flagged ship that was also carrying food aid to Somalia. Garaad later told the French Press Agency, "The aim of this attack was totally different. We were not after a ransom. We also assigned a team with special equipment to chase and destroy any ship flying the American flag in retaliation for the brutal killing of our friends."[12]

What the experts uncovered led to the conclusion: "the newly established [Puntland] administration of Abdirahman Mohamud Farole is nudging Puntland in the direction of becoming a criminal state." Farole and members of his cabinet "have received proceeds from piracy and/or kidnapping," the experts said. While acknowledging that Puntland had acted against some pirates, it was meaningless. "During the course of 2009, President Farole has publicly condemned piracy on several occasions and the authorities have arrested and convicted a number of pirates, seizing weapons and equipment. In spite of these gestures, however, pirate activity off the coast of Puntland has increased, senior pirate leaders remain at liberty and without apparent fear of arrest, and in some cases the Puntland authorities have extended protection to pirate militias."[13]

While the UN experts did not find any formal ties between pirates and militant Islamist extremists fighting in Somalia, the implications of pirate influence in Puntland were clear. Puntland had become an arms and weaponry gateway for the rest of Somalia, fueling the bloody fight for control of the country. Most of the arms came via Yemen, just across the Gulf of Aden from Bosasso. Ironically, the increase in pirate attacks had boosted the demand for small arms and ammunition by the pirates themselves, the experts noted.

The implications of the UN report were grim. The world could expect bloodshed in Somalia to continue as the militant Islamist al-Shabaab fighters solidified their grip on the country while recruiting fighters from abroad, including radicalized young Muslims from America but largely from the burgeoning Somali population in neighboring Kenya. Continued support for the fragile transitional government in Somalia was being undermined by the apparent corruption in the UN's food aid program, which some suspected was only the tip of the iceberg.

A Step-by-Step Solution

THAT PIRACY in Somalia is a symptom of a much larger problem is clear. As an outgrowth of a lawless society dominated by a kaleidoscope of armed groups, the problem of piracy in Somalia mirrors the plague of violent conflict in other troubled regions in Africa, such as the eastern Democratic Republic of the Congo. The question looms: how can chaotic and corrupted states rise from the ashes of war and become functioning nations? The answer, of course, lies in the people themselves. But only in societies where the majority of reasonable and responsible people are willing and able to take control of their lives and land can stability be achieved. It cannot be imposed from the outside, not by all the good intentions in the world, not by force, and not by a flood of money.

The reality is that the Somali people, like millions of others across Africa, are absorbed in a daily struggle to survive. Just getting through the day is a victory. Few Somalis have an education, and none have been raised with the hope or expectation that life is fair or that their future is full of possibilities. Such thinking is foreign. Few have known an organized society with law and order, where schools are open, where health care is present and available, roads are paved, and electricity is available at the flick of a switch. In this context, can a people suddenly rise up, as if stuck by a lightning bolt of awareness, and swiftly organize themselves to set things right?

Westerners typically come at such problems blinded by their own circumstances, history, and perspective. They expect a central government, functioning judiciary, transportation, and educational systems, health care, and so on. If none of that exists, then these systems are imposed; much as has been tried by the creation of the Transitional Federal Government in Somalia with strong international support. But without popular support for a centralized government, and the means and muscle to make it happen, then the government and all it tries to do are destined to fail.

Because Somalia has been without an organized government for nearly two decades, clans and clan militias control south and central Somalia and to a lesser extent Puntland. The autonomous region of Somaliland remains the sole example of a functioning, organized government in the country, but instead of exerting a positive influence on the rest of Somalia, it is being victimized by the chaos and extremists of the south and is engaged in a low-level conflict over border regions with Puntland. Expecting the fragile government in Somalia, and a more organized one in Puntland, to assume their responsibilities and exert control is certainly right, but it's largely an impossible task. For example, demanding that the Puntland government, put in power by cash infusions from pirate clans, arrest these clan leaders is absurd. One might as well ask a tiger to remove its stripes.

One would think that the major impetus to end Somali piracy and to solve the larger problem of Somalia itself would come from the global shipping companies. But these international businesses have been strangely silent. Rather than becoming active in addressing the issues that give rise to piracy, shipping companies have preferred to take their hits, pay escalating ransoms, and hide behind the wall of security provided by the NATO navies in the Gulf of Aden. A growing number have turned to armed guards for protection. This does not fix the problem of piracy. Shipping interests act as if piracy can be ignored and that it will go away. It won't.

Despite the dismal situation across Somalia, piracy can be curtailed and eliminated, just as functioning governments and societies can be re-established in Somalia. Where to begin?

Rather than first tackling the chaos and militant Islamist violence in southern Somalia, the international community should begin by solving the problem of Somali piracy. This can set the stage for a comprehensive solution for all of Somalia and will best be done with a concerted effort by the international community. The framework for this, along with some of the necessary elements, is already in place. Start with NATO's naval force already present in the Gulf of Aden. Here we have an organization with a clear mission, multiple members, a rotating leadership, and plenty of money and muscle.

Rather than a World War II–style storming of the beaches at Mogadishu, such as the U.S. forces did in 1992, a NATO-led alliance with the Russian, Chinese, and U.S. navies should set up bases of operation in Somaliland. Somaliland is eager to help, is well governed, and is crying out for international assistance. To date, those cries have fallen on deaf ears. Building up the Somaliland coast guard is an immediate first step. Somaliland also is the logical place to build up a judiciary system, complete with jails and prisons, capable of holding and trying accused Somali pirates. Somaliland is a former British colony, and restoring those strong ties to the United Kingdom would be welcomed by Somaliland officials.

Using Somaliland and the port of Berbera as a base, the NATO alliance could employ navies, marines, and special forces to exert influence on Puntland. Restoring government control in Puntland will require isolating the pirate clan leaders and severing their ties to the Puntland government. Such an endeavor would necessitate the use of force on land in Puntland, which is nothing new. The United States has repeatedly conducted strikes against suspected Islamist terrorists in southern Somalia for years and, as mentioned earlier, has conducted operations in coastal areas of Puntland. The French also have launched attacks against pirate strongholds on land.

UN reports have detailed the key pirate clans and their leaders. Their locations, activities, and accomplices are well known. There is no reason, then, why they cannot be captured and put on trial, just as the hundreds of hapless pirates themselves have been captured, tried, and jailed. The effort to end piracy must also involve the international banking community, which must end the easy money laundering and transfers by pirate financiers at work in Europe and elsewhere. It will also require the help of various countries, including the United States, to impose sanctions on the pirate backers and place them on terrorist watch lists.

An underlying problem of piracy, of course, is the pervasive poverty that exists throughout Somalia. Pirates claim they have been forced into this criminal activity because of illegal fishing in Somalia's commercial waters. As I have written, and as the UN experts also confirmed, this justification is no longer valid. Almost all of the foreign fishing vessels now working Somali coastal waters do so with permits issued by Somali governmental authorities. As the NATO commander told me, every fishing vessel that his forces had stopped had both a permit and plenty of fish. The only conclusion one can draw is that the fish are there, but the Somalis along the coast prefer not to fish. They'd rather risk life and limb on the remote chance of striking it rich by hijacking a ship and collecting a ransom. The solution is to make it increasingly risky and dangerous to be a pirate by intensifying antipiracy measures on land as well as at sea. Likewise, the Somali fishing industry needs to be revived so that the pirates have an alternative. The foreign fishing permits need to be retracted and reissued to Somali fishermen. A revival of the fishing industry in Somalia could also be enhanced by providing substantial loans to Somali fishermen for fishing vessels. Fish cooperatives, processing plants, and shipping facilities also need to be revamped and revived, and this could be done with investments from Somali businesspeople themselves or with foreign capital.

With regimes in Somaliland and Puntland recommitted to law, order, and good governance and with major pirate groups eliminated or put out of business, approximately two-thirds of Somalia would be transformed into functioning territories. This would put the international community in a position to then move toward a solution in southern Somalia, which would effectively be surrounded by antimilitant forces. To the north would be Puntland and Somaliland, both aligned with the international community. To the west would be Ethiopia, a committed, Western-backed ally whose army occupied much of Somalia as recently as 2008. To the south would be Kenya. Though unlikely to invade, Kenya could be assisted to establish a strong defense along the porous Somali border.

Sensing the inevitable, the Somali clan lords in the south could be expected to throw their support behind the Transitional Federal Government. This would give the TFG the support it needs to become a viable government for Somalia. Ensuring the support of the clan lords, however, will require doing what has been done in the past: work closely with the key Somali clan leaders and their militias. They will not want to give up their territorial controls and various economic interests, of course, but such concerns of the clan leaders could be accommodated in a new governmental organization based on regional cooperation and control. Again, this approach is nothing new. When the Islamic Courts Union was poised to take over Somalia several years ago, the various clan warlords in Mogadishu were supported and equipped by clandestine services and, with the help of Ethiopia, defeated the ICU. With clan militia support shifted to the central government, the foreign Islamist jihadists would be forced to flee. This scenario would require limited foreign military involvement on the ground in Somalia.

The final phase would be rebuilding Somalia, which will require a sustained international effort.

The United States seems to be stepping up its activity in Somalia, which is long overdue. But the United States is starting with the hardest part, not the easiest. In early March 2010, the *New York Times* reported that the United States was behind a steady buildup of forces supporting the Somali government in preparation for an offensive to drive jihadists out and to allow the transitional government to take control of Mogadishu. This would be the first phase of a drive to dislodge the al-Shabaab militants from the south.

The U.S. State Department, however, distanced itself from any possible ground action, not only fearing a repeat of the Black Hawk Down disaster but also not wanting to give Islamist militants yet another reason to rally Somalis to drive the foreigners out. "This is not an

American offensive," Johnnie Carson, the assistant secretary of state for Africa, told a *Times* reporter at the time. "The U.S. military is not on the ground in Somalia. Full stop." Carson further explained, "There are limits to outside engagement, and there has to be an enormous amount of local buy-in for this work."[14]

Despite the State Department's reluctance to discuss details, the *Times* quoted an American official in Washington who said, "What you're likely to see is airstrikes and Special Ops moving in, hitting and getting out."[15] In late 2009 and into 2010, American advisers apparently had helped in the training of Somali forces to be deployed in the offensive, the *Times* reported, and had provided covert training to Somali intelligence officers, logistical support to the peacekeepers, fuel for the maneuvers, surveillance information about insurgent positions, and money for weapons. Suppliers of humanitarian aid to Somalia, meanwhile, had been urged to move quickly into recaptured areas with food and medicine to generate Somali popular support for the government.[16]

While success of this mission would be as critical as it would be difficult, it would still leave Somaliland isolated and unsupported. It would also leave piracy in Puntland unresolved and a festering problem on Somalia's back doorstep. Without enlisting the support and active involvement of Kenya, Ethiopia, and other key players in the international community, the United States had also risked isolating itself once again and saddling itself with a military and economic burden that must be shared, if not largely shouldered by the international community. One can only hope for the best of all outcomes.

ACKNOWLEDGMENTS

AS WITH most trips to troubled regions, one is dependent on the kindness of strangers. This could not be more true than with the research of this book, and I want to thank those who paused, even for just a moment, to help me. But foremost, I want to thank Matt Brown, the Nairobi-based correspondent for the *National* newspaper, whose patience with my endless questions and whose advice and willingness to share his contacts made this book possible. I also want to thank the Nairobi office of the International Rescue Committee, especially Joanne Offer, who arranged for my stay at the Dadaab refugee camp, and Tesfay Gebrearegawi, who generously hosted me. On the home front, I want to thank my agent, Michele Rubin, who encouraged me to write this book, and all the good people at Lawrence Hill Books / Chicago Review Press, especially editors Susan Betz and Lisa Reardon. I gratefully thank my wife, Dina, whose untiring patience and support has sustained and inspired me throughout the writing of this book.

NOTES

1 Attack on the *Alabama*

1. Christo Doyle and Alan Eyres with Brian J. Kelly, "Somali Pirate Takedown: The Real Story," Discovery Channel, June 21, 2009.
2. Vincent F. Safuto, "Quinn Describes Taking of His Cargo Ship: Lakewood Ranch Man Says He's Ready to Go Back to Work," *Bradenton Times*, May 23, 2009.
3. Ibid.
4. Paul Davis, "High-Seas Terror: Shane Murphy of Seekonk Recounts Hijacking by Somali Pirates," *Providence Journal*, April 25, 2009.
5. Doyle et al., "Somali Pirate Takedown."
6. Safuto, "Quinn Describes."
7. Doyle et al., "Somali Pirate Takedown."
8. Davis, "High-Seas Terror."
9. Doyle et al., "Somali Pirate Takedown."
10. Davis, "High-Seas Terror."
11. Doyle et al., "Somali Pirate Takedown."
12. Ibid.
13. Safuto, "Quinn Describes."
14. Doyle et al., "Somali Pirate Takedown."
15. Ibid.

16. Cable News Network, "Shipmates Recount Battle with Pirates, Call Captain Brave," April 16, 2009. http://edition.cnn.com/2009/US/04/16/maersk.crew/index.html.
17. Doyle et al., "Somali Pirate Takedown."
18. "Sailors Who Thwarted Pirates Back with Families," Associated Press, April 16, 2009.
19. Safuto, "Quinn Describes."
20. Doyle et al., "Somali Pirate Takedown."
21. Davis, "High-Seas Terror."
22. Ibid.
23. Ibid.
24. Ibid.
25. Ibid.
26. Safuto, "Quinn Describes."
27. Katherine Houreld et al., "Pentagon Says Crew Retakes U.S. Ship from Pirates," Associated Press, April 8, 2009.
28. Ibid.
29. Ibid.
30. Elizabeth A. Kennedy and Matt Apuzzo, "FBI Joins Effort in Hostage Standoff with Pirates," Associated Press, April 9, 2009.
31. Ibid.
32. Ibid.
33. Ibid.
34. Ibid.
35. Robert D. McFadden and Scott Shane, "In Rescue of Captain, Navy Kills 3 Pirates," *New York Times*, April 12, 2009.
36. Julian E. Barnes and Gregg Miller, "Moment to Shoot Somali Pirates Had Come," *Los Angeles Times*, April 14, 2009, online edition.
37. Ibid.
38. Ibid.
39. Ibid.
40. Doyle et al., "Somali Pirate Takedown."
41. Barnes and Miller, "Moment to Shoot."
42. Ibid.
43. Ibid.
44. Ibid.

45. Ibid.
46. Ibid.
47. Ibid.
48. McFadden and Shane, "In Rescue of Captain."
49. Ibid.
50. Barnes and Miller, "Moment to Shoot."
51. Ibid.

2 Pirates and Prisons

1. Larry Neumeister et al., "Prosecutors Say Pirate Was Brazen Ringleader," Associated Press, April 22, 2009.
2. Ibid.
3. Ibid.
4. Ibid.
5. Mohamed Olad Hassan, Malkhadir M. Muhumed, and Carley Petesch, "Mystery Surrounds Somali Pirate's Personal Life," Associated Press, April 21, 2009.
6. Ibid.
7. Ibid.
8. Catherine Weibel, "UNHCR Emergency Team Assesses Needs in Northern Somalia's Galkayo Region," United Nations High Commissioner for Refugees (UNHCR) news story, January 15, 2007.
9. Hassan, Muhumed, and Petesch, "Mystery Surrounds."
10. Ibid.
11. Rob Walker, "Inside Story of Somali Pirate Attack," British Broadcasting Corporation, June 4, 2009.
12. Neumeister et al., "Prosecutors Say."
13. Ibid.
14. Tristan McConnell, "Interview with a Pirate: How Not to Be a Pirate—and How to Catch Them," *GlobalPost*, June 12, 2009. http://www.globalpost.com.
15. Nick Wadhams, "Drownings and Lost Ransom Won't Deter Somali Pirates," *Time*, January 12, 2009.
16. Jeffrey Gettleman and Mohammed Ibrahim, "Somalia's Pirates Flourish in a Lawless Nation," *New York Times*, October 30, 2008.
17. Ibid.

18. Wadhams, "Drownings and Lost Ransom."
19. Gettlemen and Ibrahim, "Somalia's Pirates Flourish."

3 Cauldron of Chaos

1. United Nations Environmental Programme, "After the Tsunami," National Rapid Environmental Desk Assessment, 2006, 133.
2. Ibid., 134.
3. Ibid.
4. Mahdi Gedi Qayad, "Assessment Mission to Somalia in Connection with Alleged Dumping of Hazardous Substances," Joint UNEP/DHA Environmental Unit and the UN Coordination Union (UNCU) for Somalia, June 1997.
5. Alisha Ryu, "Waste Dumping off Somali Coast May Have Links to Mafia, Somali Warlords," Voice of America News, March 15, 2005.
6. Ibid.
7. Michael Maren, "The Mysterious Death of Ilaria Alpi," unpublished manuscript. http://www.raffaeleciriello.com/site/pw/sto/39.ilaria.maren.html.
8. Ibid.
9. Ibid.
10. Ibid.
11. Ibid.
12. Ibid.
13. Ibid.
14. Ibid.
15. Bruno Schiemsky et al., Report of the Monitoring Group on Somalia Pursuant to Security Council Resolution 1676, November 21, 2006, 6.
16. Ibid., 10–24.
17. Ibid., 23.
18. Ibid., 25.
19. Ibid., 26.
20. Ibid., 12.
21. Ibid.
22. Ibid.
23. Ibid.

24. Ibid., 65.
25. Bruno Schiemsky et al., Report of the Monitoring Group on Somalia to United Nations Security Council, July 17, 2007, 17.
26. Jim Miklaszewski et al., "Attacks Against al-Qaida Continue in Somalia," NBC, January 9, 2007.
27. Barbara Slavin, "U.S. Support Key to Ethiopia's Invasion," *USA Today*, January 7, 2007. http://www.usatoday.com/news/world/2007-01-07-ethiopia_x.htm.
28. Abdiqani Hassan et al., "U.S. Navy Attacks al-Qaeda Suspect in Somalia," Reuters, June 2, 2007.
29. Zalmay Khalilzad, letter to Bruno Schiemsky, Chairman, Monitoring Group on Somalia, United Nations, June 25, 2007.
30. Tristan McConnell, "'Black Hawks' Return to Somalia," *GlobalPost*, September 15, 2009.
31. U.S. Department of State, "Remarks with Somali Transitional Federal Government President Sheikh Sharif Sheikh Ahmed," by Hillary Rodham Clinton, Secretary of State, Nairobi, Kenya, August 6, 2009.
32. "US Gives Somalia About 40 Tons of Arms, Ammunition," Reuters, June 27, 2009.
33. U.S. Department of State, "Remarks."

4 Method to the Madness

1. Matt Bryden et al., Report of the Monitoring Group on Somalia to United Nations Security Council (S/2008/769), November 20, 2008, 27.
2. Ibid., 15.
3. Dan Nolan, "Firms Reap Somali Piracy Profits," Al Jazeera, September 9, 2009. http://english.aljazeera.net/news/africa/2009/09/20099894242623358.html.
4. Douglas A. McIntyre, "Somali Pirates Are Getting Rich: A Look at the Profit Margins," By 24/7 Wall St., *Time*, April 15, 2009.
5. Bryden et al., Monitoring Group Report, 29.
6. Ibid., 30.
7. Ibid., 31.
8. Ibid., 29.

9. Ibid., 30.
10. Bruno Schiemsky et al., Report of the Monitoring Group on Somalia to United Nations Security Council (S/2008/274), April 24, 2007, 18.
11. Ibid., 19.
12. Ibid., 19–20.
13. Andrew Harding, "Postcard from Somali Pirate Capital," British Broadcasting Corporation, June 16, 2009.
14. Ibid.

5 Inside a Hijacking

1. Rob Walker, "Inside Story of Somali Pirate Attack," British Broadcasting Corporation, June 4, 2009.
2. Ibid.
3. Ibid.
4. Ibid.
5. Ibid.
6. Ibid.
7. Ibid.
8. Ibid.
9. Ibid.
10. Andrew Harding, "Postcard from Somali Pirate Capital," British Broadcasting Corporation, June 16, 2009.
11. Ibid.
12. Ibid.

6 Nightmare on the Delta

1. Sebastian Junger, "Blood Oil," *Vanity Fair*, February 2007.
2. Ibid.
3. "Toll on Civilians Still Unclear in Delta," Integrated Regional Information Network, United Nations Office for the Coordination of Humanitarian Affairs, June 11, 2009.
4. Junger, "Blood Oil."

5. Michael D. Goldhaber, "A Win for Wiwa, a Win for Shell, a Win for Corporate Human Rights," *AmLaw Daily*, June 10, 2009. http://www.law.com/jsp/LawArticlePC.jsp?id=1202431368718.
6. Ibid.
7. Chris Khan, "Shell Settles Human Rights Suit for $15.5M," Associated Press, June 8, 2009.
8. Ibid.
9. Ibid.
10. Ibid.
11. Ibid.
12. Aderogba Obisesan, "Nigeria's Main Armed Group Says to Resume Attacks," Agence France-Presse, October 7, 2009.
13. Ibid.
14. Ibid.
15. Junger, "Blood Oil."

7 Ten Months in Hell

1. Alison Bevege, "Somali Pirates Terrorized Nigerian Crew," Reuters, June 10, 2009.
2. Ibid.
3. Modupe Ogunbayo, "Nigerian Crew of a Hijacked Ship Still Held by Somali Pirates One Year After," *Newswatch Magazine*, June 2, 2009. http://www.newswatchngr.com/index.php?option=com_content&task=view&id=980&Itemid=1.
4. Ibid.
5. Ibid.
6. Bevege, "Somali Pirates."
7. Ibid.
8. Ogunbayo, "Nigerian Crew."
9. Bevege, "Somali Pirates."
10. Ibid.
11. "Ten Nigerian Sailors Freed by Somali Pirates," News Agency of Nigeria, June 22, 2009.
12. Ibid.
13. Ibid.

14. Crusoe Osagie and Onwuka Nzeshi, "Nigeria: Pirates Hijack Eight Local Vessels: Pirates Situation on Waters Getting Worse." http://allafrica.com, October 17, 2008.
15. Andrew Walker, "'Blood Oil' Dripping from Nigeria," BBC News, July 27, 2008. http://news.bbc.co.uk/go/pr/fr/-/2/hi/africa/7519302.stm.
16. Ibid.
17. Ibid.
18. Sebastian Junger, "Blood Oil," *Vanity Fair*, February 2007.
19. Ibid.
20. Ibid.

8 Malaise in Mombasa

1. Raf Casert, "EU, Kenya Agree to Prosecute Pirates," Associated Press, March 6, 2009.

9 Desperation at Dadaab

1. U.S. Department of State, "Remarks with Somali Transitional Federal Government President Sheikh Sharif Sheikh Ahmed," by Hillary Rodham Clinton, Secretary of State, Nairobi, Kenya, August 6, 2009.
2. Mugumbo Munene, "How Plot to Bomb Clinton in Kenya Was Foiled," *Daily Nation*, September 5, 2009. http://www.nation.co.ke/News/-/1056/653584/-/item/1/-/h6m244z/-/index.html.

10 Haven for Terror

1. Conor Humphries and Matthew Jones, "Russian Navy Seizes 29 Pirates off Somalia," Reuters, April 28, 2009.
2. "Russians Hose Down Somali Pirates," *Moscow Times*, Issue 4136, Maritime Bulletin, April 29, 2009.
3. "Somali Pirates Could Face Trial in Russia," RIA Novosti, April 30, 2009.
4. Ibid.
5. Ibid.

6. David Osler, "Iranians and Pakistanis Among Somali Pirates," *Lloyd's List News Bulletin*, June 2, 2009.
7. Ibid.

11 Fighting Back

1. Port Security Advisory (2-09), International Port Security Program, U.S. Coast Guard, U.S. Department of Homeland Security, May 22, 2009, 1–2. http://www.marad.dot.gov/documents/Port_Security_Advisory_2-09.pdf.
2. Katharine Houreld, "Companies Hire 'Shipriders' Against Somali Pirates," Associated Press, June 5, 2009.
3. Ibid.
4. Doreen Carvajal, "Interpol Chief Seeks Police Alliance to Fight Piracy off Somalia," *New York Times*, May 29, 2009.
5. Ibid.
6. "Netherlands Proposes International Antipiracy Tribunal," Agence France-Presse, May 29, 2009.
7. Ibid.
8. David Sharp, "Navy's Newest Warships Top Out at More than 50 mph," Associated Press, October 22, 2009.
9. Ibid.

12 Sailors Take Warning

1. Public Affairs Office, European Union Naval Force, "Longest Range Pirate Attack on Crude Oil Tanker in Indian Ocean," November 9, 2009. http://www.eunavfor.eu/2009/11/longest-range-pirate-attack-on-crude-oil-tanker-in-indian-ocean/.
2. Public Affairs Office, European Union Naval Force, "EU NAVFOR Neutralize Pirate Attack Groups in Indian Ocean," November 19, 2009. http://www.eunavfor.eu/2009/11/eu-navfor-neutralize-pirate-attack-groups-in-indian-ocean/.
3. Alan Cowell, Andrés Cala, and Mohammed Ibrahim, "Pirates Attack *Maersk Alabama* Again," *New York Times*, November 18, 2009.

4. Jason Straziuso et al., "*Maersk Alabama* Repels 2nd Pirate Attack with Guns," Associated Press, November 18, 2009.
5. Cowell, Cala, and Ibrahim, "Pirates Attack."
6. Ibid.
7. Ibid.
8. Jason Straziuso et al., "U.S. Ship Repels Pirates with Guns and Sound Blasts," Associated Press, November 18, 2009.
9. Cowell, Cala, and Ibrahim, "Pirates Attack."
10. Straziuso et al., "U.S. Ship Repels Pirates."
11. Ibid.
12. Ibid.
13. Ibid.
14. Mohamed Olad Hassan, "Somali Judge Who Jailed Pirates, Insurgents Killed," Associated Press, November 12, 2009.
15. Jeffrey Gettleman, "Pirates Seize Oil Tanker, U.S.-Bound, off Somalia," *New York Times*, November 30, 2009.
16. "Somalia: Mass Exodus as Militia Takes Control of Southern Town," Integrated Regional Information Network, United Nations Office for the Coordination of Humanitarian Affairs, November 24, 2009.
17. Mohamed Olad Hassan and Malkhadir M. Muhumed, "15 Dead After Suicide Bomber Attack in Somalia," Associated Press, December 3, 2009.
18. Mohamed Olad Hassan, "Somalia Blames al-Qaida, Somali Group for Bombing," Associated Press, December 4, 2009.
19. Ibid.
20. "Somalia: Sakhaudin Ahmed, 'My Happiest Day Turned into a Nightmare,'" Integrated Regional Information Networks, United Nations Office for the Coordination of Humanitarian Affairs, December 8, 2009.
21. "Somalia: Attack on Graduation Ceremony the 'Last Straw,'" Integrated Regional Information Networks, United Nations Office for the Coordination of Humanitarian Affairs, December 10, 2009.
22. Ibid.
23. Ibid.
24. Jeffrey Gettleman, "UN Experts Get Threats in Inquiry into Somalia," *New York Times*, December 12, 2009.

Epilogue: A Modest Proposal

1. Matt Bryden, Arnaud Laloum, and Jörg Roofthooft, Monitoring Group on Somalia, Report to UN Security Council (S/2010/91), Pursuant to UN Security Council Resolution 751 (1992), March 10, 2010, 36.
2. Malkhadir M. Muhumed, "Pirates Have Shootout over Oil Tanker Release," Associated Press, January 18, 2010.
3. Katharine Houreld and Daniel Woolls, "Private Guards Kill Somali Pirate for First Time," Associated Press, March 24, 2010.
4. Ibid.
5. Author unspecified, "France Claims Biggest Haul of Pirates off Somalia," Agence France-Presse, March 7, 2010.
6. Jason Straziuso, "US Navy Frigate Captures 5 Pirates Near Seychelles," Associated Press, April 1, 2010.
7. Bryden et al., Monitoring Group Report, 6.
8. Ibid., 35.
9. Ibid.
10. Ibid., 7.
11. Ibid., 39.
12. Ibid., 42–43.
13. Ibid., 39.
14. Jeffrey Gettleman, "U.S. Aiding Somalia in Its Plan to Retake Its Capital," *New York Times*, March 6, 2010.
15. Ibid.
16. Ibid.

INDEX

Also by Peter Eichstaedt

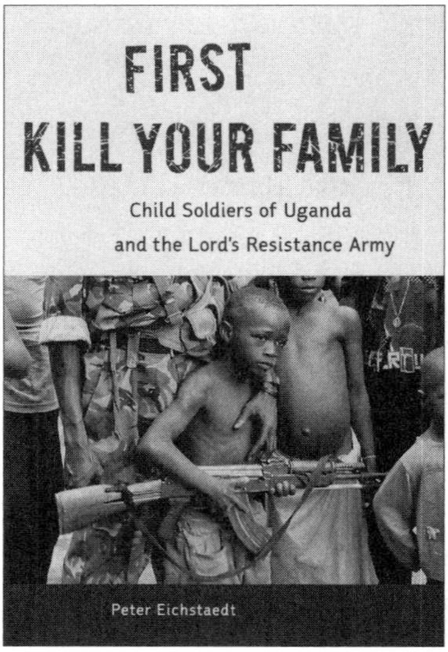

First Kill Your Family
Child Soldiers of Uganda and the Lord's Resistance Army

Winner of the 2010 Colorado Book Award for History

"You must read this powerful book. Peter Eichstaedt has given voice to the victims of the largely unheard-of tragedy of Uganda. This story calls out to our very humanity."
—Archbishop Emeritus Desmond Tutu

For the past twenty years, the Lord's Resistance Army (LRA), led by Joseph Kony, has ravaged northern Uganda with the mission of establishing a government based on the Ten Commandments. A former witchdoctor and spirit medium, Kony claims he not only can predict the future but also can control the minds of his fighters. And control them he does: the LRA consists of children abducted from their homes. As initiation, boys are forced to commit atrocities—murdering relatives and friends—and girls are forced into sexual slavery and labor. In *First Kill Your Family*, veteran journalist Peter Eichstaedt goes into the war-torn villages and refugee camps, talking to former child soldiers, child "brides," and other victims. He examines the cultlike convictions of the army; how a pervasive belief in witchcraft, the spirit world, and the supernatural gave rise to this and other deadly movements; and what the global community can do to bring peace and justice to the region.

Available at your favorite bookstore, (800) 888-4741, or www.lawrencehillbooks.com.

Sign up for the Lawrence Hill Books e-newsletter by contacting us at frontdesk@chicagoreviewpress.com.

Lawrence Hill Books